THE ITINERARIES OF WILLIAM WEY

The *Itineraries* of
WILLIAM WEY

Edited and Translated by Francis Davey

Bodleian Library
UNIVERSITY OF OXFORD

First published in 2010 by
The Bodleian Library
Broad Street
Oxford OX1 3BG

www.bodleianbookshop.co.uk

ISBN 978 1 85124 304 4

Introduction © Francis Davey
This edition © Bodleian Library, University of Oxford, 2010

Frontispiece © Detail of Doge Moro of Venice kneeling before the Virgin.
One of Add. 15816, fol. 5r Permission and © British Library.

The Bodleian Library gratefully acknowledges the editor's generous support in the making of this book.

Designed by Dot Little
Body text ypeset in 11/14pt Adobe Jenson and 9/14 Myriad
Printed in England by Cromwell Press Group, Trowbridge, Wiltshire on 80gsm Munken Premium Bookwove
Vol.17.5 sourced from an FSC accredited mill.

Mixed Sources
Product group from well-managed
forests, controlled sources and
recycled wood or fiber
www.fsc.org Cert no. TT-COC-002303
© 1996 Forest Stewardship Council

The FSC logo identifies products that contain wood from well-
managed forests, certified in accordance with the strict environmental,
social and economic standards of the Forest Stewardship Council.

British Library Catalogue in Publishing Data
A CIP record of this publication is available from the British Library

Contents

Preface

Our group had been visiting the probable site of the Battle of Edington on the edge of Salisbury Plain where King Alfred won a famous victory over the Danes in 878 AD. The coach was not leaving for another hour and the priory church of St Mary, St Katharine and All Saints looked well worth a visit. On the table inside several offprints of scholarly lectures delivered in previous years to raise funds for the church were for sale. Among them was *William Wey's Pilgrimage to Jerusalem in 1458*, by Mr John D'Arcy. Shortly after that I joined the Confraternity of St James (CSJ) and read an article in its *Bulletin* for June 1991 by Pat Quaife on "The Pilgrimage of William Wey to St James of Compostella". These two papers fired my enthusiasm to learn more about the fifteenth-century Devonian priest, who, having been a fellow of Exeter College, Oxford, became Bursar of Eton College and made three pilgrimages in 1456, 1458 and 1462.

The Latin text of Chapter 15 of *The Itineraries* had been published by Vázquez de Parga et al. in *Las Peregrinaciones a Santiago de Compostela*, Madrid 1948. I translated this into English, and in 2000 the CSJ published my version, with the Latin on the facing pages, in *William Wey, An English Pilgrim to Compostella in 1456*. While translating this chapter I found myself asking various questions. For example, who were the captains and owners of the West Country pilgrim ships at this period? Was anything left of the House of the Friars Minor in La Coruña where Wey had stayed? Who were the four English gentlemen, Austile, Fulford, Gale and Lisle, who were in Santiago Cathedral with Wey on Trinity Sunday in 1456? In pursuing the answers to these questions I consulted numerous documents in the then Public Record Office and the Record Offices in Exeter, Truro and Trowbridge. Six essays resulting from this research were included in my book and several more appeared later in the CSJ *Bulletin*, *Devon and Cornwall Notes and Queries* and *The Journal of the Royal Institution of Cornwall*. Much later, in 2006, I was invited to contribute a chapter on William Wey to the Ashmolean's book *Pilgrimage, The Sacred Journey*.

After my work on Wey's 1456 pilgrimage to Compostella I turned to his other journeys. I borrowed a copy of the Roxburghe 1857 transcription of *The Itineraries*

7

and translated the whole work. During this period my wife and I walked three of the international pilgrim routes to Santiago de Compostela, those from Le Puy, La Coruña and Oporto. This led to the publication of three *CSJ Guides* to these *Caminos*. We next decided to follow as closely as possible, and using public transport, the routes Wey took on his pilgrimages in 1458 and 1462. This led to many journeys, the two longest being those from Venice to Ulcinj along the Croatian and Montenegrin coast and up the Rhine from Cologne to Speyer. Others were from Nieuwpoort (in Belgium) via Ghent and Maastricht to Aachen; from Aachen via Trier up the Moselle to St Theobald (Thann) and Basel; from Basle to Merano, and from Merano to Venice. For all these we used combinations of bus, train, ferry and, very occasionally, taxi. Separate visits were made to Methóni, Rhodes and Cyprus.

We have tried to visit all the places Wey names. By tracing his routes we have been able to identify some of the more obscure names like Zawe (Sankt Vith in Belgium) and Hospytale (Helenenberg in Germany). Other discoveries were made by chance. At Klösterle in the Vorarlberg (Austria) we found in the basement of the Johanniter Stube the remains of the Knights Hospitaller hospice which was there when Wey passed by and which gave the village its name. Many of the places in his lists had Franciscan houses in the fifteenth century, where he might have stayed. Portions of these still exist. At Methóni the old chapel of St Leo, mentioned by Wey, still stands a mile outside the town, in the middle of a market garden. The quay, now ruined by wars and earthquakes, where his Venetian galley tied up, lies just below the surface of the clear, warm water in front of the castle and can be easily explored. The relics of St Euphemia, the Blessed Simeon and St Blaise still rest in the shrines in Rovinj, Zadar and Dubrovnik which he saw and described. Unfortunately the body of St Helena, which Wey saw, as did we in 2004, in the chapel in Venice which bears her name, has been moved recently. Our most exciting discovery, described in a separate essay, was that of the Icon of Our Lady of Philerimos and the hand of John the Baptist in Cetinje, the old capital of Montenegro.

We have not found any portraits of William Wey, but likenesses of some of the most important persons who appear in *The Itineraries*, for example Pope Pius II (Aeneas Piccolomini), Henry VI of England, Sultan Mahomet II and Raimundo Zacosta, Grand Master of the Hospitallers in Rhodes, are well known. Other contemporaries are less easy to find. An effigy of John Tiptoft, the Earl of Worcester, together with those of two of his wives, lies in Ely Cathedral. The King of Cyprus, James the Bastard, features on a medal in the Ashmolean, while his queen, Caterina Conaro, lies in the church of San Salvatore in Venice. The two doges who appear in Chapter 9, Pasquale Malipiero and Christofero Moro, also have their memorials.

The monument to the former, whose funeral Wey described, is in Venice, in the Dominican church of Santi Giovanni e Paolo, while the latter appears in a contemporary illuminated manuscript, now in the British Library, kneeling before the Virgin, reproduced here on the frontispiece.

In pursuing my hobby I have received enormous help from a great many people whose assistance I am delighted to acknowledge. Apart from the staff of the Record Offices named above I have been generously assisted by librarians, archivists and staff of the Bodleian; the British Library; Exeter College, Oxford; Corpus Christi and Newnham Colleges, Cambridge; Eton College; Lambeth Palace; the Museum of the Order of St John; the Wellcome Trust; the Worshipful Society of Apothecaries of London; the Knights of Malta in Rome; the College of Arms; and Exeter University. Individuals to whom I owe a special debt are Ms Maria Kasdagli in Rhodes; Dr William Griffiths and Ms Marion Marples of the Confraternity of St James; Dr B.J. Cook, Curator of Medieval and Early Modern Coinage at the British Museum; and Dr Nicholas Mayhew, Keeper of the Heberden Collection and Deputy Director of the Ashmolean Museum. I gratefully acknowledge the interest and support I have had from Dr Samuel Fanous and Deborah Susman of the Bodleian and Mr and Mrs Ronald Atkins of Bedford, New York. Finally, and most important of all, is my wife, Patricia Quaife, who not only started my active interest in Wey with her article in 1991 but who has accompanied me on all our journeys in Wey's footsteps and wake since then. Without her support and encouragement this book would not exist and I dedicate it to her with grateful thanks.

Patriciae

Per mare, per terram mecum per saecla petenti.
To Pat, who shared my quest across sea, land and time.

Introduction

Having been asked by devout men to compile an Itinerary of my pilgrimage to the most holy sepulchre of Our Lord, Jesus Christ, I propose to describe my journey across the various seas beyond which one must sail, the cities, towns and countries through which one must travel and the sacred places in the Holy Land, together with such things as I saw and heard both there and on the way home.

This is one of the few occasions when Wey steps out of the shadows of a narrative in the third person to address us in his own voice. His diffidence and modesty permeate his writing – that is part of his attraction – but they make it hard to get to know this adventurous fifteenth-century priest.

Firm dates of the events of Wey's life are few. Born, probably in 1407, in Devon, he died on 30 November 1476 in his seventieth year. A Master of Arts and a Bachelor of Divinity, he was a fellow of Exeter College, Oxford, from 1430 to 1442 and a fellow of Eton College from 1441 until 1467 when he retired to the Priory of Edington in Wiltshire.

It is likely that Wey was born in Devon since he was one of the eight fellows of Exeter College who, by the statutes of its founder, Bishop Stapledon, had to come from that county. It is just possible that he was the son or close relative of an older William Wey of Great Torrington who was, perhaps wrongfully, accused in February 1438 of stealing two horses. He was found guilty and although not a priest had advanced sufficiently in holy orders to plead benefit of clergy. This meant that he was imprisoned not in the city gaol but in the Bishop of Exeter's prison, where he died between 1444 and 1447, despite his plea for release by the process of compurgation.

Another contemporary in the Diocese of Exeter, who could just possibly have been the author's older brother, was Robert Wey. Robert was tonsured on 15

February 1421 and proceeded through the lower orders to the priesthood in 1427, becoming Vicar of Colaton Raleigh by December 1439. William's early education is unrecorded but it must have been a good one for him to have achieved his later success and to write as well as he did. *The Itineraries* display a knowledge of Latin, theology, finance, geography and music. Apart from academic subjects they also show the writer's sound common sense and impressive physical stamina. Robert's early career, even if he was not a close relative of William, illustrates the sort of path a young man aiming for the priesthood might have followed in Devon at this time. Robert Wey advanced through the ranks of the minor clergy in Exeter Cathedral, being a secondary in 1423–24 and a vicar choral in 1427. If William had followed a similar career in his younger days he could have acquired thereby some of the scholarship and musical ability that he displayed later.

Finally, still in the realm of speculation, one might mention the family of John ate Weye. In 1313 the De La Weye family is recorded at Way Barton in the parish of St-Giles-in-the-Wood, four miles east of Great Torrington. Since the William Wey who died in prison was named as an executor in the will of the rector of Little Torrington in June 1425 it is possible that the author's family had its origins in that part of Devon.

The writer of *The Itineraries* only emerges clearly from the shadows on 7 March 1433 when he was ordained priest by the Bishop of Salisbury, Robert Neville. In the Bishop's *Register* he is described as "Fellow of Exeter College, Oxford". The *Register* of Exeter College records that he had become a Devonian fellow there in 1430. William Wey's affection for the College, even after he had resigned his fellowship, is shown by a series of gifts he made and which were entered in *The Acts of the Rector of Exeter College*: viz. a bowl in 1440, altar cloths in 1451 and two books in 1457.

His move to Eton is intriguing. That College, founded by King Henry VI, was incorporated in 1442. While William was not one of the four original fellows appointed on 11 October 1440, his name appears seventh in the list of fellows and the likely year of his appointment was 1441. If Wey had already shown special expertise in finance, that might explain his recruitment. By the Founder's Statutes the fellows of Eton were required to appoint two of their number each year as bursars. In the years between 1441 and 1467 the Eton archives show that Wey was elected bursar eight times. The records are incomplete but it appears that Wey was one of the pair of bursars almost continuously from the time he joined the fellowship until he left to retire to Edington, with breaks in service arising from his absence on the three pilgrimages. While there were possibly some other years when he was not elected bursar, it can be assumed from the number of times he was definitely re-elected that he enjoyed the confidence of the other fellows in the discharge of these duties.

The statutes are clear about the personal, financial and administrative responsibilities of the bursars. They had the assistance of a clerk but they were not mere figureheads. Wey's competence and expertise in financial matters are shown in the first chapter of *The Itineraries*. All this leads to the questions, "How was the College able to spare him from his duties on three occasions, two of them for almost nine months?" and "Why was the King so generous in granting Wey leave of absence without financial penalty for such long periods?" Apart from any financial talent he possessed, may one perhaps assume that it was because he was a loyal Lancastrian who enjoyed the king's favour that Wey was invited to become a fellow of the new Royal College at Eton?

While enmity between Yorkists and Lancastrians had been simmering for some time, the first pitched battle between them did not take place until May 1455 at St Albans where the Lancastrians were defeated. The details of the Wars of the Roses are complicated and will not be recounted here. Quite apart from the series of battles between 1459 and 1461 (Blore Heath, Northampton, Mortimer's Cross, St Albans – again – and Towton) where victories were variously gained by each side, there was endless intrigue. Success depended on money and alliances and Henry's queen, Margaret of Anjou, niece of Charles VII, King of France, played an important role in seeking both of these. The name of one of her agents in 1457 is known. This was Dolcereau, employed by her former admirer Pierre de Brézé, an important figure at the French court. In her search for military assistance she used Dolcereau to carry sensitive messages to Richard de Beauchamp, Bishop of Salisbury, England's ambassador in France. Five years later, in 1462, another of her supporters, John de Vere, Earl of Oxford, led a group of conspirators who were planning a Lancastrian invasion and the overthrow of Edward IV, who had replaced Henry as king on 28 June 1461. Unfortunately for de Vere his courier was a Yorkist double agent and his plot was discovered. In February 1462 he was tried by Wey's fellow-pilgrim of 1458, Sir John Tiptoft, Earl of Worcester, convicted of treason and sentenced to an especially gruesome death.

The two dates 1457 and 1462 straddle the years of Wey's longer pilgrimages. In *The Itineraries*, although wars involving German bishops, Turks and Hungarians are mentioned, there is scarcely a hint of the dreadful events and intrigues occurring in England at this time. The five battles listed above all took place between 1459 and 1461 and resulted in thousands of casualties, yet Wey's story goes serenely on. It would be surprising if Wey had remained unaffected and uninvolved in what was happening around him. In the whole of *The Itineraries*, Wey gives the names of only five Englishmen, Tiptoft, Austile, Fulford, Gale and Lile, who travelled with him on one or other of his pilgrimages. Two of these were executed in spectacular fashion during the Wars of the Roses. Sir Baldwin Fulford, a Lancastrian, was executed in 1461 after the Battle of Towton, and his head was placed on Micklegate Bar, York. Ten years later Sir John Tiptoft, the Earl of Worcester, a Yorkist, was tried and condemned by John de Vere's son. He was beheaded in the Tower on 18 October 1471.

Wey set off for his final pilgrimage on 26 February 1462. Edward IV had been crowned king eight months before. The deposed King Henry VI was trying to muster support in Scotland and Queen Margaret was plotting with the new king of France, Louis XI, at Amboise. If Henry or Margaret had needed an agent William Wey would have fitted the part ideally. His cover as a pilgrim was impeccable; the records show that many pilgrims acted as spies in the Middle Ages. Wey's powers of observation and attention to detail would have been further recommendations. This additional employment could also explain the apparent ease with which Wey obtained extended leave of absence from his duties at Eton and why he undertook two lengthy Jerusalem pilgrimages. Money to fund armies was a vital concern for both sides in the Wars of the Roses, and Queen Margaret's efforts to obtain foreign alliances show the importance of diplomacy. In those areas, too, Wey and the contacts he might make in his travels could have been useful. Edward IV, pressed for money, was minded to close Eton College, but was dissuaded by William Waynflete, the Bishop of Winchester. This must have been an anxious time for the provost and fellows of Eton, and not least for their bursar, William Wey. The threat to the royal foundation could have been another reason for Wey to absent himself from Windsor for the greater part of the year.

While Wey was astute enough to avoid partisan pronouncements in his book, there is one tiny possible hint of his sympathies in Chapter 9 of *The Itineraries*, when he records the singing of the hymn *Miles Christi gloriose* on 18 July 1462 in the ruined church at Lydda. This was an antiphon of Thomas of Lancaster, who had been executed by Edward II in 1322. His brother Henry had tried to have him canonized. The Lancastrian connection might have been emotionally significant to William Wey.

Wey finally retired to Edington in 1467. Henry VI was imprisoned from 1465 until 1470 and was restored to the throne in October of that year. Then he lost it again a few months later, after the battle of Tewkesbury in May 1471. A week after that, on 21 May, he was murdered in the Tower.

Wey lived on at Edington for another five years, surrounded by his treasured possessions and the mementoes he had collected. He built a very handsome chapel "made in the likeness of the Sepulchre of Our Lord at Jerusalem" as an annexe to Edington Priory. While only the foundations of this remain, on the outside of the south side of the chancel, its elegant doorway, now blocked, can still be seen on the inside of the church. To judge from these remains Wey's extension must have been expensive. His wealth enabled him not only to build the chapel but to furnish it with handsome hangings and costly vestments of silk and velvet as well as a silver chalice and pewter articles. Then there were his books, maps and the relics listed in his "List of Gifts". His pilgrimages also, especially the two to Jerusalem, would have been costly. Even if Wey had enjoyed free hospitality at monasteries and friaries along the way he would have had to pay passage money across the Channel and along the rivers where he used boats. He does not give the figures for these but his contemporary, Richard of Lincoln, gives the charges in great detail, and they come to a considerable total. Finally there were the two return voyages by galley from Venice to Jaffa of forty ducats. It seems probable from one of Wey's statements that he took a servant with him, which would have added to his costs. One can only speculate how he might have afforded all this; was there perhaps a paymaster behind the scenes who contributed towards his expenses?

As one of the brethren called *boni homines* or *Bonhommes* at Edington, Wey was required to observe the Statutes of the House and the Rule of St Augustine. As one of the canons William would have professed obedience to the rector and worn the grey habit of tunicle, a scapular with hood and, for outdoors, a cloak and a hat. Despite his wealth the only linen garment permitted was drawers. Perhaps Wey was only too pleased to adopt this new persona and accept these restrictions. Peace and obscurity in the Priory in Wiltshire might have come as a relief after a busy and, on occasion, dangerous life at home and abroad.

THE JOURNEY

In William Wey's time and later, reformers began to question the traditional doctrine of Purgatory, and the means of alleviating it by indulgences gained through pilgrimages to holy sites and relics. Wey devotes two chapters, 5 and 6, to ten *materiae*, underlying causes, which inspire Christians to undertake pilgrimage. Opportunities to go on pilgrimage and to visit shrines and to venerate holy relics en route were not to be missed, and a number of these are mentioned in all three

Itineraries. The virtues of certain sites are described at length, for example Trier in Chapter 9 and Padrón in Chapter 15. Some of the saints he names were famous and of long standing, like St Mark and the Blessed Simeon; others, like St Francis from the thirteenth century, were more recent; while one, St Christina, was almost contemporary, having died in Spoleto in 1458, only weeks before Wey arrived there.

The desire to strengthen faith (see *materiae* numbered 3 and 5 in Chapter 5) lies beneath Wey's interest in continuing or recurrent miracles like the perennial lamp at Casope and the spring near Bethlehem which bubbled up at Epiphany. Equally important to him was the physical evidence of Christ's time on earth, such as apparent footprints and splashes of blood on marble. By the extension of grace described by St Bridget and repeated in *materia* number 4, indulgences gained by pilgrims could be transferred to their deceased relatives. If the earlier William Wey described above, who died in the Bishop of Exeter's prison in the 1440s, was related to the author, it is just possible that he hoped that his pilgrimage would release his luckless kinsman from Purgatory.

Having resolved to undertake a pilgrimage the aspirant pilgrim had to decide his destination and how and with whom he would travel. In view of the hazards of the journey many also made their wills. In the Middle Ages, three destinations towered above all the rest, Jerusalem, Rome and Compostella. Some people, like Chaucer's Wife of Bath, who had visited all three places, including Jerusalem "thrice", were inveterate pilgrims. Wey's tally of four (Compostella, Rome and Jerusalem twice) was impressive, not least because he returned safely on each occasion.

The journey to Compostella in north-west Spain was known as *ad limina Sancti Jacobi*. The relics of St James the Greater, after several miraculous transfers, were finally enshrined in the church and later cathedral dedicated to him in Santiago de Compostela. This destination became very popular from the eleventh century onwards and several routes to it across the Iberian peninsula were soon established. Some of these allowed detours to be made to other shrines, thereby earning further grace for the pilgrim. A popular route for English pilgrims to St James took them by sea to La Coruña since, weather permitting, it could be quick and easy. It was not obligatory to suffer en route to obtain the indulgences, reaching the holy destination in the right spirit being the most important objective. Holy Years, when St James's Day, 25 July, fell on a Sunday, were the most popular for this pilgrimage since extra indulgences were granted. Wey chose one of these, 1456, for his own journey. His route from Plymouth to Galicia was among those most frequently taken by English pilgrims, and his description in Chapter 15 of ships in the harbour at La Coruña shows that pilgrims from many other northern regions also travelled by sea. Those, like parish clergy, who had to seek leave of absence from their superiors to go on pilgrimage were normally allowed a generous three months to complete it. Weather in the Bay of Biscay could be menacing but, even with a four-day delay for bad weather, William Wey completed the round trip from Plymouth back to Plymouth in twenty-three days.

For English men and women the pilgrimage to Rome was a much lengthier undertaking. While some pilgrims used ships in the Mediterranean, most followed the Via Francigena from the Western Alps to Rome overland. In 1454 a predecessor of William Wey, Richard of Lincoln, took a direct route across the English Channel and the Low Countries to reach the Rhine at Cologne. Unfortunately for William Wey parts of this Rhine route were not available in 1458 and 1462. He must, for example, have been very disappointed not to visit the famous Shrine of the Magi in Cologne. His alternative routes, however, can be followed from his lists and narratives. In 1462 he used the Moselle from Trier to Epinal as the main artery south towards the Alps. At a time when many roads were ill maintained and dangerous, travel on a river must have been an inviting alternative. Wey does not say explicitly that he used river barges, but the names of the places he gives in Chapter 9, and the distances between them, indicate convenient landing places at comfortable distances for ultramontane pilgrims travelling to Italy by boat. For the modern traveller, hydro-electric schemes, locks and weirs prevent any definitive judgement, but the presence, even today, of towpaths and the evidence of contemporary drawings and paintings show how much barge traffic there was in the Middle Ages and how it was managed. Not least, the presence of friaries or monasteries at the places named is a strong indication of Wey's mode of travel.

The pilgrimage to Jerusalem was even longer and more hazardous than that to Rome. After the fall of Constantinople in 1453 the safest route was by sea from Venice to Jaffa. Some pilgrims, like Wey, first went to Venice overland; others, like Roberto de Sanseverino, a fellow-pilgrim in 1458, who started from Milan, travelled to Pavia and then took a barge down the River Ticino and the Po nearly all the way to Venice. Wey's account of his stay in Venice and the arrangements to be made for the passage by sea to Jaffa are clearly set out in Chapter 9 and Chapter 2. One can still follow the route of his galley, the *Morosina*, across the Adriatic to Pula and then south along the coast to Corfu, to the major ports of Methóni, Heraklion, Rhodes, Paphos and Jaffa.

The timing of Wey's pilgrimages depended on the season and weather, especially snow and wind. While Chaucer says that April was a good time for pilgrimage, those travelling across the Alps and through the Eastern Mediterranean had to think of more than spring showers. The main obstacle was the snow on the Alpine passes. There was no point in trying to cross these, on the outward journey, before the snow melted or, on the return homewards, after the first snows of winter. This gave a window of about six months from March to September. In 1462 William left England on 13 March and reached Venice on 22 April, where he stayed for a whole month. He does not give many of his arrival and departure dates in 1458, but since, in that year, he visited Rome before he reached Venice, he probably did not spend quite as long in Venice. It is likely that he left England in mid-March in 1458 also.

Climate also affected the sailing season for the Venetian galleys. Pilgrim ships set sail from Venice at the end of May to take advantage of the wind known as the Maestro or Maestrale (not the Mistral of the Golfe du Lion), which blows from the north-east at Trieste but then from the north-west in the central and southern Adriatic. It is a wind which appears remarkably punctually around the third week of May and blows fair for the first 1,000 miles of the voyage along the coast of Croatia, Montenegro, Albania and Greece.

THE BOOK AND THE TRANSLATION

Remarkably little is known about the history of this book, which Wey called *Matters of Jerusalem*. His request that the book should remain in the monastery at Edington was fortunately not fulfilled. If it had stayed there it would probably have disappeared along with the other bequests whose whereabouts are unknown.

The Roxburghe editor describes *The Itineraries* as follows, "A small quarto volume, probably written by Wey himself, on vellum with rubricated letters, but not illustrated, in an excellent state of preservation." On the flyleaf at the end is written the hexameter couplet:

> *Si fore vis sapiens sex serva quae tibi mando.*
> *Quid loqueris, et ubi, de quo, cui, quomodo, quando.*
> Edyngden Abbeye

"If you want to be wise, pay attention to the six things which I tell you; what you say, where, about whom, to whom, how and when." While one cannot be certain, these lines could well have been written by Wey himself.

The next known owner was a "Master Tempest", who disposed of the book in 1624 with the words "Ex dono Mri Tempest 1624" ("Presented by Master Tempest,

1624"). It is not certain whether the word *Magister* refers to academic or social standing. It is not known to whom or to which body the volume was presented.

The only other name connected with the manuscript is that of John Edwards, which appears at the end with the note *pro ligatura hujus libri et 47tem literis iiid* – "for the binding of this book and 47 letters, 3 pence".

Edington Priory was dissolved in 1539. In 1533 John Leland, who had been appointed keeper of his libraries by Henry VIII, was given authority to search monastic and collegiate libraries. Accordingly, between about 1535 and 1542, he journeyed around England to inspect these, visiting Edington between 1535 and 1539. Ker, in *Medieval Libraries of Great Britain*, lists five books which were at Edington at this time; one is now in Cambridge, three, including *The Itineraries*, are in Oxford and one in Salisbury. It is likely that Wey's book stayed at Edington between his death in 1476 and 1539. Ker describes the period 1540–1640 as "the golden age of the English private collector" and perhaps Mr Tempest was one of these.

The first printed catalogue of books in the Bodleian that includes MS Bodl. 565 is Edward Bernard's *Catalogi librorum manuscriptorum Angliae et Hiberniae in unum collecti* (Oxford 1697). Two later catalogues, those of Madan and Craster (*Summary Catalogue*, Oxford 1922) and Richard Hunt (*Summary Catalogue*, Oxford 1953) naturally assumed that the 1624 donation was to the Bodleian, but the former properly expressed some slight doubt.

The identity of "Tempest" is similarly elusive. Foster's *Alumni Oxonienses* (Oxford and London, 1891–92) includes three men of that name who might have been alive as adults in 1624. The likeliest of the three to have been the donor is Thomas Tempest, who matriculated at Queen's College on 23 November 1610 aged 16. He became a barrister, attorney-general of Ireland in 1640 and was knighted on 30 December that year. There is a faint, but piquant, possibility that this Thomas was the Sir Thomas Tempest whose thirteenth-century volume of French and Latin poetry passed to Richard Rawlinson, who, in turn, presented it to the Bodleian in 1756 (MS. Rawl. poet 241 S.C. 14732). This volume of poetry is described as "from the library of Sir Thomas Tempest, baronet". Perhaps he was a collector of medieval manuscripts, who at some time owned both of these books.

(Note: I am deeply indebted to Dr B.C. Barker-Benfield, Senior Assistant Librarian, Department of Special Collections and Western Manuscripts at the Bodleian, for his most helpful and scholarly research on the provenance of *The Itineraries*, used above.)

There remains a span of about ninety years when the whereabouts and the ownership of Wey's manuscript are not definitely known.

For this book the present writer has used the transcription by Bandinel published by the Roxburghe Club in 1857. On a very few occasions where there are misprints or dubious transcriptions the original manuscript has been consulted. Sometimes the problem has been resolved when Wey has repeated himself in his own text.

Although the writer has translated the whole work for his own satisfaction, the present edition does not include the complete translation of all fifteen chapters. Chapter 10, which consists of word lists, has been briefly summarized. The lengthy *materia* number 8 of Chapter 6, which appears again in Chapter 7, has been omitted.

Wey's spelling, including that of proper names, is not consistent. No attempt has been made to standardize this feature of the original but it is hoped that the index entries of *variae lectiones* will avoid confusion.

The Itineraries is one of a number of accounts of pilgrim journeys in the fifteenth century. That by Margery Kempe, who made her pilgrimage to the Holy Land in 1413 and Compostella in 1422, together with those of Samuel Purchas's Pilgrim (to Compostella, Rome and Jerusalem, probably in the 1420s), Felix Fabri (to Jerusalem in 1480 and to Jerusalem and Sinai in 1483) and Canon Casola (to Jerusalem in 1494), are the best known and most easily accessible. A recently discovered work, now in the Wellcome Trust, MS 8004, is a book by Wey's contemporary, Richard of Lincoln. Richard, pilgrim, doctor and astrologer, went to Jerusalem in 1454. His is a much shorter work – about one-tenth of the length of *The Itineraries*. It is written in Danelaw Middle English, not Latin. There are no word lists or tables of currency and little of the "advice to the traveller" found in Wey. The work is of interest, however, as it follows much of Wey's route and deals with many of the places and shrines he visited, and the two were travelling only a few years apart. Since Richard was a layman, his account provides a contrast with that of the priest, William. Wey's book has an additional interest since, as Bandinel says, it foreshadows "Mr Murray's most useful handbooks", and therefore deserves a worthy place in the history of travel writing. In one direction his approach recalls that of Herodotus, the enquiring traveller and acute observer; in the other he looks ahead to Murray's and Baedeker's *Handbooks*, which are the ancestors of today's Michelin *Green Guides*, *Guides Bleus* and *Rough Guides*. All of these contain information about currency and exchange rates, word lists and practical advice to ensure the traveller's heath and safety. Wey's book is one of the first to include all these.

Lewis
S. Kilda
Rockall
Western Is.
S. Uist
Skye
Thurso
Wick
Murray Firth
Peterhead
Inverness
Aberdeen
SCOTLAND
Mull
Perth
Islay
Edinburgh
Berwick
North Chan.
Malin Hd.
Glasgow
Carlisle
Newcastle
Londonderry
Donegal B.
Belfast
Durham
R. Tees
Erris Hd.
Achil Hd.
Sligo
I. Man
York
Slyne Hd.
IRELAND
Liverpool
Hull
R. Humber
Galway
Dublin
Holyhd.
Manch.
Chester
Boston
Limerick
R. Shannon
Waterfd.
Wales
Norwich
Dunmore Hd.
Queenstn.
Cork
ENGLAND
Pembroke
LONDON
Bantry B.
C. Clear
St. Georges Chan.
Bristol Chan.
Bristol
Southampton
Dover
Plymouth
Exeter
I. Wight
Lands End
Scilly Is.
Falmouth
ENGLISH CHANNEL
Cherbg.
Guernsey
Jersey
Caen
Dieppe
Rouen
Seine
PARIS
Ushant
Brest
Rennes
Chartres
Orleans
Nantes
Tours
R. Loire
Belle I.
I. Dieu
FRANCE
I. Re
Oleron
Rocht.
Limoges
Bay of Biscay
R. Garonne
Bordeaux
R. Dordogne
Lyon
Bayonne
Agen
Avignon
Toulouse
Marseille
Toulon
C. Ortegal
Corunna
Ferrol
Oviedo
Gijon
Santander
Bilbao
C. Finisterre
Santiago
Pyrenees
R. Ebro
Leon
Pampeluna
Burgos
Vigo
R. Minho
Braganza
R. Duero
Oporto
Salamanca
Saragossa
SPAIN
PORTUGAL
Coimbra
MADRID
Berlingas
R. Tagus
Cuenca
Elvas
R. Guadiana
LISBON
Badajos
Cordova
Guadalquivir R.
Granada
C. S. Vincent
Sevila
Murcia
Cartagena
Cadiz
Malaga
Almeria
Gibraltar Str. & F.
Alboran
Tangier
Ceuta
Tetuan
Melilla
Mehedia & R. Sebú
Sali & Robat
Teza
Azamore & R. Omerbeg
Mekinez
Fez
Tedla
C. Cantin
Safi
R. Tansift
MAROCCO
Mogador or Suera
C. Ghir
Agadir
Terodant
Tafilelt
Tabelbelt
Figig
Sidi Hesham
Tatta
Garara
MADEIRA Is.
Madeira
Pto. Santo
Funchal
Desertas
Salvage Is.
Lancerota
Fuerteventura
Teneriffe
C. Nun
Egersund
The Naze
NORTH SEA
Heligoland
Sylt
Emden
Groningen
Zuyder Ze.
Amsterdam
Haag
Rotterdam
NETHERLANDS
RHEIN PRUSSIA
Brussels
BELGIUM
Calais
Mons
Amiens
Mezieres
Soissons
Troyes
Dijon
Nevers
Basel
Nancy
Strasb.
SWITZ.
Geneva
Turin
G. of Lyons
Perpignan
C. Creus
Barcelona
Taragona
R. Ebro
Minorca
Majorca
Valencia
Iviza
C. Nao
CORSICA
Ajaccio
Str. of Bonifo.
Sassari
SARD.
Oristano
MEDI
ALGIERS
Bujeya
Stora
Bona
Tenez
Medea
Setif
Constantine
Philip.
Shelif
Oran
Mascara
Tlemsen
Busada
R. Jedi
Biskra
Tibesa
ALGERIA
Vjda
Stiten
Abeid
Aguat
Temerna
Gardaia
Metlili
Beled el Je
Tugurt
Gerata
Wergala
Galea
Tuimmun

1456 to Santiago de Compostela

1458 to Rome, Venice, Jaffa and Jerusalem

1462 to Venice, Jaffa and Jerusalem

I

Changes of Money from England to Rome and Venice

SYNOPSIS

Although Wey says in his heading that he will deal will currencies in use in countries between England, Rome and Venice, he does include also those encountered by pilgrims sailing from Venice to Jaffa – that is, coins in use in Corfu, Methóni, Candia, Rhodes, Cyprus and "Syria".

TRANSLATION
Author's Introduction
(Roxburghe, pp. 1–3)

At Calais you will get 24 *placks* for an English *half-noble* or for a *ducat*. That is the best money until Bruges.

At Bruges you will get the same number of *placks* for a *half-noble* or a *ducat* as you got at Calais. You get 19 *placks* for a *gildern*, and for a *liliaris gildern* 23 *placks* and 17 *mites*. For a *half-noble* or for a *ducat* you will receive 31 *liliaris* which is Brabant money.

In Brabant *placks* are called *styfers*. A *plack* is worth 2 Flemish *groats* called *pennies*. There are two *obols* to a *groat*. There are 2 *farlyngs* 48 *mites* to an *obol*. For a *plack* the rate is *penny Flemish obol*. A *liliar* is worth 36 *mites*. Three *placks* are worth 5 English *pennies* (*d*). 5 *gilderns* and a *plack* are worth 2 English *nobles*. A *gildern* is worth 2 *shillings* (*s*) 8 *pence* (*d*) in English money. The aforesaid money will serve until Cologne.

At Cologne you will have Rhenish *gilderns* and Cologne *pennies*. There are 24 Cologne *pennies* to the *gildern*. A Cologne *penny* is worth 12 *hallards*, or *myrkenys*, – it's all one, – and they will serve until Mainz. A Cologne *penny* is worth half of an English *obol*.

When you change money at Bruges take *gilderns* with a round ball and a cross above: they will be good as far as Rome and are the best all the way. Do not take any English gold with you from Bruges because you will be the loser in the exchange. Indeed, for most of the way they will not change it. All along the route they know Rhenish *gilderns* well and with them you suffer little or no loss.

At Mainz you will find *bemysch* and *blaffards* and a different kind of *hallards*. A Rhenish *gilder* there is worth 21 *blafferdys* and the same number of *bemysch*. A Venetian *ducat* is worth 26 *bemysch* and 3 *hallards*. A *bemysch* or a blaffard is worth 11 *hallards* there. They will last as far as Kempton. *Bemysch* will serve well as far as Rome. 7 *bemysch* are worth 11 English *pennies*.

At Kempton you will have *ferars*. There are 5 *ferars* to the *crowser* and 40 *crowsers* to the *gilder* and a *ferar*.

At Trent you will all have *katerines* and *markets*. One *bemysch* is worth 9 *katerines* and 4 *markets*. There are 2 *katerines* and 2 *bagantines* to a *market*. A *market* is a *galley halfpenny*. This is called a *solde* [shilling] in Venice.

At Bologna you will have *boliners* and another sort of *katerines* and *bayoks* and *boliners*. A *boliner* is worth 6 *katerines* as far as Rome, and in Rome too. In Siena a Roman *boliner* is only worth 5½ *katerines*, although the same *boliner* is worth 6 *katerines* at Rome. In Bologna a *ducat* is worth 46 *boliners*. A *guildern* in Bologna is worth 35 *boliners* - it is good silver. There are 48 *bayoks* to a *guildern*. A *bayok* is worth 4 *katerines*. An old Bologna *boliner* is worth one English *penny*. These are the best coins from Bologna to Rome.

In Rome you will have Roman *bolendines* and *bayoks* and a different sort of *katherines*. There are 48 *bayoks* to one Venetian *ducat*. There are 2 *lylior* to a Roman *ducat*. There are 48 *bolendines* to a Florentine *ducat*. There are 36 *boliners* to the *gildern*. There are 54 *bayoks* to the *guildern*. There are 10 papal *groats* to the *ducat*. Of *bolendines* at Rome 4 *bayoks* to a papal *groat*. There are 4 *katerines* to a *bayok*, there are 12 *pichelynes* [*piccolini*], called *dinars* in Rome, to a *katerine*. The rate varies in different lordships. The *katerine* of one lordship will not be accepted in the next lordship.

In Venice there are *groats*, *grossets*, *galley halfpennies*, which are there called *soldi* [shillings] and *bagantines*. There are 15 *groats* or 30 *grossets* to the Venetian *ducat*. The rate for a Roman or Florentine *ducat* is one *groat* less. There are 8 *soldi* to the *groat* and 4 *soldi* to the *grosset*. There are 12 *bagantines* to the *solde*. You will get 5 pounds and 14 *soldi* for a Venetian *ducat*. A pound is worth 20 *soldi*, also called *galley halfpennies*. There are 12 *bagantines* to the *solde*.

At Corfu in Greece you will have black coins called *torneys*, – the rate is 24 to the *grosset*. In Venice you get six for a Venetian *solde*. At Corfu, Methóni and Cande in Crete a *solde* of *torneys* is only worth 4 *torneys*. You must therefore be careful and, if you purchase anything, ask whether they mean a *solde* of *torneys* or *of silver*. At Methóni you will only get 5 *torneys* to the *solde* on some occasions, but on other occasions more. At Cande you will get 5 *torneys*, but, on occasion, 6, according to the rate set by the king. There they have *besants* called *pepper*. A *pepper* is worth 32 *torneys*.

In Rhodes you will find *gilots*, also called *jouet[t]s*, and *aspers*. One *gilot* is worth one *jouet*; half a *jouet* is worth 32 Rhodian *dinars*. An *asper* is worth half a *jouet*, i.e. 16 *dinars*. The *jouet* and the [*j*]*asper* are Rhodian silver. The *asper* is a Turkish coin made of silver. A Venetian *ducat* is worth 19 *jouets* and [...] *dinars*.

In Cyprus you will find silver *groats* and half *groats* together with a different sort of *dinar* of black money and *besants*. Half a *besant* is worth 48 *dinars*. There are 7½ *besants* to a Venetian *ducat*. A Cypriot *groat* is worth 38 *dinars*. A Venetian *ducat* is worth 9½ *groats*. Half a *groat* is worth 19 *dinars*. A Venetian *groat* is worth 16 *dinars* there, while a *solde* is worth 4 *torneys*.

In Syria you will find *dremes* and half *dremes*. 2 *dremes* are worth 3 Venetian *groats*. One *dreme* is worth 6 Venetian *soldi*. A Venetian *ducat* is worth 19 *dremes*. Venetian *ducats*, *groats*, *grossets* and *soldi* are acceptable in Syria, that is to say in the Holy Land, but no other currency, except at a great disadvantage in the exchange.

This is the variety of coinage as you travel from England to Syria in the Holy Land.

COMMENTARY

It is not surprising that Wey, who was so often re-elected as one of the bursars at Eton, devotes the first chapter of his book to money. To the ordinary pilgrim with no special financial expertise the problems of money-changing would have been daunting. Once the pilgrim arrived at Venice, however, the task became a little easier. The Venetian ducat and its subdivisions sufficed for transactions in the Venetian colonies and trading posts throughout the eastern Mediterranean as well as the Holy Land. In Chapter 2 Wey advises the traveller to change up to 34 ducats into the smaller Venetian coins, *grotes*, *grossets* and *soldi*, "also called *galley halfpennies"*. From the figures he gives, one can work out that the commission charged by the money-changers in Venice was 5 per cent.

One immediate question arising from this chapter is, "Did Wey personally carry this weight of coins with him?" It would have been considerable. He does hint that he had a servant with him and in Chapters 2 and 9 he mentions the purchase of a lockable chest, or even two or three, to prevent the theft of valuables by the *galeotti* or by fellow pilgrims. During the fortnight ashore in the Holy Land the pilgrims could leave their chests aboard the galley with the *patronus* for safe keeping, but the question remains of how this weight of money was transported between Flanders and Venice. Although river barges were probably used for some of the way, there were long stretches where the pilgrims rode horses or mules with the risk of loss or theft.

Wey does not mention one answer to this difficulty, which Richard of Lincoln, who made his pilgrimage to Jerusalem in 1454, only four years before Wey's first visit, provides: "Who that will to Jerusalem go must make his change at London with the Lombards." As Bursar of Eton Wey was no novice in matters of finance and it is odd that he did not tell his readers about Letters of Credit, a service provided by the Lombards.

The following quotation illustrates the practical tone of this chapter: "When you change money at Bruges take *gilderns* with a round ball and a cross above; they will be good as far as Rome and are best all the way. Do not take any English gold with you from Bruges because you will be the loser in the exchange. Indeed, for most of the way they will not change it. All along the route they know Rhenish *gilderns* well, and with them you will suffer little or no loss."

This chapter mentions thirty-nine types of money. The full list is:

asper	bagantine	bayok	bemysch	besant
blaffard	bolendine	boliner	crowser	dinar
dreme	ducat	farlyng	ferar	galley halfpenny
gildern	gilot	groat	grosset	half-noble
hallard	jouett	katerine	liliar	
lylio	market	mite	myrkeny	noble
obol	penny	pepper	pichelyne [piccolini]	plack
pound	shilling	solde	styfer	torney

2

A Provision

SYNOPSIS

This is one of the three chapters (numbers 1, 2 and 3) written in Middle English. Most of it is to be found, in Latin, in Chapter 9, but neither version is an exact translation of the other. It contains much sensible advice and shows Wey as a seasoned traveller who knew how to keep himself comfortable, healthy and safe. The shrewdness in finance he exhibits in Chapter 1 appears here also.

TRANSLATION
(Roxburghe, pp. 4–7)

When a man is at Venice and purposeth by the grace of God to pass by the sea to the port of Jaffa in the Holy Land and so to the Sepulchre of Our Lord, Christ Jesus, in Jerusalem, he must dispose him a good provision in this wise.

First, if you go in a galley, make your contract with the *patron* in good time. Choose for yourself a place in the said galley on the highest deck, because below, in the lowest, it is right smouldering hot and stinking. If you are going to get a good place and be comfortable in the galley and be well looked after, you will have to pay forty ducats for your galley and for your meat and drink to the port of Jaffa and back to Venice. When you make the contract ensure that the *patron* is bound to you in the presence of the Doge or Lords of Venice in the sum of one hundred ducats to observe in full the agreement with you, namely:

That he will convey you to certain harbours on the way to refresh you and to get you fresh water and fresh bread and meat.

Further that he will not stay longer than three days at the most at any harbour without the agreement of all of you.

Further that he will not load on the vessel, either on the outward or homeward passage, any kind of merchandise without your consent which would inconvenience you in your berths and prolong the length of time at sea.

Further, if you so wish, that he will take you to Pula, 100 miles by water from Venice; from Pula to Corfu 600 miles; from Corfu to Methóni 300 miles; from Methóni to Candia [Herakleion] 300 miles; from Candia to Rhodes 300 miles; from Rhodes to Baffa [Paphos] in Cyprus 400 miles; and from Baffa to Port Jaffa 300 miles, and no further. (Make an agreement that you do not visit Famagusta in Cyprus at any price, for many Englishmen and others too have died because the air thereabouts is so corrupt and the water is bad as well.)

Further that your *patron* shall give you hot meat twice a day, at two meals, dinner in the morning and supper in the afternoon; that the wine that you will drink shall be good and your water fresh, provided that it is obtainable, and also biscuit.

You must also obtain for yourself and your servant, if you have one, three barrels each of a *quart*, – a *quart* holds ten gallons. Two of these barrels will serve for wine and the third for water. Put red wine in one barrel and keep it in reserve. If possible, do not broach it until the return passage, unless you have to because of illness or some other necessity. Remember especially, if you suffer from the flux, that, even if you were prepared to give twenty ducats for a barrel, you will not be able to get any after you have gone far past Venice. The other barrel will be useful to refill at the next port you come to when you have finished your drinking wine.

You must also purchase a chest to put your things in. If you have a servant with you get two or three. I would buy a chest as broad as the barrel is long. In one end of it I would have a lock and key and a little door. I would then place the barrel which I would use first at the end where the door is. If the galleymen or pilgrims get to it too many will tap it and drink it. They will also steal your water, which you would not often miss for your wine. In the other part of the chest you can put your bread, cheese, spices and everything else. You must arrange to have your biscuit with you because, even though you may eat at your *patron's* table, you will nevertheless have need to use your own victuals, bread, cheese, eggs, fruit and bacon, wine and other things to make a meal. On occasion you will get poor bread and wine and stinking water, and you will often be glad to eat your own supplies.

I advise you to take with you from Venice confections, confortatives, laxatives, restoratives, gingever, rice, figs, raisins, – both large and small, – which will give you much ease on the way, pepper, saffron, cloves and mace, – as few as you think necessary, – together with *powder duke* [*poudre douce*].

Take with you a small cauldron and frying pan, dishes, platters, wooden saucers, glass cups, a grater for bread and such essentials.

When you reach Venice you can buy a bed near St Mark's Church. You will pay three ducats for a feather bed, a mattress, two pillows, two pairs of sheets and a quilt. When you return bring the bed back to the man from whom you bought it and you will get a refund of one and a half ducats, even if it is broken and worn.

Change your money at Venice. Take at least thirty ducats in *grotes* and *grossines* with you. You will get twenty-eight and a half new *grossets* in Venice [*sc.* for one ducat]. Once you have passed Venice you will [only] get twenty-six or twenty-four *grossets* in some places. In addition take three or four ducats with you in *soldes* which are Venetian *galy* halfpence; one *grosset* is worth four shillings. Also take a ducat or two in *Torneys* with you from Venice; this is brass money from Candia and it will be acceptable for purchases all along the way. In Venice, Methóni and Candia you will often get eight for a shilling; but elsewhere four, five or six at the most for a shilling.

Buy a cage for half a dozen hens or chickens to have with you in the galley; you will often have need of them. Buy half a bushel of Venetian millet seed for them as well.

Take a barrel with you as a close stool for your chamber in the galley; it is very necessary if you are so sick that you cannot come into the open air.

When you come to harbour towns you can buy eggs, if you wish. Provided you get ashore quickly you can get them good and cheap. They are very good in the galley either fried with olive oil or as a *caudel*. When you come to harbour towns, if you are going to stay there three days, get ashore quickly to secure lodgings before the others, because they will be taken quickly. Similarly if there is any good food there you must be quicker than the others. When you come to the various harbours be wary of different fruits in case they do not suit you and cause a bloody flux. If an Englishman gets that sickness it is a marvel if he escapes it and does not die.

When you reach the port of Jaffa take with you, when you land from the galley, two gourds, one with wine and the other water. Each of these should hold a *potel* at least because you will not get any more until you reach Ramys. The wine there is weak and expensive. At Jerusalem it is good and expensive. Make sure that the *patron* takes charge of your kit in the galley until you return. You will stay in the Holy Land thirteen or fourteen days. Take good care of your knives and the other small things which you carry on your person. The

Saracens will walk with you, talking and being friendly, but they will rob you of anything you have which they can manage to steal.

When you hire your donkey at the port of Jaffa do not be too far behind your companions. If you get there early you can choose the best mule or donkey and you do not pay any more for the best than for the worst. You must give your assman a tip of a *groat* or a Venetian *grosset*. Do not be too far ahead or too far behind your companions for fear of *screws*.

When you ride to the River Jordan take with you from Jerusalem bread, wine, water, hard cheese and hard eggs and such other supplies as you have for two days, since there is no one, either there or on the way, to sell you food. Fill one of your bottles or gourds with wine for when you come from the River Jordan to Mount Quarantine. If you go up to the place where Our Lord Jesus Christ fasted forty days and forty nights, it is extremely hot and very high. When you come down again, on no account drink any water. Rest for a little and then eat bread and drink clean wine without water. After that extreme heat water produces a great flux or a fever or both, and so a man may perhaps lose his life as a result.

Remember all these things written above and, with God's grace, both going and coming, you will speed well on your journey to please God and to increase your bliss, which Jesus grant you. Amen.

COMMENTARY

This chapter may be an early draft later incorporated in Chapter 9. It is likely that the English one was written first because it gives the full list of ports to be visited – that is, Venice, Pula, Corfu, Methóni, Candia, Rhodes, Paphos and Jaffa – while in the Latin version the list runs: Venice, Pula, Corfu, Methóni, Candia, Paphos and Jaffa, omitting the stages Candia to Rhodes and Rhodes to Paphos.

Wey's advice falls into clear categories. First is the importance of a proper contract between the pilgrim and the *patronus* which specifies what accommodation and food the pilgrim will have on the voyage and the obligations of the *patronus* and his crew to their passengers. Then there is a list of what food and equipment the pilgrim should provide for himself. Next follow useful hints on what to do when the galley reaches a harbour and finally some advice on how to survive the rigours of the tour in the Holy Land.

This chapter provides a clear idea of some of the hazards faced by the pilgrim. "Choose for yourself a place in the said galley on the highest deck, because below, in the lowest, it is right smouldering hot and stinking. If you are going to get a good place and be comfortable and well looked after, you will have to pay forty ducats for your galley and for your meat and drink to the port of Jaffa and back to Venice." Each of the two Venetian galleys which sailed for the Holy Land in May carried about one hundred pilgrims. Prescott (*Jerusalem Journey*, p. 59) describes the pilgrims' cabin as "a kind of hall where the berth space of each pilgrim was chalked out on the deck; one and a half feet were looked on as a fair allowance. In two long lines at the feet of the pilgrim stood each man's chest."

The clauses in the contract stipulating the route and the maximum duration of the stay in each intermediate port and restricting commercial merchandise were necessary to protect the pilgrims' interests and comfort. The crew of the galley, the *galeotti*, traditionally indulged in private trading: "When the galley entered a port they took [their] merchandise ashore and established a sort of fair" (Newett, *Canon Pietro Casola's Pilgrimage to Jerusalem*, pp. 58 and 161).

Apart from barrels for wine and water and chests for such victuals as bread, cheese, eggs, fruit and bacon, the pilgrim was advised to provide himself with comfortable bedding:

> When you reach Venice you can buy a bed near St Mark's Church.
> You will pay three ducats for a feather bed, a mattress, two pillows,
> two pairs of sheets and a quilt. When you return bring the bed back
> to the man from whom you bought it and you will get a refund of
> one and a half ducats, even if it is broken and worn.

Richard of Lincoln, travelling in 1454, gives the same prices as Wey: forty ducats for the passage with board and one and a half ducats for bedding.

The mention of equipment for a "servant" suggests that Wey was not travelling alone.

Wey has helpful advice for pilgrims going ashore between Venice and Jaffa:

> When you come to harbour towns you can buy eggs, if you wish.
> Provided you get ashore quickly you can get them good and cheap.
> When you come to harbour towns, if you are going to stay there
> three days, get ashore quickly to secure lodgings before the others,

because they will be taken quickly. Similarly, if there is any good food there you must be quicker than the others. When you come to the various harbours be wary of different fruits in case they do not suit you and cause a bloody flux. If an Englishman gets that sickness it is a marvel if he escapes it and does not die.

Wey gives a special warning about Famagusta: "Make an agreement that you do not visit Famagusta in Cyprus at any price, for many Englishmen and others too have died because the air thereabouts is so corrupt and the water is bad as well." On the outward and return voyages he made between Venice and Jaffa in 1458 and 1462 William Wey only visited Famagusta once, on the return from Jaffa in 1458. Then he landed at Salinis (near the modern Larnaca) on 8 July and stayed in Cyprus until 14 July. On the other three journeys he landed at Paphos. In the Middle Ages Famagusta was notoriously unhealthy because of the proximity of a large marsh. Nicole de Martoni, who visited the island in 1394, refers to this and also to the large number of courtesans to be found there. Another visitor, Ludolf, a priest from Westphalia, who visited Cyprus between 1336 and 1341, says: "Drugs are as common there as bread is here and are sold as commonly. There are very many wealthy courtesans."

Two more excerpts show that thieves were another nuisance, both on the galley and ashore:

> You must also purchase a chest to put your things in. … In one end of it I would have a lock and key and a little door. I would then place the barrel which I would use first at the end where the door is. If the galleymen or pilgrims get to it too many will tap it and drink it. They will also steal your water …

> [I]n the Holy Land … [t]ake good care of your knives and the other small things which you carry on your person. The Saracens will walk with you, talking and being friendly, but they will rob you of anything you have which they can manage to steal.

Purses and knives, being suspended from the belt, were especially vulnerable to "cutpurses". In Chapter 15 Wey describes how a Breton robbed a Compostellan pilgrim by this means: *Unus de navi nostra habuit bursam absissam ab zona sua*, "One from our ship had his purse cut from his belt."

Where Wey stayed is an interesting question. The present writer has followed Wey's routes across Europe from the English Channel to Venice and down the Adriatic coast. In many of the places Wey names there was a Franciscan house where he might have stayed. Santo Brasca, a pilgrim in 1480, wrote: "I must tell you that in the Levant there is no comfortable lodging to be found, whatever you would be willing to pay for it, except in the monasteries of the observant friars of St Francis" (Newett, *Canon Pietro Casola's Pilgrimage*, p. 397). It is likely that priests, like William Wey and his two companions, would have been made especially welcome since, as Prescott says, "To members of other religious orders the Franciscans were very ready to show hospitality" (*Jerusalem Journey*, p. 119.) When noblemen went ashore they were frequently entertained and given accommodation by family friends or those of similar social status (Mitchell, *The Spring Voyage*, p. 77).

3

In This Book Contained is the Way to Jerusalem and the Holy Places in That Same Country

SYNOPSIS

This chapter consists of a poem, in Middle English, 352 lines long in 176 rhyming couplets. It deals with the sites Wey visited in the Holy Land in 1458 and describes in Latin prose in Chapter 7. In Chapter 7 he adds a few details of the voyage from Venice to Jaffa, and, once in the Holy Land, some account of the help given by the Franciscans, the distances travelled by donkey and the dimensions of important sites. These features do not appear in the poem.

TRANSLATION
(Roxburghe, pp 8–19)

From Venice to Port Jaff by the sea
It is two thousand mile and hundreds three;
And in that sea there is a place
Where the whale swallowed Jonas.
5   There is in the same, beside that,
A stone that Saint Peter fished at.
Also at Jaffa there was a place
Where Dorcas from death raised was.
From thence to Ramys we do ride,
10   And there two days we do abide.
In the city of Ramys born was
Joseph that took Christ from the cross.
There dwelt also, without strife,
Helkana and Anne, his right good wife.
15   Two mile from the city of Ramys
Is a city called Lydda Diaspolis.

33

There was a church and a devout place,
Where Saint George beheaded was.
In a place to that church nigh
20   Aeneas was healed of his palsy.

From Ramys we ride to Jerusalem

By the way to Jerusalem, as I you tell,
Is the sepulchre of Samuel,
The which is nigh to the castle of Emaus,
There Jesus spake with Saint Lucas.
25   Also at that castle and that place
Is buried Saint Cleophas.
Thence go we forth and rightly
By Sylo and Abaramathy;
And, when we be past that place,
30   We shall see Jerusalem in short space.
Then kneel we down upon our knee,
When we that holy city see;
For to all that thither come
Is give and grant full remission.
35   Before the temple door lieth a stone,
That Our Lord Jesus fell upon;
For he bare His cross with so great woe,
That the manhood might no further go.

Holy Places within the Temple of Jerusalem

The first place within the door
40   Is Our Lord's holy sepulchre.
The next that is without failing,
Is a chapel of Our Lady where friars doth sing.
There was Our Lady in her prayer
When Christ was risen from his sepulchre,
45   And He full lowly, when he come thither,

Said unto her, "Hail, Holy Mother".
And in that same chapel is
Of the pillar a great piece
That Christ Jesu was bound unto,
50 When Pilate him beat, and wrought him woe.
There is in that place a stone also
That a dead man by the cross was raised from.
Without the chapel door,
Right in the temple floor,
55 There is a stone, round and plain,
Where Jesus as a gardener met with Magdalene.
In that stone by Christ was made
An hole wherein he put his spade.
Beyond, as pilgrims gone,
60 They find two holes in a stone;
In those holes Christ's legs were put,
And with chains fast knit.
There is by a vault within,
Which is called Christ's prison.
65 Next that in our procession
Is a place of great devotion.
There at the dice knights began play
Who should bear Christ's tunicle away.
Beyond there is a pillar also,
70 Upon which Christ sat naked though;
Where the knights, to his scorn,
Set on His head a crown of thorn.
Beyond is a chapel, it is right low,
Twenty pace down as men it know;
75 In that chapel under the ground
There was the holy cross found.
There is full remission in that place
To all men that thither go for grace.
The next is of fifteen steps high,
80 Is called the Mount of Calvary.
There is more pardon in that hill,
Than any Christian man can tell;

For all the pardon that is at Rome
There is the well, and thence it come.
85   The mortice is a foot of breadth,
Who will mete it with a thread.
There beside is a great rock,
That for Christ's death asunder broke.
Beneath the mount, as I you tell,
90   There is a little chapel;
The name thereof is Golgotha.
There be buried conquerors two;
The one is Godfrey duke of Bolonia,
The other king Baldwin called also.
95   Also in the temple is a place,
As all pilgrims may see,
Where Mary saw Christ Jesu, his face,
When he lay dead upon her knee.
Also there nigh to man's feet
100   Is the midst of the world set.

Holy Places in the city Jerusalem

Furthermore in that city
Be pilgrimages both fair and free.
The first tokening of all
Is at the corner of a wall;
105   There Jesus met with His Mother Mary,
There sorrowed together both He and she;
And there the women of Jerusalem
Wept on Christ when that he came.
Beyond that, in a street,
110   Is the school of Our Lady sweet.
Beside that, in a temple small,
That sometime was Saint Anne's hall,
A little forth in the way,
Is Herod's hall as I you say.
115   Beside that is a place,

Where Mary Magdalene had great grace:
Men calleth that Simon leper's hall,
That Christ forgave Magdalene her sins all.
Beyond that there is a place than
120   Where Dives lived, the rich man.
Two stones there be above men's head,
And be laid in a wall on high:
Upon them Christ stood judged to be dead,
And to be crucified at Calvary.
125   Now leave we a city full of sin,
And go forth by the gate of Saint Stephen.
So come we to that same place
Where Saint Stephen stoned was;
Right there by is Torrent Cedron,
130   Where the tree lay that Christ died on.

Holy Places in the Vale of Jehoshophat

In the midst of the vale, as I you tell,
There is a fair round chapel.
Surely in that same place
Our Blessed Lady buried was;
135   A cave under earth there is fast by
Where Christ knelt verily
When He sweat both blood and water,
And made His prayer unto His Father,
Nigh unto that place He was arrested
140   And grievously shaken by His holy breast.

Holy Places in the Mount of Olivet

The Apostles in a close by slept together
When Jesus prayed unto His Father,
And thereby is a great stone
There Our Lady girdle fell upon

145　When she was brought to her dear Son
　　In joy and bliss with Him to live.
　　In that mount is a rock and a place
　　Where Christ with His Apostles was,
　　And as He stood among them
150　He wept upon Jerusalem.
　　Beyond that a place we sought
　　Where an angel Our Lady a palm brought
　　Afore three days that she should die
　　And come to the joy of Heaven on high.
155　There a little is not far thence
　　Where men may have full indulgence.
　　Then go we up as men may see
　　To the town or place of Galilee.
　　There is a chapel that standeth right high
160　From the which Jesus to Heaven did fly,
　　The steps of His feet be there in a stone,
　　Which men may see that thither have gone.
　　Further we have gone by sufferance
　　And see where Saint Pelage did her penance,
165　And nigh thereby to your great meed
　　The twelve Apostles made the *Creed*.
　　A little beyond, and not full far,
　　Christ Jesu made the *Paternoster*.
　　In the descent of that hill
170　Christ preached unto his people;
　　Unto Egypt anon to go
　　With the child Jesus and His Mother also.
　　Without Bethlehem a place there is
　　Where angels sang *Gloria in Excelsis*.
175　From thence at Thene two mile and more
　　At a castle was Amos the prophet born.

Holy Places in the Mountains of Jury

In the mountains of Jury is a place
Where Philip baptised Eunuch of Candace;
In the mountains also a place is set
180 Where Mary and Elizabeth met.
Our Lady *Magnificat* there did say
To their both hearts greatest joy.
When Herod sought to slay Saint John
Then was he there received of a stone.
185 By there too is the place
Where John circumcised was,
And high in a chapel, as we do read,
Zachary *Benedictus* made indeed.
Near to Jerusalem John was born
190 In a place that is now forlorn.
Nigh thereto is Simeon's place
In whose arms Christ named was.
Furthermore in our way friars we saw,
And see where Christ's Cross did grew.

Holy Places to *Flum* Jordan

195 Beyond Betany, as I you tell,
Joachim with shepherds did dwell
Forty days and forty night,
Until he saw an angel bright.
Beyond is a wilderness of quarantine
200 Where Christ with fasting His body did pine,
In that holy place, as we rede,
The devil would had of stones bread;
Above that wilderness right far and high
The fiend to Christ showed *regna mundi*,
205 And said "If thou wilt me worship do
All these shalt thou have thy lordship to".
Beneath is a flood, Marath it is,

That Samuel turned from bitterness.
At Jericho Zache did dwell,
210 There is the place as I you tell.
Beyond is a monastery of Saint John
Where he baptised Christ and many on.
Two mile from the Dead Sea,
In Jordan Pilgrims washed be;
215 In the other side of the *flum*
Was the monastery of Saint Jerome.

Holy Places in Bethany

At Bethany in an old castle
Is Lazarus' tomb made full well;
Also at Bethany is a stone
220 Upon which Martha kneeled on,
And said to Christ, with mild cheer,
"My brother had not died and you had been here."
Martha there a house had and Magdalene fair,
Where they did Our Lord good service and cheer,
225 In meat, drink, and lodging also,
Until He gan to His passion go.
Now have I told you of the places all
That pilgrims seeketh both great and small.
Further we go unto a stone
230 There Our Lady rest upon.
There be also nine caves beside
Where the Apostles did them hide
At the time [th]at Christ did die,
For they dared not Him come nigh.
235 The place that of this mount is near
Is where Saint James Younger did fast,
Therein is buried Zachary,
Son to the bishop Barathy.

Holy Places in the Vale of Syloe

	There is a well a little thence
240	There Our Lady Christ's clothes did cleanse;
	Above that is a water by it one
	That healed the blind man.
	Fast by, against the law,
	Manasses to death did Isaiah saw,
245	And high from thence a field there is,
	Called *Ager Sanguinis*,
	But for them that Latin lack
	It is called Acheldemac.

Holy Places in the Mount of Syon

	There is a church also fast by
250	Called the House of Cursed Counsel certainly
	The first place where Jews would have bringed
	Our Lady's body when it should be buried;
	The second where St Peter wept
	When Christ in His Passion was kept;
255	The third where Christ was brought
	To fore Anaias and set by naught
	From that place led He was
	To the House of Caiaphas,
	There blindfolded and bound
260	To a pillar that is all round.
	In that hill a church there is
	Called the Church of St Francis,
	A fair church soothly to say,
	Where friars sayth Mass every day.
265	When that church was great and holy,
	It was called Holy Mary of Ladder to Heaven by.
	At the altar of that church
	Jesu did great works work;

There gave He His body and blood,
270   To His Apostles that were right good,
Under the form of wine and bread,
And this us to take to our good speed.
Beneath the church and this altar
King David lieth that made the Psalter.
275   Nigh to this altar the Apostles sat
When our Lord Christ did wash their feet;
By then this altar even by
There were in number one hundred and twenty
There received they the Holy Ghost
280   That very God is of might most.
Beneath the cloister as men do sit
There be two doors that were shut,
Through Christ entered, as He may now,
And to His Apostles said, "Peace be to you."
285   In a hole of the treasury is also
Of the pillar that Christ was bound unto.
At the east end of that place
Stephen the martyr buried was;
There also the water was heat
290   With the which Christ washed Peter's feet.
There also was roasted a lamb
Which to Christ's supper came.
At that church's west end
Mary her prayers to Heaven did send.
295   In the north side is a great stone
Where Christ stood and preached upon.
Upon a rock thereby unhid
Our Lady stood when Christ preached;
And nigh by unto this place
300   Saint Mathew Apostle chosen was.
From thence a cast of a quoit and somewhat less
Mary dwelt and heard her Mass.
There is thereby also a stead
Where they smote off Saint James's head;
305   And thereby as men may see,

Our Lord to Marys said *Avete*
Fast also that place by
Our Lady looked to Calvary.

Pilgrimages to Bethlehem

Without Jerusalem not full far
310   The three kings saw the star;
Beyond that there is a place
Where Elijah by an angel fed was;
Nigh thereby Elijah hid himself right well
For he would not be slain by Jezebel.
315   Also further where Jacob lay
From earth to Heaven a ladder he saw.
In the right hand after our lore
Is the place where Elijah was bore;
There beyond, as I you tell,
320   Is the sepulchre of fair Rachel;
Nigh to Bethlehem marked was
Where Mary descended off her ass.

Holy Places in Bethlehem

In a deep chapel, tell you I will,
Where Saint Jerome translated the Bible;
325   Also places where he said Mass,
And lay full hard and nothing soft.
By this there is a place right near
Of Innocents slain the sepulchre.
In the north side of the chancel without
330   Kings of their coffers took jewels out,
And offered to Jesu, heaven King.
Gold, myrrh and incense, right low kneeling.
Under the chancel a chapel there is
Of fifteen steps in deepness,

335   At which east end Our Lord was born
         To save mankind that was forlorn.
         Thereby there is a church of stone
         In the which Our Lord was laid on.
         The star also the kings did lead
340   Fell down in an hole to that stead.
         In the south aisle is a stone
         That Jesu was circumcised upon.
         Besides this place, and somewhat nigh,
         An angel bade Joseph to hie;
345   The which be of great devotion,
         And is granted to have great pardon.
         To eighteen places marked with crosses
         Full remission of all sins.
         And to all other holy places
350   Is granted seven year and seven Lents.
         This pardon to have God send us grace,
         And in Heaven hereafter to see His face. Amen.

COMMENTARY AND NOTES

In Chapters 4, 6 and 7 the pilgrimage to Bethlehem is described *before* the visit to the mountains of Judaea, the River Jordan and Bethany. In Chapter 3, however, the poem describes the visit to Bethlehem *after* that to the mountains of Judaea, the River Jordan and Bethany.

The 1462 pilgrimage to the Holy Land, described in Chapter 9, did not include a visit to the River Jordan or the Mount of Temptation because of the political situation, *Sic quod peregrini illo tempore non poterant ire ad Jordanem neque ad montem Quarantene.*

Almost every place or event in the poem of Chapter 3 appears in Chapter 6 *materia* 8 and Chapter 7. The notes below indicate places where there are significant differences between the narratives of Chapter 3 on the one hand and Chapters 6 and 7 on the other. In these Wey revises or corrects something he wrote in the earlier narrative, perhaps because he decided, after reflection, that information he was given at the site required further thought.

l. 52   The experiment to prove which is the True Cross. In Chapter 3 the corpse raised is that of a man, in Chapter 7 it is that of a woman.

l. 117   The House of Simon. In Chapter 3 he is called "Simon the Leper", but in Chapters 6 and 7 the house is that of "Simon the Pharisee". "Simon the Leper" appears in Chapters 6 and 7 in a house in Bethany.

l. 170   There appears to be a fault in the text after line 170. Lines 171–6 do not make sense in their present position. They should appear after line 344, when they would follow the sequence, which appears in Chapters 6 and 7, in the section "Pilgrimages outside Bethlehem",

    (a) the angel's warning to Joseph;

    (b) the *Gloria in excelsis Deo*;

    (c) Thene Castle and Amos.

l. 276   In Chapter 3 the sequence of locations visited and the events associated with them is:

    (a) Christ washes the Disciples' feet, (John 13:5) etc.

    (b) the meeting of the 120 which led to the selection of Matthias (Acts 1:15)

    (c) the appearance to Thomas (John 20:26).

    In Chapters 6 and 7 the sequence runs:

    (a) Christ washes the Disciples' feet;

    (b) the descent of the Holy Ghost at Pentecost (Acts 2:1);

    (c) the appearance to Thomas.

4

Mnemonic Verses

SYNOPSIS

This is the strangest chapter in *The Itineraries*. It consists of twenty-nine Latin hexameters, divided into thirteen sections, which deal with various sites visited by pilgrims in Jerusalem and elsewhere in the Holy Land. The scansion of the verses does not always measure up to the Vergilian canon, and individual words are frequently and severely abbreviated. The result looks like a code, but, by giving a superscript gloss in Latin over each word or abbreviation, Wey explains what each syllable or group of syllables means.

TRANSLATION
(Roxburghe, pp. 19–25)

The Number of Days of the Pilgrims' Visit in Jerusalem

1st day at Jaffa	2nd day to Ramath	3rd to Lidda	4th to Jerusalem
Ad Jaff prima via	*se Ram*	*ter Lidda*	*Jeru quart*

5th day to the Stations	6th to Bethlehem	7th day to the Mountains of Judaea
Quint sta	*Beth sexta*	*Sep ad montana Judee*

8th day they stay in Jerusalem	9th to the Jordan	10th day to Bethany
Oc remanere Jeru	*non Jurdan*	*decima Betha*

11th they stay in Jerusalem	12th to Ramatha	13th to Joppa and Galea on the way home
Unde Jeru	*duo Ram*	*via tercia decima Joppen*

The Names of the Holy Places in the Holy Land Sought by Pilgrims

1st place	2nd place	3rd place	4th place	5th place	6th place	7th place	8th place
Jaff	Lid	Emaus	Jehoshophat	Oliveti	Sylo	Syon	tem

9th Road to Bethlehem	10th Bethlehem	11th Bethlehem	12th to the Mountains	13th to the Jordan	14th to Bethany
Et via	Beth	extra	Montan	Jordan	Bethania

The Sites of Miracles from Jaffa to Jerusalem

The rock on which St Peter stood to fish	The place where Dorcas was brought back to life	The town of Lydda where Saint George was beheaded
1	2	3
Pe petra pis	Dorkas	Geor

In Lydda Aeneas was cured of paralysis by St Peter	Emaus Castle where Christ was recognized by the Disciples in the breaking of bread
4	5
Enea paral	Emaus

Betulia, the town of the widow Judith	The place where Judith beheaded Holophernes	Anathot, the town of the prophet Jeremiah	The place where Hely stayed
6	7	8	9
Betulie	decoll	Anathot	Sylo

The town called after Aramathia
10
cum Joseph Ara

Holy Places at the Stations in Jerusalem

The stone, marked with crosses, on which Christ fell with His Cross	The road along which Christ went to His Passion	The house of the rich man who refused to give crumbs to Lazarus	Where Christ fell with His Cross
1	2	3	4
Lap	stat	di	trivium [not trimum]

The place where the women wept for Christ	The place where the widow, or Veronica, placed a handkerchief on Christ's face	The place where the Most Blessed Mary fainted
5	6	7
Flent	sudar	sincopizavit

The gate through which Christ passed to His Passion		The pool in which the sick were healed at the time of Christ		The stones on which Christ stood when He was condemned to death	
8		9		10	
Por	+	pis	+	lap	+

The place where the Blessed Mary went to school		The house of Pilate		The house of Herod	The house of Symon, the Pharisee
11		12		13	14
que scola	+	domus	+	Her	Symonis pharysei

The place of birth of the Blessed Mary	The Temple of Our Lord		The door through which Mary went when she was purified		The pinnacle of the temple from which St James was thrown	
15	16		17		18	
Nati	+ tem	+	porta	+	Ja	+

The tomb in the Temple where St Symeon was buried		The Temple of Solomon		The Golden Gate through which Christ entered, seated on an ass		The gate of St Stephen
19		20		21		22
Sepul	+	Sal	+	aurea	+	Stepha

The place where St Stephen was stoned	The brook Cedron		The tomb of the Blessed Virgin Mary	The cave where Christ sweated blood	The garden where Christ was betrayed
23 [sic]	2		3	4	5
Steph	+ torrente	+	sepul	cavernula	tradicionis

The garden where Peter cut off the ear		The garden where John, Peter and James slept		The garden where Christ said to the Apostles, "Sleep and Rest"		The place where the Virgin gave her girdle to Thomas
6		7		8		9
Auri	+	Jo	+	dormi	+	cin

The place where Christ stood and wept over the city		The place where the angel gave the green palm to Mary		The place where Galilee once was	
10		11		12	
Fletus	+	palma	+	Galile	+

The places where they can see Holy Sites in Jerusalem		The Chapel of the Ascension of Our Lord, Jesus Christ		The Chapel of Saint Pelagia	The place called Bethfage
13		14		15	16
Indulgens	+	Ascen	+	Pel	+ Beth

The place where the Apostles composed the *Creed*		The place where Christ taught the *Our Father*		The place where Christ preached		The place where the Blessed Virgin sat when she visited the Holy Places
17		18		19		20
Cre	+	*Pa*	+	*Pre*	+	*la Marie*

The cave where Christ appeared to St James		The place where St Barathias was buried		The small caves where the Disciples hid at the time of the Passion
20 [*sic*]		21		22
Apparet Jacobo	+	*Sepul*	+	*antrum discipulorum*

Holy Places in the Valley of Syloe + +

The spring where Mary washed Christ's clothes before her Purification		The spring where the man, blind from birth, received his sight		The place where Isaiah was sawn
1		2		3
Fons	+ +	*nat Sylo*	+	*secant*

The place called Acheldemak		The caverns where Holy Christians performed penance		The place called the House of Evil Counsel
4		5		6
Achelde	+	*cavernule*	+	*Consi*

Holy Places on Mount Syon + +

The place where the Jews wanted to seize Mary's body		The place where Peter wept after his denial of Christ		The house of Annas, the high priest	The house of Caiaphas, the high priest
1		2		3	4
Rap	+	*Petri fletus*	+	*An*	*Cay*

The church on Mount Syon where Christ ate with the Apostles		The place there where He washed the Apostles' feet		The chapel where the Holy Spirit appeared in tongues of fire
5		6		7
Ce	+ +	*Pe*	+	*Spiritus almus*

The chapel which Christ entered though the doors were closed		Part of the column to which Christ was bound	The place where the Blessed Virgin Mary used to pray		The stone on which Christ preached
9 [*sic*]		10	11		12
Clausa	+	*columpna*	*rogat*	+	*in pre*

The stone where the Most Blessed Mary sat when Christ preached		The tomb of David, Solomon and the other kings
13		14
Pre	+ +	Se + Salamonis

The place where the Paschal Lamb was roasted for Our Lord's Supper	The place where the water was heated to wash the Apostles' feet	The place where St Stephen and others were buried
15	16	17
Agnus +	et unda +	Stepha

The place where St John celebrated Mass before the Blessed Mary	The house where the Blessed Mary used to live	The place where Matthias was chosen to be an Apostle
18	19	20
Mis + +	domus +	fuit elec

The place where the cock crowed thrice	The place where Saint James was beheaded	The place where Christ said "Hail" to the women	The place where the Blessed Virgin looked back at Calvary
21	22	23	24
Gallus +	decollat +	"avete" +	respice Calva

Holy Places in The Holy Temple of the Christians

The chapel where Christ appeared to His mother after the Resurrection	The column where Christ was scourged	On which the woman was restored to life by the Cross of Christ
I	2	3
Cap +	columpna +	lapis +

The stone with the hole where Christ put His spade	The stone with two holes in which Christ was imprisoned	The altar where they cast lots for Christ's tunic
4	5	6
Petra +	carceris + +	altaque sortes

The deep pit in which the Holy Cross was hidden	The column on which He sat when He was crowned	The hole where they placed Christ's cross
7	8	9
Fossa + +	corona + +	fora

The stone broken at the departure of Christ's Spirit	The great stone on which they anointed Christ Jesus	The tomb of Christ	The place which divides the centre of the world
10	II	12	13
Frac +	mir la +	sepul	mediumque

Holy Places on the Road to Bethlehem + +

The place where the star appeared to the Wise Men	The church of Elijah	The place where Elijah hid	Jacob's Ladder	Rachel's Tomb
1	2	3	4	5
Stell +	*Hely* +	*latet*	*sancta*	*Rachel*

The place of Elijah's birth	Where Mary dismounted from the donkey
6	7
Hel +	*des asinoque*
+	+

Holy Places in Bethlehem

The chapel of Saint Jerome	The tomb of the Innocents	The place where the treasures of the kings were opened	The holy place of the Nativity	The place of the manger of Our Lord Jesus
1	2	3	4	5
Jero +	*sepul*	*tezau* +	*Nati* +	*pre*

The altar where Jesus Christ was circumcised	The place where the star was plunged into the material from which it was made
6	7
Cir + +	*quoque stella* + + +

Holy Places outside Bethlehem

The place where the angel told Joseph to flee into Egypt	The place where the angel appeared to the shepherds	The place where the prophet Amos was born
1	2	3
Fugit in Egiptum Joseph +	*patet angelus* +	*Amos*

Holy Places in the Mountains + + +

The spring where Candaces' eunuch was baptised	The place where Mary greeted Elizabeth	Where Mary composed the *Magnificat*
1	2	3
Fons + +	*El* + +	*Magnificat*

The rock which opened to receive the Baptist from Herod's executioners	The place of the Baptist's circumcision	The place where Zecharias prophesied the *Benedictus*
4	5	6
Petra + +	*Cir* + +	*bene*

The place of birth of St John, the Baptist		The house of Simeon who held Christ in his arms			The place where the Holy Cross grew	
7		8			[9]	
Nat	+ +	*Symeon*	+ +		*et crux*	

Holy Places near the Jordan + + +

The place where Joachim was with the shepherds before the birth of Virgin		The Mount of Forty Days where "Command that these stones"		The Mount above the Forty Days where the devil showed the kingdom
1		2		3
Pastori Joachim	+	*mons quarentena*	+	*super mon*

The house of Zachaeus in Jericho		The monastery of the Baptist		The River Jordan	The desert of Jerome	The monastery of St Jerome
4		5		6	7	8
Zacheus	+	*baptist*	+	*Jordanus*	*Jero*	*monast*

Holy Places in Bethany + + + +

The tomb where Lazarus was raised from the dead		The stone where Martha met Christ		The home of Martha and Mary	
1		2		3	
Lazarus in tumba	+	*Martha currente*	+	*Maria*	+

COMMENTARY

Since the verses which form Chapter 4 appear again in Chapters 5 and 6 below, any particular comment arising from them is made in the notes to those chapters.

These twenty-nine lines are described by the Roxburghe editor as a *memoria technica* "in the most unmelodious hexameters". Later he dubs them a record of "medieval superstition and barbarous Latinity". This is unfair to William Wey and fails to understand his purpose.

Wey's use of Latin hexameters as a mnemonic is paralleled elsewhere. Several fifteenth-century manuscripts survive, some of them from Exeter, which show how Latin was taught in English schools when William Wey was a boy (Orme, *Medieval Schools*). Short tracts dealing with aspects and problems of grammar or syntax were written in verse to make them easier to learn. This device was continued in Kennedy's *Revised Latin Primer* up to the twentieth century. The prosody of some of the hexameters contained in grammar books produced after 1100 is as rough as

Wey's. One line, quoted by Orme, which deals with the paradigms of first-declension Latin nouns, runs:

Quintus in a dabitur post es tamen e reperitur.

The appearance of a quadrisyllable at the end of the line is as un-Vergilian as some of Wey's lines.

Alexander de Villa Dei, Villedieu in Normandy, wrote his *doctrinale* in about 1200. This is a verse treatise, used to teach Latin grammar and composition, consisting of 2,650 hexameter lines. This or similar teaching manuals would have been familiar to Wey. Alexander not only uses Latin hexameter verses as aids to remember grammatical rules, but he also employs abbreviations of Latin words to fit the scansion, even at the cost of false quantities which would not be acceptable in a hexameter of the "Golden Age". An example which is highly reminiscent of William Wey's lines is:

Cre, do, se, nex, iu, sta, la, mi, ve, to, fri, pli, ne, cu, so.

This line is in a code that uses only the first few letters of those Latin verbs of the first conjugation which form their perfect tense in an irregular way. *Cre, do* and *se* represent respectively *crepo, domo* and *seco*, while *iu, sta, la* stand for *iuvo, sto* and *lavo*. The full list appears in Kennedy's *Latin Primer*.

Hexameters as a mnemonic were used not only in schools but in higher studies also. Such a poem, which would have been familiar to students of logic, deals with the various moods of categorical syllogisms. It commences with the line: *Barbara, celarent, darii, ferioque prioris*, where the position of the vowels in each word is significant in the analysis of various propositions.

The code which Wey uses in Chapter 4 is a personal one and he did not intend his mnemonic lines to be used by anyone but himself. *The Itineraries* contains several layers of composition. Straight repetitions are noted elsewhere. The most obvious example is the repetition of Chapter 2 in Chapter 9. Another is the "Ten Questions and their Solutions" which Wey enumerates and answers in Chapter 9 and again in Chapter 11.

Wey's aim was to describe his pilgrimage in the Holy Land. The exigencies of the journey meant that he would not have carried with him a vast quantity of stationery. His "journal" would have consisted of the tersest of notes reinforced by his memory and biblical scholarship. The twenty-nine hexameter lines of Chapter

4 were probably the earliest draft of his proposed book, later forming the basis of Chapter 5, *materia* 6 ("The things which we shall do each day while we are in the Holy Land"), Chapter 5, *materia* 7 ("The names of the holy places which are visited by pilgrims in the Holy Land") and Chapter 6, *materia* 8 ("Various holy places to be visited by pilgrims with the indulgences granted at these sites, together with verses composed about these places").

In these three *materiae* Wey deploys his mnemonic lines again, using six of the lines in Chapter 5 and twenty-three in Chapter 6. He introduces them with the words, "So that the things which we shall do in these days may be held in the mind I have composed these verses" – *ordinavi versus*. This is one of the few occasions when Wey uses the first person and shows that the device was his own.

The following is an example of one of the lines (complete with a false quantity!), and Wey's superscript explanation. A translation of the latter is given below.

locus ubi S. Stephanus erat lapidatus	*torrens Cedron*	*sepulchrum B. Marie virginis*	*caverna ubi Christus sudavit sanguinem*	*ortus ubi Christus erat traditus.*
Steph	*torrente*	*sepul*	*cavernula*	*tradicionis*
The place where St Stephen was stoned	The brook Cedron	The tomb of the Blessed Virgin Mary	The cave where Christ sweated blood	The garden where Christ was betrayed

5

Reasons for Pilgrimage to the Holy Land

SYNOPSIS

In Chapters 5 and 6 Wey lists ten *materiae*, a technical term in logic which meant "material causes" – that is, "basic reasons" – for pilgrimage, and then elaborates each separately. *Materiae* 1 to 7 appear in the fifth folio and numbers 8 to 10 in the sixth folio of The *Itineraries*. The information given in *materiae* 6 to 10 is repeated, in some places *in extenso* and verbatim, in the pilgrimage narrative of Chapter 7.

TRANSLATION
(Roxburghe, pp. 25–30)

In this section are contained ten material causes which inspire devout Christians to visit the Holy Land of our redemption.

The first is the complaint of Christ over ungrateful persons who are unwilling to visit it.

The second which inspires pilgrimage is the command of Christ.

The third is the exhortation of St Jerome.

The fourth is the indulgence and forgiveness for sins granted to those who come there and to their relatives in Purgatory.

The fifth which inspires Christians to go there is the Letter of St Leo to Bishop Juvenilis for the confirming and strengthening of our most holy faith.

The sixth concerns those things which we shall do every day while we are in the Holy Land, and the number of days of our stay there in the Holy Land.

The seventh concerns the names of the holy places which are sought out by pilgrims in that same Holy Land.

The eighth concerns the indulgences granted by the holy sites in the Holy Land.

The ninth concerns things of note in the Holy Land.

The tenth concerns the relics in various places along the road to the Holy Land.

The First Material Cause Inspiring Christians to Travel to the Holy Land is the Complaint of Christ over Ungrateful Persons who are Unwilling[1] to Visit those Holy Places

In the seventh book of the *Revelations of St Bridget*, Chapter 13,[2] Christ said to St Bridget,

"The princes of the world do not heed these things which you have now seen and the other things which I endured, neither do they value those places where I was born and suffered."

The Second Material Cause Inspiring Christians is the Command of Christ to Various Persons

First, Christ commanded St Paul by an angel to visit the Holy Places in Jerusalem. In the Life of St Barnabas[3] it is written that the angel said to St Paul,

"Do not prevent Barnabas from going to Cyprus since the Grace of God is prepared for him there to enlighten many and achieve holy martyrdom. You, however, continue to Jerusalem to visit the holy places. Hasten quickly to Jerusalem and make no delay, since the brethren eagerly wait for your arrival."

In the seventh book of the *Revelations of St Bridget*, Chapter 9,[4] it is written that Christ commanded St Bridget and her friends to go to Jerusalem with the words,

"Why do you make excuses about your age? I am the creator of nature. I have power to weaken and strengthen nature as I wish. I shall be with you. I will direct your way. I will lead you to Rome and back again, and I will provide for you the things you need in greater measure than you have ever had before."

Again, in the Life of Basilis,[5] the Lord said to Basilis,

"Go and take one of your brothers, and see your parents and make them come with you to the Holy City of Jerusalem. I will give you the crown of life. Go with joy and I am with you to the end of time." + + + +

The Third Material Cause is the Exhortation of St Jerome to Desiderius

This is in a letter which encourages visiting the Holy Land and commences, "When the sermon has been read".[6] It says,

"I encourage and beg you, through the charity of Our Lord, to grant us a sight of you and enrich yourselves at the same time by the great gift of the holy places. Truly if your fellows do not please, it is part of the faith to see, as it were, fresh traces both of the Nativity and of the Crucifixion and the Passion."

The Fourth Material Cause is the Indulgence and the Forgiveness of Sins Granted to Those Who Come There and to Their Relatives in Purgatory

In the seventh book of the *Revelations of St Bridget*, Chapter 11,[7] it is written how Christ, when talking to St Bridget in the Christians' Temple said,

"When you enter My temple, dedicated by My Blood, you are cleansed from all your sins as if you were at that moment lifted out of the font of baptism. Because of your labours and devotion some souls of your kindred which were in Purgatory have today been set free and have entered into Heaven in my glory. For all who come to this place with the true intention of leading a better life according to their better conscience and have no wish to sink back into former sins, for them all their former sins are forgiven and the grace of achieving perfection will be increased."

Christ displayed to St Bridget His Passion on Mount Calvary, when He said to her,

"Behold, the foot of My Cross was set in that hole in the rock at the time of My Passion."[8]

The Most Blessed Virgin Mary showed St Bridget Christ's Nativity in the holy cave at Bethlehem. When Bridget was going out of that cave in the Valley of Jehosophat this same Most Blessed Virgin Mary said to her,

"You should know that there is no human body in Heaven except the glorious body of my Son and my own body. Do you therefore return to the lands of the Christians, amend your lives for the better and live in future with the greatest care and attention, from this time when you have visited these holy places where my Son and I lived our bodily lives and where we died and were buried."[9]

The Fifth Material Cause is the Confirmation and Strengthening of Our Faith

This is shown in the Letter of Pope Leo to Juvenilis, Bishop of Jerusalem,[10] when he writes:

"No priest should be ignorant of that which he preaches, since he who is ignorant will be ignored. More inexcusable than any ignoramus is a Bishop of Jerusalem who, to learn the truth of the Gospel, is instructed only by the eloquence of written pages and not by the evidence of the places themselves. Something which, in another place, has to be believed, in that place, cannot fail to be seen. Why should the mind toil when the sight instructs? Why are things read or heard matters of doubt in the place where so many human proofs of salvation flourish both to sight and touch? Our Lord, as it were, still employs His human voice, and says to any who are still in doubt, 'Why are ye troubled and why do questions arise in your hearts? Behold my hands and my feet, because I myself, etc.' Therefore, My Brother, use the most incontrovertible proofs of the Catholic Faith and the preaching of the Evangelists. Defend yourself with the evidence of the Holy Places in which you live. In your land is Bethlehem where shone the saving babe, born of the Virgin of David's line: He whom the manger held wrapped in swaddling clothes in the lowliness of an inn. In your land the infancy of Our Lord was declared by angels, worshipped by the Wise Men and pursued by Herod through the deaths of many. In your land is where his boyhood grew up, where his youth advanced to manhood, and through all the physical stages the nature of the true man advanced towards the perfect man. Not without food when hungry, not without sleep when weary, not without tears when sad, not without terror when afraid. For He is the one and the same who both, in the form of God, wrought miracles of great virtue and, in the form of a slave, suffered the cruelty of His Passion. The cross itself declares this to you without ceasing; the stone of the sepulchre, where Our Lord lay in his human condition and from which He arose with divine power, cries this aloud to you. When you approach Mount Olivet, the place of His Ascension, to worship, does not that angelic voice, which was heard at the elevation of Our Lord by the amazed bystanders, echo in your ears? 'Men of Galilee, why do you stand looking up into Heaven? This Jesus who has been taken from you into Heaven will thus come etc.' The true cross confirms the true birth of Christ. Since He was born in our flesh, who was crucified in our flesh, who, with no sin intervening, unless He had been of our nature could not have been mortal, received all flesh to redeem all life."

The Sixth Material Cause Concerns These Things Which We Shall Do Each Day While We Are in the Holy Land and the Number of Days[11]

On the first day we shall arrive at the port of Jaffa and we shall wait in the cave there.

On the second day we shall ride to Ramatha and stay the whole night in the Christians' hospice.

On the third day we shall travel to Lidda, where St George was beheaded, and we shall return to Ramatha.

On the fourth day we shall ride to Jerusalem. When we arrive there we shall go to the holy Temple of Christ. We shall not enter the Temple but we shall see the stone in the centre of the pavement before the gates of the Temple on which Our Lord rested with his cross.

On the fifth day at about the second hour of the night we shall traverse the Stations through the streets of Jerusalem and through the Valley of Jehosophat, Mount Olivet, the Valley of Syloe and to Mount Syon. We will have a meal there with the devout Brothers. On the following night we shall enter the holy Temple of Our Lord and leave it the next morning.

On the sixth day we shall ride to Bethlehem and we shall spend the whole night visiting the holy places there.

On the seventh day to the Mountains of Judaea, visiting the sacred sites there. Thence we shall return to Jerusalem and enter the holy Temple of Christ at nightfall.

On the eighth day we shall stay in Mount Syon and Jerusalem until nightfall. In the evening we shall ride towards the Mount of the Forty Days. After we have come down from the Mount of the Forty Days we shall eat in a glade in the valley and then sleep.

On the ninth day, after coming down from the Mount of the Forty Days, we shall ride to the River Jordan and lie that night in Jericho.

On the tenth day, in the morning, we shall ride to Jerusalem by way of Bethany seeing the holy places there. When we reach Jerusalem we shall enter Christ's holy Temple at nightfall.

On the eleventh day we shall stay in Jerusalem and Syon. That night we shall lie in the monastery of the Holy Brothers on Mount Syon.

On the twelfth day we shall ride to Ramatha.

On the thirteenth day we shall go to Jaffa and embark on the galley in the morning.

So that the things which we shall do in these days may be held in the mind I have composed these verses:[12]

1	2	3	4
Ad Jaff prima via	se Ram	ter Lidda	Jeru quart

5	6	7
Quint Sta	Beth sexta	sep ad Montana Judee

8	9	10
Oc remanere Jeru	non Jurda	decima Betha

11	12	13
Unde Jeru	duo Ram via	tercia decima Joppen

The Seventh Material Cause Concerns the Names of the Holy Places Which are Sought and Visited by Pilgrims in the Holy Land

The first place is Joppa, the second Lidda, the third Emaus, the fourth the Valley of Jehosophat, the fifth Mount Olivet, the sixth the Valley of Syloe, the seventh Mount Syon, the eighth the holy Temple of Christ, the ninth the road to Bethlehem, the tenth the monastery at Bethlehem, the eleventh the road to the Mountains of Judaea, the twelfth in the Mountains of Judaea, the thirteenth the River Jordan, the fourteenth is Bethany. To keep these places in mind the following verses have been composed:

1	2	3	4	5	6	7	8
Jaff	Lid	Emaus	Jehoshophat	Oliveti	Sylo	Syon	tem

9		10	11	12	13	14
et	via	Beth	extra	Montan	Jordan	Bethania

COMMENTARY

In this chapter Wey quotes five times from the *Revelations of St Bridget*. These quotations are considered individually below. Wey gives most of them verbatim, with one or two slight inaccuracies of reference. It appears that he had ready access to a copy of her *Revelations*, possibly in Syon Monastery itself, which stood less than twenty miles down river from Eton. The Monastery, founded at Twickenham in 1415, moved to new buildings at Isleworth in 1431, ten years before Wey became a fellow of the newly founded College at Eton.

There is reason to believe that Wey used Syon Monastery's famous library. *The Catalogue of the Library of Syon Monastery*, one of the prized possessions of Corpus Christi College, Cambridge (MS 141), shows the names of benefactors and gives the name of (William) Wey, author and, possibly, donor, of a volume of *Sermones dominicales super Euangelia per totum annum* and *Sermones de festis principalibus et sanctis cum aliis multis sermonibus generalibus*, together with four *Tabulae* which deal with the contents of the sermons.

The following notes contain much detail of the original works from which Wey quotes. The present writer's purpose was to discover how closely Wey was following his sources. If his quotations were paraphrases or loose recollections one could conclude that he was writing from memory. In the event his quotations are so accurate, both in naming the loci of quoted passages and in repeating the words of the original, one can reasonably conclude that he was writing with the original works within easy reach. The three sources named at the end of Chapter 6 can be examined similarly. If a catalogue of a fifteenth-century library were discovered which contained most of Wey's named sources, it might indicate where Wey did much of his writing.

The number of pre-1470 copies of the quoted works which survive is not large. The present writer thanks the staff of the Lambeth Palace Library for their help in finding the earliest editions available, some of which appeared within a century of Wey's death. Since Wey was writing at the very dawn of printing, many of the books he used would have been in manuscript. This explains the trivial variations which occur in Wey's quotations.

NOTES

1   *Nolunt* ("they are unwilling") makes much more sense than the *volunt* ("they are willing") of the Roxburghe transcription. This amendment is validated by Wey's own use of the word *nolentes* ("being unwilling") in the synopsis immediately above (*super ingratos nolentes illam visitare*).

2   Wey's quotation is extremely close to the original; he inserts the word *tu* and slightly re-arranges the last four words. The quotation, however, is not from Book 7, Chapter 13, as Wey states, but from Book 7, Chapter 16, line 3, according to the Nuremberg edition *Rev. sanc. Birg.* by Anton Koberger, of 21 September 1500 (Lambeth Palace Library).

3   When Wey names as a source the Life of St Barnabas he is referring to the section of *The Golden Legend* entitled De Sancto Barnaba, which appears as Life LXXVI in an edition of the *Legenda Aurea Sanctorum*, by Jacobus de Voragine, published in Strasburg in 1483, and which, one assumes, does not differ materially from the edition Wey used twenty years or so earlier. This book also is to be found in the Lambeth Palace Library. In it the relevant passage runs: *"Angelus quoque domini Paulo apparuit dicens, 'Festina venire Hierosylima quia quidem fratres adventum tuum praestolantur ibidem.' Cum ergo Barnabas Cyprus vellet pergere…"*
(The angel of the Lord appeared to Paul saying, "Make haste to come to Jerusalem since the brethren wait for your arrival there." Therefore since Barnabas wished to go to Cyprus…) Wey's verbal echo of *fratres praestolantur adventum* is very striking.

    It is not surprising that Wey was familiar with the *Golden Legend*, which had already been in circulation for more than a century before his birth. Known in the Middle Ages as *Legenda Sanctorum*, it is one of the most famous books of the period, and William Wey quotes from it again, using that form of the title, in his account of St George and the Dragon which appears in Chapter 11.

4   Wey's reference here to *Revelations of St Bridget*, Book 7, Chapter 9, is correct and his transcription of St Bridget's words is exact.

5   This quotation from the *Vita Basilidis* does not appear in the *Life of Basil* by Jacobus de Voragine. Jacobus, however, in the very first line of his *Vita Basilidis*, says that a life of St Basil "was written by Amphilochius" (Bishop of Icona). It may be that Wey was here referring to this work.

6   The Exhortation of St Jerome to Desiderius. In the Lambeth Palace Library there is a copy of Erasmus's 1516 edition of *St Jerome's Letters*, which belonged to Archbishop Whitgift, *Opus Epistolarum*, reprinted at Basle in 1524. Wey's reference enables the researcher to discover his exact source since, in the *Index Iuxta Ordinem Literarum*, the phrase *Lecto sermone* indicates *Epistola familiaris ad Desiderium*; To.3; fo. 201.

    The translation of the Basle text runs:-

> Therefore that which the venerable Paula has asked me to do, I do of my own free will. I urge and pray you for the love of Our Lord to give us a sight of you. Enrich us with such a great gift, on the occasion of your visit to the Holy Places. Indeed, even if you do not like our company, it is part of your faith to worship where Our Lord's feet stood and to see the traces of His Birth, Cross and Passion, as it were, still fresh.

Wey's version of the original passage is so close to the wording in the sixteenth-century Basle edition that one feels he had a copy of Saint Jerome's text (in an earlier but similar edition) in front of him as he was writing. There are several other references to Saint Jerome and his writings in *The Itineraries*.

7   Wey's wording in this quotation from the *Revelations of St Bridget* has only three, trivial, differences from that given in the Lambeth Library text. These are *quum* for *quando*, *residinare* for *recidivare* and *perficiendi* for *proficiendi*. Wey gives the reference source as Book 7, Chapter 11; it is in fact Book 7, Chapter 14, line 2.

8   This quotation comes from the *Revelations of St Bridget*, Book 7, Chapter 15, line 9. Here again the differences in wording are insignificant: Wey writes *quia* for *quod* and *illo* for *isto*.

     Wey had a keen interest in this particular stone, which he describes, with its mortise, in Chapters 6 and 7. He took careful measurements of it and recorded them, together with other dimensions, on "a board" which he kept behind the choir at Edington Priory. Its association with Adam's skull and Christ's crucifixion, together with the belief that it was the centre of the world, fascinated Wey as priest and geographer.

9   Wey's final quotation from St Bridget, for which he does not give the reference, is also from Book 7, from Chapter 26, line 1. Again there are only three, insignificant, verbal differences between Wey's version and the original.

10   The Letter of Pope Leo to Juvenilis. The Library of Lambeth Palace has two relevant volumes: *Opera D. Leonis Magni*, Antwerpiae 1583, and a translation, *The Letters and Sermons of Leo the Great*, Oxford 1895. Wey copies out approximately half of Epistola LXXII, Beati Leonis Papae ad Juvenalem Hierosolymitanum Episcopum – 48 lines out of 107. Here again the fidelity to the original is most striking. There are only half a dozen variations between the texts of Wey and Leo and these are mainly matters of orthography (e.g. *potencia* for *potentia*), or synonyms e.g. *involutum* for *obvolutum*. The bulk of Wey's paragraph is an exact copy of what Pope Leo wrote. It is such a long passage that it is unlikely Wey wrote it out from memory; he probably had an early copy of the book beside him as he was writing.

11   At this time thirteen days seems to have been the normal length of visit permitted to pilgrims: see Chapters 7 and 9.

12   These mnemonic verses are a curious feature of Wey's book. Together with explanatory, superscript, glosses in Latin they form his Chapter 4. The verses then appear again, separately, in Chapter 5, in the 6th and 7th *materiae* and in Chapter 6 under the 8th *materia*.

6

Reasons for Pilgrimage to the Holy Land (ctd)

SYNOPSIS

In this chapter Wey deals with the last three of the ten *materiae* listed in Chapter 5. The lengthy *materia* 8 forms the kernel of Chapter 7 and also includes some mnemonic verses from Chapter 4. Some sentences or phrases from *materiae* 9 and 10 are reused in later chapters. In *materia* 10 Wey gives the names of three of his sources, Robert Grosseteste, Petrus Comestor and Bede.

TRANSLATION
(Roxburghe, pp. 30–56)

The Eighth Matter Deals with the Various Holy Places to be Visited by Pilgrims with Their Names and the Indulgences Granted at These Sites, Together with Verses Composed about These Places[1]

The Ninth Matter Deals with Things of Note in the Holy Land

The first notable thing concerns the thirteen sects in the Lord's Temple. They are as follows:

Latins, Greeks, Armenians, Indians, Jacobites, Gorgians, Syrians, Georgites, Maronites, Nestorians, Andians, Abbacians and Pessines.

Near Hebron, which is eleven miles from Bethlehem, is Mount Mable, where there is an oak tree, so I have read, which the Saracens call Dryp.[2] It existed in the time of Abraham and is called the "Dry Tree". Some say that it existed from the beginning of the world and that it used to be green and had leaves, until the death of Christ and then it became dry. Some maintain that a Prince will come from the West who, with the help of the Christians, will gain the Holy Land and cause Mass to be said under that tree, which will then become green and will bear leaves and fruit. Then shall many of the Jews and Saracens be converted to our faith because of that miracle.

Also in Hebron, which is called Carea-thaba by the Saracens and Arboth by the Jews, lie Adam, Abraham, Jacob, Eve, Sarah, Rebecca and others.[3] There Abraham saw the three and prayed to one of them.[4] There too is a cave where Adam and Eve lived after their expulsion from Paradise.[5] The Vale of Hebron starts there and continues almost to Jerusalem.

In Jerusalem there is neither stream nor spring. Water is brought to Jerusalem by a conduit from Hebron.

On the north of Jerusalem is the Kingdom of Syria.

In front of Christ's tomb there is a lamp which, so it is said, is extinguished of itself on Good Friday and lights itself again in the hour when Christ rose again.[6]

There is a hole for the cross in white marble tinged with red flecks. Adam's head was found in that hole after the flood as a sign that therein lay redemption. On that stone is written, "Here God achieved salvation in the centre of the earth"; likewise is written, "That which you see is the foundation of the whole world and of this faith."[7]

Two miles from Jerusalem is the Mount of Joy where lies the prophet Samuel. That is where pilgrims can gain their first sight of the city of Jerusalem.[8]

The Tenth and Final Matter Deals with the Relics of Saints in Various Places along the Road from the Holy Land

In Jerusalem is the Temple of Our Lord. This is a round church which Christians do not enter.[9] It used to contain the Ark of the Lord, which Titus took to the city of Rome, where it is now, in the church of St John Lateran.[10] Near the church at Bethlehem is the church of St Nicholas, where the Blessed Mary dropped some milk from her breasts on to red stones; and, so I have read, the marks of the milk remain on the stone.[11] The body of St Anne, the mother of the Most Blessed Mary, was translated to Constantinople by the Queen, St Helena. In the same place is one of the jars from Cana in Galilee which looks like marble. I have read that this jar always drips water and refills itself once each year.[12] Also in Constantinople was the lance and the sponge on which they placed the vinegar mixed with gall when Christ was hanging on the cross. The Emperor of Germany has the spear shaft which Longinus held in his hand when he struck the body of Christ.[13]

Twenty miles from the port of Salamis (in Cyprus) is the cross of the Good Thief, which is said to be hanging up in a chapel without any other fastening.[14] In Rhodes there is a thorn from Christ's crown. This flowers for an hour on Good Friday while the story of Christ's Passion is being read. In the same place there is the left arm of St Katherine, Virgin and Martyr. There is also a cross made from the bowl in which Christ washed the feet of his Apostles, together with one of the thirty pence for which Christ was sold by the traitor Judas.[15] At Candia is the head of Saint Paul's disciple, St Titus.[16] At Casope there is a lamp in front of the Most Blessed Mary which is filled with oil once a year and then burns for a whole year with that oil.[17] At Ragusa there is an arm of St Blaise.[18] At Jarra in Dalmatia is the uncorrupted body of Simeon, the Just, who held Christ in his arms, together with the body of the Confessor, Zoyolus, and the body of the Martyr, St Anastasia.[19]

The following relics are in Venice and nearby: first the body of St Lucy, Virgin, then the thigh bone of St Christopher, the body of St Zacharias, father of St John the Baptist, the body of St Sabina, the body of St Pancras, the body of St Marina, the left arm of St George and a statue of the Most Blessed Virgin Mary made from the rock which Moses struck in the desert and from which he produced water. In St Mark's church is a statue of Christ Crucified. This was stabbed by a Jew with a dagger five times and dripped blood. That blood was kept and is displayed twice a year at which times there is full remission.[20] Also there is a statue of the Most Blessed Mary after a picture by St Luke the Evangelist.[21] In a holy monastery near Venice there is the uncorrupted body of the most holy Helena, mother of the Emperor Constantine, and daughter of Coel, King of England, who built many churches in the Holy Land and discovered the Holy Cross.[22] There too are the body of St Theodore, an arm of St Blaise, the body of St Secundus, one chest full of the bones of the Innocents of Israel, the body of St Nazarenus, the body of the martyr, Claudius, and the head of the confessor Stephanus. In another place, near Venice, is the right arm of St Katherine, one jar from Cana in Galilee, and the pastoral staff and sandals of St Nicholas.[23]

At Padua lie Lucas and Matheus, Antonius the Franciscan, Antony the Pilgrim, St Justina and twenty-eight saints beneath an iron grille.[24] At Viterbo is the uncorrupted body of the virgin, St Rosa.[25] At Assissi there lies the body of St Francis and the body of St Clare. In that place also is the statue on the

Cross which told St Francis to build a house for St Clare and the other nuns in Assisi.[26] On Mount Alvernia St Francis received the stigmata on his hands, feet and heart.[27] At Spoleto is the body of the virgin, St Christina.[28] Twelve miles from Ancona and three miles from Reconato is the house called Loreto (now it is a chapel of St Mary made of stones), which was once built in the Holy Land by St Helena. Because the Most Blessed Mary was not honoured there the chapel itself was lifted up by angels, with the Most Blessed Mary seated on it, and carried from the Holy Land to Alretum [Loreto]. Farmers and shepherds witnessed angels carrying it and placing it on the spot where it is now and where the Most Blessed Virgin Mary is held in the highest honour.[29]

Once a certain Englishman was about to set out for the Holy Land, eager to see the marvels of that country; he accordingly hired a Saracen to show him the wonders. Among these there occurred this one. When he was passing through a very beautiful wood with tall trees, a delightful sight, he heard no bird singing. Looking up he saw several birds lying dead on the branches of the trees, with their wings spread out in the form of a cross. When he asked the Saracen the reason for this the Saracen replied, "There is a very large number of birds in this wood all through the year and their song is of the sweetest, but during the week in which your Prophet, that is Christ, suffered they all die." It was Holy Week at that time. The Saracen added, "They start to die on Passion Sunday, and on the Sunday a fortnight later, that is on Easter Day, they come back to life and start singing again. As though dying for grief at the death of Christ and rejoicing together for His Resurrection they rise again with Him and sing their sweetest song." The reference for this is the Lincoln Author on "Repent", Chapter 56 near the end.[30]

Epiphanius said that when Senacherib returned from Egypt he sent his army ahead to besiege Jerusalem. The army pitched camp near the pool of Siloam to use its waters. The pool was, as it were, common since both citizens and enemies were able to go down to it. Isaiah, however, prayed to the Lord and obtained his wish that when the citizens went out the waters were there as before, but when the enemy drew near the waters dried up utterly. Thus it was that the Assyrians were amazed whence came the water supply in the city. As a perpetual memorial of this deed the waters of Siloam do not bubble forth continually but only at certain times. The reference for this is in *The Master of the Histories* in 4 Reg [now known as Kings II]; Chapter 20.[31]

In Luke, Chapter 4, verse 24, it is written that when Jesus said at Nazareth, "No prophet is accepted in his own country" all were filled with anger and thrusting him out of the city led him to the brow of a mountain that they might cast him down headlong (verses 28 and 29). This mountain is one mile from Nazareth and is called "The Lord's Leap". Bede [in his commentary] on this text says, "When the Lord slipped from their hands to descend from the top of the mountain and wishing to hide under the cliff, suddenly, at the touch of Our Lord's garment, that rock yielded beneath Him and melted like wax and made a sort of hollow in which the aforementioned body could be received. In this place all the outlines and creases of His garment and His footprints are still visible on the rock, as those who have seen them bear witness."[32]

On the road to Bethlehem, where the star appeared to the Three Kings of Cologne, water bubbles out of the ground and runs on the road from the first Vespers of Our Lord's Epiphany until the second Vespers and then stops, and it does this every year.[33]

COMMENTARY

Since *materia* 8 reappears almost in its entirety in Chapter 7 and is there translated, it has been omitted from the translation that follows. *Materiae* 9 and 10, however, are translated in full.

The duplication of *materia* 8 is the longest of Wey's repetitions. It is a much drier and less personal account than the very slightly longer version that appears in Chapter 7, since it does not mention the sermon that Wey preached nor the several Masses "with organ accompaniment" provided for the Earl of Worcester, John Tiptoft. It does not give the actual dates when the various sites were visited, which are recorded in Chapter 7. Finally it does not mention the sad death of the French priest who was buried beside the road from Jerusalem to Jericho.

Materia 8, however, has two references to the miraculous transport of stones from Mt Sinai, which Wey leaves out in Chapter 7. The first is to a stone by the tomb of the Blessed Virgin Mary in the Valley of Jehoshophat "which an angel carried to the most Blessed Mary from Mt Sinai. It is the same colour as the stone of St Catherine's tomb." The second is to the red stone in the Franciscan monastery church on Mount Zion which "was brought from Mt Sinai by the hand of angels in answer to the prayers of St Thomas on his return from India."

The final paragraphs of *materia* 10 are especially interesting as, like Chapter 5, they give the names of some of Wey's sources.

NOTES

1   Verses: a reference to the mnemonic verses of Chapter 4.

2   Dryp: the Greek for an oak tree is δρῦς, *drus*.

3   "Sarah died in Kiriath-arba, that is Hebron." Genesis 23:2. See also Chapter 7. For the other burials, see Genesis 49:31.

4   Abraham and the three: Genesis 18:2.

5   The Expulsion from Eden: Genesis 3:23.

6   The lamp on Christ's tomb, one of the "recurrent miracles", features also in Chapter 11.

7   This description appears again in Chapter 11.

8   First sight of Jerusalem. On the pilgrimage to Compostella the place where pilgrims on the Camino Francés had their first glimpse of the cathedral was called variously Mons Gaudii, Mont Joie and Monte del Gozo. It was the scene of various ceremonies and celebrations. The first pilgrim in a group to see the towers of the cathedral was appointed "King" for the final stage into the city.

9   The Temple: Solomon's Temple was destroyed by the Babylonians in 586 BC. It was rebuilt as the "Second Temple" in 520. This was desecrated by Antiochus Epiphanes but rededicated under Judas Maccabeus. Herod the Great erected more magnificent buildings but Jerusalem was destroyed by the Romans in 70 AD. The Muslim shrine known as the "Dome of the Rock" was built in the area towards the end of the 7th century. This is the "round church which Christians do not enter". St John Lateran: see Chapter 14. (*ODCC* s.v. Temple).

10   Titus, Roman Emperor: see Chapter 14.

11   Marks on stone. Wey's guides often interpreted marks on marble stones as evidence of milk, blood, tears, footprints etc. See also Chapters 7, 9 and 11.

12   The jar from Cana: Chapter 11.

13   Longinus's spear: Chapter 11.

14   The Good Thief, Dismas: Chapters 7 and 9.

15   The relics on Rhodes: Chapters 7 and 9.

16   St Titus: Chapter 14.

17   This recurrent miracle is described again in Chapter 7.

18   St Blaise: Chapters 7 and 9.

19   Simeon: Chapters 7 and 9. Seyole (Zoyolus) and Anastasia: Chapter 7.

20   Relics in Venice and the stabbed statue. In Chapter 9 Wey tells a similar story about a picture.

21   St Luke as an artist: Chapters 9 and 14.

22   St Helena: Chapter 9. .

23   More relics in or near Venice. Some of the relics listed here (e.g. Secundus and Theodore) appear in Chapter 9. For Cana, see also Chapter 11.

24   Padua is only 20 miles from Venice. Wey passed through it in 1458 on the way back from Venice to England. See Chapter 8. Apart from the cathedral, Padua has the Basilica di San Antonio

(Il Santo) and the Capella degli Scrovegni. The former is a thirteenth- to fourteenth-century basilica containing the saint's tomb, a major pilgrimage site. Here Wey could have seen two important works by Donatello within a decade of their completion: the high altar in San Antonio (1443–50) and the bronze equestrian statue known as the "Gattamelata" (1447–53) in the square outside. In the Scrovegni chapel are the frescoes painted by Giotto between 1304 and 1306 (see note below). Close by is the church of the "Eremetani" where Mantegna painted his frescoes between 1454 and 1457. Wey could have seen them also, just one year after their completion.

25 Viterbo appears in Chapter 8 in the list of places Wey passed through on his route south between Bolsena and Rome. Fifty miles from Rome, its church of Santa Rosa contains the mummified body of St Rosa, who died in 1261. The church of San Francesco contains the tombs of two thirteenth-century popes, Clement IV (d.1268) and Hadrian V (d.1276).

26 Assisi was visited by Wey after his pilgrimage to Rome, while he was travelling northwards to Ravenna to take ship for Venice. In Chapter 8 he makes one of his brief marginal notes, "St Francis lies there and Clare". St Francis was born in Assisi in 1182 and died in the Portiuncola oratory in Santa Maria degli Angeli near Assisi in 1226. The saint's tomb is in the crypt of the San Francesco basilica where Wey could have seen the famous paintings by Giotto (d.1337) in the Upper Church. The "speaking cross" now hangs in the Capella del Crocefisso in the church of "Santa Clara". St Clare, foundress of the "Poor Clares", was the first abbess of San Damiano. She died in 1253 and was canonized by Alexander IV in 1255.

27 St Francis received the stigmata on Mount La Verna (Alvernia), a place of retreat given him by the Lord of Chiusi in 1224.

28 Spoleto was another of the places he visited on his route north from Rome. Among the buildings still standing which were there in Wey's time are the cathedral, rebuilt in 1175, and the Rocca, formerly the residence of the papal governor.

  St Christina is also mentioned in Wey's marginal note in Chapter 8. According to Butler's *Lives of the Saints*, she was Augustina Camozzi, the daughter of a physician, who "led a rather disorderly and very tempestuous life," but "died after making expiation by the austerest penance" at Spoleto on 13 February 1458. Wey left Venice for Jaffa on 18 May 1458, which means that he passed through Spoleto within a few weeks of her death. This may explain his references to her.

29 The Holy House of Loreto is south of Ancona and three miles west of Porto Recanati (Wey's Reconato), on the Adriatic coast. The event described by Wey is said to have occurred in 1295. Another version says that the house was transported to Italy on board a Crusader ship.

30 The Lincoln Author, called by Wey "Lincolniensis", is Robert Grosseteste, the great thirteenth-century Bishop of Lincoln, who died in 1253. He was a polymath and a prolific writer. Part of a fifteenth-century edition of his work, formerly owned by Syon Abbey, is in the Bodleian Library (Barlow 49).

31 The Master of the Histories, Magister Historiarum, is Petrus Comestor.

32 Bede on St Luke: The Venerable Bede *c*.673–735.

33 The spring and the star: one of the "recurrent miracles" which so fascinated Wey. He includes this site in his "Gazetteer" in Chapter 12. He has another story about the Magi and the star in Chapters 7 and 11.

7

The 1458 Pilgrimage to Jerusalem

SYNOPSIS

In 1458, two years after his pilgrimage to Compostella, Wey made the other two major pilgrimages, to Rome and Jerusalem. In this chapter he describes, in some detail, the thirteen days he spent in the Holy Land.

Wey probably wrote this account soon after his return to Eton in December 1458 since in Chapter 9, which deals with his second journey to Jerusalem in 1462, he avoids repetition by referring his reader to his 1458 account: *sicut in precedenti itinerario meo dixi* – "As I have said in my earlier Itinerary".

TRANSLATION
(Roxburghe, pp. 56–79)

In the name of God, Amen. In the Year of Our Lord 1458 I, William Wey, Bachelor of Sacred Theology,[1] Perpetual Fellow of the Royal College of the Most Blessed Mary of Eton at Windsor,[2] having been asked by devout men to compile an itinerary of my pilgrimage to the most holy sepulchre of Our Lord, Jesus Christ, propose to describe in my itinerary my journey across the various seas beyond which one must sail, the cities, towns and countries through which one must travel, and the sacred places in the Holy Land together with such things as I saw and heard both there and on the way home.

To begin with, I crossed three seas. The first one is called the Adriatic Sea and it starts at Venice and ends at Corfu. The second is named the Mediterranean Sea; it begins at Corfu and ends at Cande[3] in Crete. The third is known as the Aegean Sea; it begins at Cande and ends at the port of Jaffa, or Joppa, in the Holy Land. The distance across these seas from Venice to the port of Jaffa is 2,300 miles.[4]

71

I left Venice and the harbour between the two towers beside the church of St Nicholas[5] on 18 May, arriving on the 20th in the land of Parenzo[6] in Istria, 100 miles from Venice. On the 24th of the same month I came to the city of Ragusa[7] in Slavonia, next to the kingdom of Hungary. In that city there is an arm of St Blaise, bishop. It is a wealthy city with a fine wall set on the coast. The silver money there is very good. On the last day of May I came to the city of Durrës[8] where I heard that the Venetians maintain sixteen galleys in the Adriatic Sea. These are fine vessels armed and equipped to protect the cities, towns and lands which they have in those parts. I also heard that in that month 50,000 Turks had been killed by the Hungarians near the city of Belgrade. The Turk had retreated from there to besiege the city of Negroponte[9] which is in Greece. Next I came to Casope,[10] a city which had been destroyed by a crocodile. There is a chapel of the Most Blessed Mary there where a lamp burns for a whole year on one filling of oil. On 4 June I came to Corfu and then to Turkey. On 7 June I reached Cande, a large city beside the sea on the island of Crete, where there was once a king called Minos.[11] St Paul once preached there on a high mountain. He was chased away from there by the Cretan Greeks, and from this event comes the saying about them, "The Cretans are always liars, evil beasts."[12]

Next I came to the city of Rhodes on the island of Colosa, where the Knights of St John the Baptist[13] live. In that place there is one of the thorns[14] which was on Christ's head; it flowers on Good Friday. On the 16th day of the same month I reached the port of Paphos[15] in the land of Cyprus. Paul was imprisoned in that town beneath the church. Pilgrims purchase gourds[16] there to carry wine to the Holy Land. On the 18th, the Day of the Holy Martyrs Marcus and Marcellinus,[17] I came to the harbour of Joppa, or Jaffa, at the hour of Compline.[18]

The voyage from Venice to the port of Jaffa lasted four weeks and four days. Two men were dispatched from the galley to the Warden[19] of the Franciscan Brothers, the Consul and the Saracen commanders for permission to enter the Holy Land. On 19 June the Saracens pitched two tents by the seashore before noon and then, after noon, pitched their tents on Mount Jaffa near the tower. After obtaining permission to enter the Holy Land I disembarked from the galley at Jaffa about midday on 21 June. After the pilgrims had been counted I spent the whole of the night in one of the subterranean caves.[20] The number of pilgrims from the two galleys[21] was 197. On first entry to the Holy Land from Jaffa there is remission of all sins for those who come on pilgrimage and have confessed and are contrite. + Note that wherever a cross is inserted there is full indulgence from punishment and guilt; where there is no cross there are seven years and seven Lents. These indulgences were granted by the Pope, St Sylvester,[22] in response to the prayers of the Emperor, Constantine the Great, and his mother, St Helena.[23] Such indulgences, which are to endure for ever, are granted to all who are truly penitent, who have confessed and are contrite, and who come to those holy places for reasons of piety and pilgrimage.

The city of Jaffa was built by Japhet, the son of Noah.[24] It used to have a good harbour with a wall, but now it has been destroyed except for the three caves in which the pilgrims are put to be counted by the Saracens. There is also a small tower on Mount Jaffa by which sailors recognize the harbour and the country. That land once belonged to the Philistines but now it is called Syria, as is all the Holy Land. There is a spot in Jaffa where the Apostle, St Peter, raised Tabitha,[25] the Apostles' disciple, from the dead. There too is the harbour where the Prophet Jonah went down to flee from Tarshish from the face of the Lord.[26] One mile from Jaffa is the great rock where St Peter used to stand to fish; it is now under the sea. On the morning of 22 June we pilgrims took our donkeys to ride to Rama,[27] which is ten Welsh miles[28] from Jaffa. We stayed there for the rest of that day. One should note that it is a good idea to be among the first to arrive at the place to choose a room and to get fresh water. It will also be sensible to purchase a rush mat from the innkeeper to put between us and the ground to sleep on, because there are no bedclothes there. After we had slept in that hospice for the first night the Warden of the Franciscans came before daybreak on the morning of 23 June and had a Mass said. Before Mass was begun the Warden asked the pilgrims if they all had permission from the Lord Pope to come to the Holy Land. He rebuked those who did not have permission for their disobedience to the Catholic Church, but said that he had authority to absolve them. He urged them to confess and to have the true charity by which the indulgences of the Holy Land may be obtained. When Mass was over the pilgrims travelled, walking or riding as they wished, the two miles to the town now called Lydda but which was once named Diaspolis. At one time it was a great city but now it is almost in ruins; it is in the land of the Philistines. Pilgrims make their offerings to St George[29] in the church of the Greeks. This used to be large and beautiful but now for the greater part it is in ruins. St George was martyred there. It is also the place where St Peter healed the paralysed Aeneas.[30] The pilgrims then returned to Rama and stayed in the hospice that day and the following night.

On the 24th, St John the Baptist's Day, we rode from Rama to Jerusalem. Early that same morning Saracen cavalry came against us in a large number, as though ready to fight. They had trumpets and a standard on which was displayed a chalice with the consecrated host. This was to insult Christians because one of the Frankish kings, who had been captured in war, deposited the sacrament with the Sultan as a pledge which he was never willing to redeem afterwards. So we rode to Nova Porta,[31] twelve miles from Rama. We rested there and ate those provisions which we were carrying with us. We had water from a large cistern. It is twelve miles from Nova Porta to Jerusalem, and the road is rough, rocky and steep. It is a good thing therefore to have water mixed with wine in your gourd to drink on the way. Before one reaches Jerusalem, seven miles along the way beside the road on the right, in the mountains, was the church which was once called Emaus Castle, where the two Disciples recognized the Lord in the breaking of bread.[32] On the plain near the mountains was the city of Betulia from which came St Judith who beheaded Holophernes.[33] The place where she beheaded him is nearby. As one goes up towards Jerusalem there was the town of Amatoth, the birthplace of the prophet St Jeremiah.[34] After that, on the mountain, is Sylo, the place where Eli, the priest, lived and the boy Samuel who served there before the Lord.[35] Near there is the tomb of Cleophas[36] and also the tomb of the prophet Samuel. Close by also was the city of Aramathea from which came the noble Joseph who begged for the body of Jesus.[37]

It is five miles from Sylo to Jerusalem, which we entered on St John the Baptist's Day. As we entered boys threw stones at us. Entering the city we came to the square in front of the Temple of the Christians and we kissed the stone covered with crosses on which Our Lord rested with his cross. Then we entered the hospice for dinner. We passed the whole night there lying on the ground. On the morning of 25 June the Franciscan Brothers from Mount Syon arrived,[38] two hours before sunrise, and escorted the pilgrims to those holy places which pilgrims are most eager to visit. On the road to Jerusalem there are the six sites, described above, Emaus, Bethulia, where she beheaded Holofernes, Sylo, where Eli was priest, the tomb of Samuel, the tomb of Cleophas and Aramathea.

Pilgrimages to the Sites of the Stations

First they go to the Church of the Holy Sepulchre.[39] There is a square in front of this which is about a stone's throw in size; it is well paved. In the middle of this pavement there is a square stone of white marble, engraved with many crosses.[40] It is about a foot and a half long. Christ rested on it when he was weary with carrying the cross on His shoulders from Pilate's house to Mount Calvary. Beside that square, beneath the flight of steps by which one climbed up to Mount Calvary, is a chapel of St Mary and St John the Evangelist. They stood in that place at the time of Christ's crucifixion; Indians minister there. Near it is a chapel of St Michael and All Angels; Jacobites minister there. Near that is the chapel of St John the Baptist where Armenians minister. These three chapels are on the east side of the aforesaid square. On the west side is the large, beautiful chapel of St Mary Magdalene; Nestorians minister there. In Constantinople there was once a great doctor called Nestorianus from whom arose that false traitor Mahomet.[41] These Nestorians still persist in their sect and claim they are Christians, but, rather, they are heretics and schismatics. They have the custom of shaving the whole head except the very crown where they allow their hair to grow long according to their rite. The Mahomedans shave their whole head like a coronet and let their long hair hang around their ears. They all have beards. Permission[42] will not be given at that time to enter the Church of the Holy Sepulchre but the Franciscans lead pilgrims to other holy sites.

These are the Pilgrimages to the sites of the Stations[43]

As one crosses from the place of the Holy Sepulchre there is first, on the east, a street up which Christ climbed with His cross to suffer. Along this short road one comes to the house of the rich man who denied crumbs to Lazarus.[44] A little distance from here is the crossroads where the Jews forced Simon of Cyrene[45] to carry Jesus' cross. This is the spot where Jesus said to the women, "Daughters of Jerusalem, do not weep for me", etc.[46] On the right is the place where Jesus pressed his face on to the cloth and handed it to Veronica.[47] Not far away is the site where the Blessed Virgin Mary fainted when she saw her Son coming with His cross. The church which the Christians called St Mary de Spata used to be there but it has now been destroyed. Further on is the gate of the old city through which Christ was led to His death. Not far away is the Pool of the Sheep[48] where an angel stirred the water once each day. Near there, in the arch of a vault which has been built over the square from one side to the other, are two white stones on which Christ stood when he was condemned to death.[49] Then close by is the school of the Blessed Mary in which she learnt her letters and the Scriptures.[50] Through that gate on the other side of the road is the house of Pilate[51] in which Christ was flogged, crowned and condemned to death. + Further on in the same square is the house of Herod[52] where Christ was mocked and clad in a white garment[53] by Herod. Further on, towards the north, is another square where is the house of Simon the Pharisee, where the many sins of Mary Magdalene were forgiven.[54] Near the Pool of the Sheep is the house of St Anne[55] where the Blessed Virgin Mary was born. + This house was the monastery of St Scholastica, virgin,[56] but it is now a Saracen hospital. Next, opposite, on the south, is the temple of Our Lord, where Christ performed many miracles and in which the Blessed Virgin Mary was presented and betrothed to Joseph. That is where Christ was presented on the day of Purification and on another occasion was discovered among the doctors.[57] + Next to that temple, on the south, is the gate through which the Virgin Mary entered with the boy Jesus when she presented him in that temple. It was from a pinnacle of this temple that St James the Less[58] was hurled. Near this temple is the tomb of St Simon the Just, but his body now lies at Jarra in Dalmatia.[59] Not far off is the Temple of Solomon where Christ preached on Palm Sunday.[60] Near it is the Golden Gate through which Jesus entered on Palm Sunday sitting upon an ass. Heraclius[61] entered through the same gate. In this very gate Joachim and Anna met when it was announced that Mary would be born to them. Near St Anne's house is a gate facing east through which St Stephen was led to be stoned.[62]

Pilgrimages in the Valley of Jehoshophat

As one goes down to the Valley of Jehoshophat there is a stony place on the road on the left-hand side where the Jews stoned Stephen. In the middle of the Valley of Jehoshophat is the stream Cedron, which is produced by the great amount of rain coming down from the mountains of Olivet. It is said that the wood of the Holy Cross lay across the stream for a long time like a bridge, but when the Queen of Sheba came to Solomon in Jerusalem she was loath to walk over it because she knew in her spirit its future miraculous power.[63] In the

Valley of Jehoshophat, on the right, there is a large chapel of the Blessed Virgin Mary. On its eastern side, beneath a well-made chapel, is her tomb, beautifully decorated with stones of white marble.[64] + This chapel has one entrance, to the south. There is a flight of forty-eight steps leading from that entrance to the floor of the chapel. In front of the south-east corner of the chapel is a large stone cave where Christ prayed three times to the Father on the night of the Last Supper and his sweat was like drops of blood dripping to the ground.[65]

Pilgrimages on Mount Olivet

A stone's throw to the south from the oratory, or cave, is the garden and the place where Judas betrayed Christ with a kiss and where Christ was arrested and bound.[66] Not far away is the spot where Peter cut off the ear of the high priest's servant whose name was Malchus.[67] Outside the garden, as one climbs the mount, is the place where Christ sent Peter, James and John away with the words "Watch and pray", etc. A little further up the mount is the place where the Disciples slept while Christ prayed.[68] Nearby is the spot where the Most Blessed Mary gave her girdle to St Thomas, the Apostle, when she was taken up into heaven.[69] As one climbs the mount there is a long narrow road and beside the road is the place where Christ looked at the city of Jerusalem and wept over it saying, "If thou also hadst known," etc.[70] Further up the mount is the place where the angel presented the Blessed Mary with a palm telling her the day of her death and her assumption into heaven. On the mount on the left-hand side is the site where once was the town of Galilee. That is where Christ appeared to the twelve Disciples on the day of His Resurrection and said to them, "I will go before you into Galilee."[71] A short distance from there is another place where are contained all the indulgences which arise from those places which pilgrims cannot enter, namely Pilate's house, the Lord's Temple, Solomon's Temple, the house in which the Most Blessed Virgin Mary was born and the Golden Gate. Pilgrims are not allowed to enter any of those places. + On the same mount the city of Jerusalem can be seen in its entirety as well as the aforementioned Golden Gate.

From there one goes over Mount Olivet towards the south where there is a church, in the middle of which there is stone which bears the print of Christ's foot as He ascended into heaven.[72] The men of that town were standing with Christ's disciples looking up to heaven and two men clad in white garments beside them said, "Men of Galilee, why are you amazed?" etc. On the stone mentioned, which is of white marble, there remains the imprint of Christ's right foot.[73] Outside the church, on the left, is another chapel in which St Pellagia[74] performed penance for her sins, together with the place called Bethfage to which Christ sent two of His Disciples saying to them, "Go to the village which faces you," etc.[75] Near the mount, as one descends, was a chapel of St Mark the Evangelist where the Apostles composed the Creed.[76] Close to it is the place in whose wall is the large stone on which Christ taught the Apostles the Lord's Prayer, Our Father.[77] Again close by there is a stone in the middle of the road where Christ taught the eight Beatitudes, that is "Blessed in spirit", etc.[78] Lower down the mount is the place where the Blessed Virgin Mary rested because she was tired when she was visiting these holy places.[79]

Other Pilgrimages in the Valley of Jehoshophat

Further down the mount on the left still stands part of that tree on which Judas hanged himself.[80] Going down to the Valley of Jehoshophat is the Tomb of Absolon, son of King David. Nearby is the spot where Christ appeared to James the Less on the Day of Resurrection and set bread before him saying, "Rise, my brother, and eat."[81] Zacharias, the son of Barachias, was buried in the same place. He was slain between the temple and the altar. Near that place are the Apostles' hiding places where they concealed themselves at the time of Christ's Passion.[82]

Pilgrimages in the Valley of Syloe

On the other side of the bridge of Syloe, which divides the Valley of Jehoshophat and the Valley of Syloe, is the way down into a dell hidden in a valley, at the bottom of which is a spring with excellent water. The Most Blessed Mary washed the clothes of her son, Jesus, there when she presented Him in the Temple.[83] As one goes further on from there, on the right, is the Pool of Syloe in which the man who was blind from birth washed his eyes and received his sight.[84] In front of that pool there is a place near the road where the Jews cut the Prophet Isaiah through the middle with a wood-saw.[85] His tomb is close by. As one goes further one climbs up on the right to the sacred field of Acheldemach which was purchased with the price of Christ's blood for the burial of pilgrims.[86] It is now called the Armenians' Field. It is a square field a stone's throw in width. It is slightly hollowed with nine pits in which the bodies of the dead may be placed. Around that spot are many hiding places in which, when the land was in the hands of Christians, many Christian hermits performed their penances. A little higher up is the House of the Evil Plan. It has this name because it was there that the leaders of the priests, with others, devised the plan of handing Jesus over to death. It was there that Judas went to betray Christ.[87] Once there was a monastery of St Cyprian in that place.

When we had visited these sites we came to the holy mount of Syon, to hear Mass and after Mass had been said we took a meal with the Brothers. After the meal we went across to the holy places of Mount Syon.

Pilgrimages on Mount Syon

On Mount Syon is the place where the Jews wanted to seize the body of the Most Blessed Virgin when it was being carried by the Apostles to burial.[88] There is also the place where St Peter wept bitterly because he had denied Christ.[89] There is also the church of St Angelus.[90] It is the house of the priest Annas where Christ was examined and slapped;[91] later it became a monastery of the Armenians. On Mount Syon is the beautiful monastery of the Franciscans; there is a flight of eight steps up to the church. At the high altar in that church Our Lord, Jesus, had supper with His Disciples and performed the Holy Sacrament.[92] + Near this altar, on the right, is an altar where Christ washed His Disciples' feet.[93] Outside the church, to the south, is a square raised from the ground near the church courtyard. One goes across it to the upper room which is behind the high altar. There was a chapel there with one altar and it is where the Apostles and others received the Holy Spirit on the Day of Pentecost.[94] Then one goes down into the cloister, in the corner of which there is a small chapel to St Thomas. There Christ offered himself to St Thomas to be touched and it is where Jesus entered although the doors were closed.[95] + Below it, in the sacristy, is a portion of the column of Christ's flagellation secretly shut up in the wall. Next to the western side of the church is the place where the Blessed Mary was wont to pray.[96] On the north side of the church is the stone where the Most Blessed Mary sat when He preached. In the wall of the church, on the north, is the tomb of David and other kings, and it is called the Chapel of King David.[97] Outside the east side of the chapel is the place where the Paschal Lamb was prepared for the Lord's supper,[98] and there too the water was warmed for washing the Apostles' feet. Then, going further north a short stone's throw, is the place where St Stephen, Nicodemus,[99] Gamaliel and Abibon were buried in turn. Then another stone's throw to the west is the stone where St John the Evangelist said Mass for many years in front of the Most Blessed Virgin after Our Lord's Ascension. Near there, further south, is the place where the Most Blessed Virgin Mary lived for sixteen years and where she departed this earthly life.[100] + A little further on to the south-east is a red stone surrounded with other stones where St Mathias was appointed an Apostle on the Day of Pentecost in place of the traitor Judas.[101] All these sites described on Mount Syon were below the great church which was called St Mary of the Ladder to Heaven.[102] A stone's throw to the north is the Church of Our Saviour; Armenians minister there. On the high altar of this church lies that stone which was rolled to the mouth of Jesus Christ's tomb:[103] it is really large, being more than 2 fathoms long and 1½ feet thick. It is made of white marble. Next to the southern edge of the altar is a cell in the wall where Christ was tied to the column the whole night. This church used to be the house of the priest Caiaphas, and is where Christ was scorned, examined, spat upon, robed, struck on the head, denied by Peter three times and shut up in the cell afore mentioned until Good Friday morning until he could be sent to Pilate.[104] The entrance to this church is on the west side. Near it, on the right as one enters, in a hole in the wall, higher than a man, lies that stone on which the cock stood when it crowed before Peter denied Christ. Outside the entrance is the tree where Peter stood when he denied Christ in Caiaphas's house. Next, as one crosses from Mount Syon towards Jerusalem, on the right of the road, is the Armenians' church. There is a small chapel on the east side of this where the Apostle St James, the brother of St John the Evangelist, was beheaded by Herod.[105] Next, as one goes north towards Jerusalem, about two stones' throws, is a large stone on the right side of the road near a wall. All around this stone in the wall are many crosses which are kissed by pilgrims. It was there that Christ appeared to the three Marys who were returning from the tomb on the Day of Resurrection and said "Hail".[106] There, facing it on the west, about a stone's throw away, is the Castle of David surrounded by a ditch. A short distance from the Castle of David is the spot where the Most Blessed Virgin Mary used to sit and look back at Mount Calvary.[107]

After visiting all these places one returns to Jerusalem and pilgrims stay there in the hospice until Vespers, guarded by Saracens. After Vespers, Brothers come to them from Mount Syon and take them to the Church of the Holy Sepulchre. When they arrive Saracen leaders gather from Jerusalem and count the pilgrims and write their names down.[108] Then they shut them up until morning. When we are in the Church we shall enter together, with candles lit, into the Chapel of the Most Glorious Virgin Mary and commence the procession to these sacred places described below.

Pilgrimages and the Holy Sites in the Church of the Holy Sepulchre

The Chapel of the Most Blessed Virgin Mary is on the north. There Christ is believed to have appeared after His Resurrection to his Most Blessed Mother on Easter Day. In the same chapel is part of the column[109] to which Christ was bound when he was flogged in Pilate's house. It stands on the right side of the chapel under a wooden grating. In the same chapel is the altar where the Holy Cross was kept for a long time. A small portion of the cross of Our Lord, Jesus Christ, is still held there. In the middle of this chapel lies a round, marble stone. On this stone they placed a corpse and then laid the three crosses on top of it. When Christ's cross was placed on the dead woman's body, she, who was previously dead, immediately rose up.[110] In front of the entrance to this chapel lies one round stone of white marble veined with black. It contains a hole in the centre three fingers long. When Our Lord appeared to St Mary Magdalene on the Day of Resurrection in the guise of a gardener He made that hole in the aforesaid stone with the spade which was in His hand and said to Mary, "Do not touch me."[111] One then goes through the north wall of the church eastwards where there is the entrance to the chapel which is called "Christ's Prison". Christ was put there when they prepared the cross. It contains a stone with two holes where they placed Christ's feet.[112] Close by is the entrance to the chapel on the left, where there is an altar on the spot where the executioners cast lots for Christ's seamless tunic.[113] Not far from this altar, on the left, there is a flight of twenty-nine steps leading down to the chapel of St Helena, mother of the Emperor Constantine. Inside this chapel there is another flight of ten steps down to a pit or grotto. On the eastern side of this is the place beneath a stony rock where were discovered Christ's holy cross, the crown, the nails [and] the point of the lance which had been hidden together with the thieves' crosses.[114] + Outside that entrance to Helena's chapel, on the left, is an altar under which is a column, about one ell long, on which Jesus sat when He was crowned with thorns in Pilate's house. As one continues around it one comes to the southern edge of the high altar. There there is a flight of twelve steps leading up to a beautiful chapel with three windows on the south side. On the east side of the chapel there is a round hole in the rock which is more than half an ell deep while its width at the top is about a palm's breadth each way. + About 5 feet away from here towards the south is that cleft of which it is said "And the rocks were rent."[115] This is 1½ palms in length and 4 feet long. It runs east and west. When one comes from Mount Calvary, outside, a little to the west, on the left-hand side as one returns eastwards, beneath the rock of Mount Calvary, is the site of Golgotha. There is a chapel there in which Gorgians minister. In it one can see the cleft in Mount Calvary from top to bottom. There is an altar on the spot where Adam's head was discovered.[116]

In this chapel there are two tombs. Over the first is written this epitaph:

"Here lies Godfrey, Duke of Buillon,[117] who gained all this land for the Christian faith. His soul reigns with Christ, Amen."

Above the second tomb is this epitaph:

"King Baldwin,[118] a second Judas Machabeus,
The Hope of his Country, the Strength of the Church, and the Glory of Both,
Whom Cedar and Egypt, Dan and murderous Damascus feared,
To whom they brought gifts in tribute,
Alas, in a modest tomb is here enclosed."

As one crosses to the tomb of Our Lord there is a black marble stone on which the body of Jesus Christ was laid when they took Him down from the cross to bury Him with spices and wrapped Him in linen cloths for burial.[119] + One next returns, on the right, to the Holy Sepulchre of Our Lord. This is situated in the centre between the choir and the west end of the Church in a little chapel about 28 feet long and barely 8 feet wide. The room of the Holy Sepulchre is almost square except for half a foot. It stands between two rooms which are connected to the Tomb, one to the east and the other to the west. In the eastern room is a wooden door whose keys are kept by the Franciscans. Between that door and the entrance to the Sepulchre there is a round chapel, about 8 feet in width and almost the same in height. [In] that chapel in front of the entrance to the chapel of the Holy Spirit, a little to the right, is a white stone. This stone is about one and a half feet long and one and a quarter feet wide; the angel sat on it when he said to the women, "Do not be afraid", etc.[120] The entrance to the Holy Sepulchre is there on the west. That entrance, like the first entrance, is made of white marble stones, but there is no means of closing it because the stone which had been placed at the mouth of the Holy Sepulchre is now on the altar of the church of the Holy Saviour on Mount Syon. This entrance is one ell less 3 inches high, and a little over half an ell wide. Below that entrance, next to the north side of the chapel, is the tomb of Our Lord cut out of white marble stone, properly polished and decorated. It is about three-quarters of an ell in depth, 8 feet long and 3 feet wide. Its edges run precisely from east to west. A handsome stone lies on top of it, the same kind and colour as the Sepulchre. It is attached to it with cement to prevent it being opened. The Chapel of the Holy Sepulchre is almost the same length as the Sepulchre and its width is almost the same as its length; the height, however, below the Sepulchre is about 9 feet from the floor to the top of the same. The pinnacle of the Holy Sepulchre is round and constructed like a dovecote. It is covered with lead and the roof of the Temple over the Sepulchre is open. The following verses are written over the pinnacle of the Holy Sepulchre of Our Lord, Jesus Christ, in golden letters and run as follows:

Life was willing to die and lay in this tomb.
Because Death was Life, in victory it destroyed our death.
For He, the strong lion, who broke the regions of Hell in pieces
And subdued them to Himself,
By leading His forces and being Himself leader of His company,
And gaining the victory, rose from this place.
For this reason Hell groans and sorrowful Death is robbed.[121]

The third little building is a chapel with an altar on the west side of the Sepulchre. The entrance to this is on the west. Gorgians minister there. When a priest celebrates in the Sepulchre of Our Lord he can only have three others and no more with him to hear Mass. Fourteen Knights[122] were appointed this year in this Holy Sepulchre. Below the choir, about 40 feet away, there is a stone a little above the ground with a hole in the centre, where, it is said, Our Lord Jesus designated the centre of the world to be.[123] Next one arrives at the high altar towards the east in the same choir: Greeks say the Mass there. The Latins and the Franciscans celebrate Mass throughout the whole year at the altar to the south of Mount Calvary in the Chapel of the Most Blessed Virgin Mary in the Holy Sepulchre and on Mount Syon. Behind the Holy Sepulchre is the chapel in which Jacobites minister. On the right-hand side is the chapel where Indians minister. In the chapel where the Holy Cross was discovered Gorgians minister.

When we had seen and visited all these things in the Church of the Holy Sepulchre we had dinner and after dinner we lay down on the ground to sleep. About midnight we rose to say Matins, to hear Confession, to say Mass and to give the Sacrament to the pilgrims. That same night Lord John Tiptoft, Earl of Worcester in England,[124] stood with his retinue to sing the Mass of the Holy Cross, with organ accompaniment, on Mount Calvary. When this Mass and the others were over we left the Holy Church at dawn for our hospice. We had a meal there in the Consul's house and, after our refreshment, at about three o'clock in the afternoon, we took our donkeys to ride to Bethlehem. This is 26 July [sic].

Pilgrimages on the Road to Bethlehem

It is five miles south from Jerusalem to Bethlehem. There the Wise Men were first entertained. About half-way is the well with a round stone where the three Kings, seeing the star, rejoiced with exceeding great joy and said one to another, "This is the sign of a great king; let us go and offer him gifts, gold, frankincense and myrrh.[125] Further on, on the left, is the church of St Elijah, the prophet. Here, under the shade of a juniper tree, St Elijah was fed by an angel with bread "baked on the coals".[126] There too is the place where the same prophet hid himself when Queen Jezebel was pursuing him.[127] As one goes down further along the road there is the place where Jacob saw the ladder whose top touched heaven.[128] There used to be buildings there but now they are in ruins. Even further along the road, on the right, is the tomb of Rachel,[129] the wife of Jacob and mother of Joseph and Benjamin. This is well maintained. On the right one is shown the site where the prophet Elijah was born.[130] Leaving the road which goes to Hebron is a small road on the left which leads to Bethlehem. Near Bethlehem is the spot where the Most Blessed Virgin Mary dismounted from her donkey[131] and sat down and rested when she came on her wanderings with her husband Joseph for the taxation of the whole world and to give birth in Bethlehem.[132] Then one reaches the city of Bethlehem, the birthplace of King David. In the castle in this city, that is in the north-east corner, there is the church of the Most Blessed Virgin Mary. It is holy and very beautiful. The Franciscans live there. Pilgrims, after choosing their places to sleep in the cloister and after leaving their things there, make their way to the Franciscans' choir, on the north side of the church, where they start their procession.

Pilgrimages within the Site and Church at Bethlehem

The pilgrims go first into the cloister on the north side of the church. There is a flight of eighteen steps there, on the east, called St Jerome's Staircase, which leads down to the chapel. There is a place in the wall where he used to sit when he translated the Bible from Hebrew into Latin.[133] He used to celebrate Mass in the same chapel. There is also the place where he used to sleep and where he was later buried. His body has now been translated to the church of Santa Maria Maggiore in Rome.[134] On the other side of the chapel is another grave where many of the bodies of the Innocents slain by Herod[135] were thrown. The pilgrims then move into the church on the north side of the choir. In the eastern corner is an altar where the Wise Men, after opening their caskets, prepared their gifts for offering.[136] Sixteen steps lead down into a chapel under the choir 30 feet long and about 10 feet wide. At the east end of this is an altar and beneath it the place where Our Lord, Jesus Christ, was born of the Virgin Mary. A little west from this altar, about 10 feet away, is the stone manger where Jesus was laid between the ox and the ass by the Most Blessed Virgin after His birth.[137] + A little further to the east, about 5 feet away, is another altar. These two altars, with the manger, are virtually under one rock. In the west wall of the chapel, in the north-west corner, there is a small hole about half an ell deep and more than half a foot wide where it is said that a dry, barren tree once stood. At the time of the Nativity it flourished and was green and formed one of the timbers of Christ's cross.[138] After that one climbs about sixteen steps southwards. There next to the west wall is the altar where Our Lord, Jesus Christ, was circumcised on the eighth day.[139] + Beneath this church is the well where, so some say, the star which appeared to the Wise Men was changed back into the pre-existent material from which it had been created.[140]

This church is very splendid both above and below. It contains four rows of marble columns with ten columns in each row. There are ten more at right angles to them so that there are fifty altogether. The story is told that once when a great and powerful lord wanted to rob this church and cart away some of its marble stones, a dreadful beast in the shape of an asp or a serpent appeared and made a great cleft in the wall with its tail. The cleft is still visible. It came and stood in front of this lord glaring balefully at him. He was terrified at the sight of the creature and, not daring to do any mischief to this church, beat a hasty retreat with all his companions.[141] In addition, just as we said Masses in the Church of the Holy Sepulchre, so we did in the Church of His Nativity in Bethlehem. The Earl of Worcester, whom I have mentioned above, had the Mass of Our Lord's Nativity, with organ accompaniment, at the altar of Our Lord's Nativity. After Mass we left the holy church in Bethlehem at dawn on the seventh day of June [sic], taking our donkeys and riding to the sites in the mountains of Judaea.

Pilgrimages outside Bethlehem

A stone's throw south from the holy church at Bethlehem is the church of St Nicholas, where the angel appeared to Joseph in his dreams telling him to flee from Bethlehem into Egypt with the boy Jesus and His mother Mary.[142] Two miles east, in a valley, is the place where the angel appeared to the shepherds with a multitude of angels telling them of Christ's birth.[143] In the same place there was a monastery where Paula and Eustochium stayed.[144] Three miles north from Bethlehem is Thene Castle, the birthplace of the prophet Amos.[145] There, too, many dead bodies of the Holy Innocents were buried. There used to be a church there but it has been destroyed. As we were riding thus towards the mountains we met Saracen men and women on the road making their way to the valley of Mambre to the tomb of Abraham and Sarah.[146] + +

Pilgrimages in the Mountains of Judaea

One travels four miles north-west from Bethlehem to the mountains of Judaea. On the road is the spring where Philip baptised the eunuch.[147] Next, on the north flank of the mountain, is a church with an altar in the south-east corner where the Blessed Virgin Mary greeted Elizabeth, and the infant Jesus leapt in her womb. There the Blessed Virgin Mary sang the psalm, "My Soul Doth Magnify the Lord".[148] In the south wall of this church is a huge rock which opened itself in answer to Elizabeth's prayers and received the infant John the Baptist to prevent him being killed along with the other Innocents by Herod's servants.[149] He was taken from there by an angel into the desert where he grew and was nurtured until the time of his preaching. One climbs a stone stairway towards the south up to a sort of large stone courtyard. On the north side of this is a chapel with an altar where St John was circumcised on the eighth day.[150] On the south side, near the edge of the altar, is a small place big enough to hold two men standing, where Zacharias' mouth was opened and he prophesied, saying, "Blessed is the Lord God of Israel", etc.[151] About a quarter of a mile from there, on the road by which they return to Jerusalem, on the right hand side, is a church where the Saracens keep their animals. The entrance to the chapel is on the north side. On its eastern side is an altar on the spot where St John the Baptist was born.[152] + That was Zacharias' third house. The house of St Simeon the Just, in which he was given the answer by the Holy Spirit that he would "not see death until," etc., is near Jerusalem. As one goes on, closer to Jerusalem, in a valley on the left, is the monastery of the Holy Cross where Gorgians minister. Behind and beneath the high altar is a hole where the wood of the holy cross grew. From there we crossed to Jerusalem to our hospice for a meal. After the fourth hour we entered the Church [of the Holy Sepulchre], staying there the whole night, saying Masses and visiting the holy sites as before. After midnight the lord, the Earl of Worcester, had Mass with organ accompaniment on Mount Calvary. At dawn on the eighth day we left the Church for our hospice and stayed there until the fourth hour. Then we went to the House of Syon and that same night took our donkeys to ride to the Desert of the Forty Days.[153]

These are the Pilgrimages from Jerusalem to Jordan

One next travels from Jerusalem to Jordan. That is a really hard, rough road because of the heat, the number of mountains and the lack of water and other things necessary to sustain the body. The advice therefore is that no one should go on that road on foot. Quite often many persons die there since they can find nothing on that route to eat or drink before the return to Jerusalem. It is accordingly necessary to carry with one bread, water, hard-boiled eggs, wine, cheese and other necessary things, especially restoratives. From Jerusalem to Jordan is a good thirty miles.[154] Along the road is the place where St Joachim lived with his shepherds when he was driven out of the Temple.[155] It is there that the angel announced to him the future birth of Mary.[156] From that place there are two roads. One leads to the Mount of Temptation (the Mount of the Forty Days), the other to Jericho. There are high mountains on both roads. After descending eastwards from the mountains they go about four miles northwards to the Mount of Temptation. This is a high mountain, hard to climb, which stands on the eastern edge of the other mountains. On its eastern side there is a path almost halfway up the mountain towards the south, where there is a cave in the mountain face with two chapels, a lower and an upper. We celebrated Mass there. It is the place where Our Lord Jesus fasted forty days and forty nights. + It is also the place where He was tempted by the devil with the words, "If thou art the Son of God, command", etc.[157] After Mass the pilgrims descend and go to a grove of trees near the foot of the mountain towards the east. Through the middle of this grove there is a stream of fast-running water which flows towards the Jordan. It comes from the river Marath behind the north flank of the mountain. In response to the prayers of the sons of the prophets it was cured of its bitterness and barrenness by Elisha by the scattering of salt on the river.[158] Pilgrims rest in this grove beside the water and refresh themselves with food and drink. After that, those who so wish climb the aforesaid mountain by the earlier road. When they reach the north flank of the mountain they turn left towards the south. They then climb to the top of the mountain where the devil tempted Christ with the words, "All this will I give thee."[159] Here stand three walls of a chapel, namely the north, the east and the south walls, about 8 feet wide and the same length. One then comes down from the mountain to Jericho to the house where Jesus was received as a guest by Zachaeus.[160] He restored a blind man's sight there.[161] That city is now destroyed, apart from the houses of some country people still standing there. Pilgrims sleep there that night on the stones. It is about five miles from the Jordan. Further along the road to Jordan stood the monastery of St John the Baptist. It is said that Christ was baptised there because at one time the Jordan came up to that place.[162] Now the river has retreated about a crossbow shot. After that one arrives at the Jordan where the pilgrims bathe. This is a beautiful, deep river which runs into the Dead Sea. The Dead Sea has no visible outlet. It is a good eighty miles long and is two miles from the place where the pilgrims bathe.[163] It is not advisable to stay long in the water of the Jordan. One should bathe because of the indulgences and then get out quickly. Near the Dead Sea, on the other side, was the monastery of St Jerome. He performed his penance in that vast desert before he went to Bethlehem, as he himself bears witness in one of his letters. Near the Sea also is the statue in salt of Loth's wife.[164] After visiting these sites we arrived that night at Jericho where we lay for four hours on the stones. A French priest died that night and was buried halfway along the road from Jerusalem to Jericho. After sleeping we got up to ride to Bethany and Jerusalem. We reached Bethany on the morning of the tenth day.

These are the Pilgrimages in Bethany

In Bethany the first site is an old castle in which is the fine tomb of St Lazarus whom Christ raised from the dead.[165] The monastery of the virgin, St Scholastica, was there. Outside the castle is the place where Martha ran to meet Christ and fell at His feet saying, "Master, if thou hadst been here my brother would not have died."[166] The house of the holy women, namely Martha and Mary, was there as well as the house of Simon, the leper. Christ was often entertained in these houses.[167] Above Bethany towards Mount Olivet is the site of Bethfage where Christ sat on the foal of the donkey to ride into Jerusalem on Palm Sunday.[168] One should note that Mount Olivet towers in height over all the region. On this mount the Lord was at pains to teach His disciples as well as those who flocked to Him from the city. One should note too that in the times of Christ there was a little town named Gethsemane where Christ was seized and arrested. After seeing all these places we came to Jerusalem and waited in the hospice until the hour of Vespers.

We then entered the church and heard a sermon there from an English priest from the Royal College of the Blessed Mary at Eton. His text was, "Thou art a pilgrim in Jerusalem."[169]

There were twenty-seven Englishmen with the lord, the Earl I have mentioned above.[170] In the morning he had Mass sung, with organ accompaniment, in the Chapel of the Most Blessed Mary. In Our Lord's Temple there are twelve sects,[171] Latins, Greeks, Armenians, Indians, Jacobites, Gorgians, Syrians, Maronites, Nestorians, Aridians, Abbatians and Pessines. All of them have places in the church to worship God.

On 1 July we left the Church at dawn for the hospice. The next night we lay on the ground in the House of Syon. At dawn on 2 July, after Mass, we rode to Rama. On 3 July, after Mass, we rode at dawn to Jaffa and embarked on our galley. Thus we were in the Holy Land for thirteen days. We set sail on 5 July, arriving in the harbour of Salinis.[172] in Cyprus on the 8th. There, on a high mountain, is the cross of the Good Thief.[173] It is suspended up in the air and it cannot be moved from that place; sometimes it appears white and sometimes red. There is also a river of white salt there. The King of Cyprus[174] pays the Sultan of Babylon 10,000 ducats as tribute each year in cloth called "camlet".[175] St Katherine[176] was born in the same country, near Famagusta. She was converted to Christianity by a holy hermit.

We set sail from Salinis on 14 July and arrived at Rhodes on 22 July, Mary Magdalene's Day. We heard there that, before our arrival, 250 Turks had been brought to Rhodes by sea, and had been dealt with in the following manner. When they entered the city they were preceded by Christian boys, who had been Turkish prisoners, dressed in white and carrying white crosses in their hands. These dragged with ropes the apostates whose nostrils had been pierced and others whose hands were tied behind their backs. Of these prisoners eighteen had stakes driven into the anus which came out through their backs or chests; ten were dragged naked across a plank full of iron goads; two were beheaded after baptism; one was flayed and another was thrown from a tower and hung up by the genitals. The rest were hanged, some by the feet and some by the neck, on either side of the city so that they should be in full view of all passers-by.[177]

At this time the Great Sultan was in the Morea.[178] He took 30,000 men, women and children of that land to colonize the land and city of Constantinople.

In Turkey there is an island on which there are 20,000 Greek monks who eat neither meat nor fish. No member of the feminine sex lives among them.[179]

We reached Cande on 4 August. There we saw the head of St Titus,[180] Paul's disciple, who was archbishop of Cortina [Gortyn], the metropolis of the island of Crete, where there are nine bishops. Mallasetum,[181] cypress and sugar[182] grow there. We arrived at Corfu on 24 August. On 2 September we reached Jarra in Dalmatia where St Simeon lies. His body is uncorrupted. He it was who held Christ in his arms. In the same church lies St Zoyolus,[183] confessor, while in the cathedral lies St Anastasia, virgin and martyr.[184] She is remembered on the Day of Our Lord's Nativity because on that day she endured martyrdom by burning. We came to Venice on 6 September. Thus we spent nine weeks and a day on the return voyage from Jaffa to Venice. We spent sixteen weeks on the complete return journey from Venice to the Holy Land and from there back to Venice. In this we were attended with God's aid and we render Him eternal thanks for showing us His mercy so graciously. Amen. +

The total time taken on my return journey from Eton back to Eton was thirty-nine weeks.

COMMENTARY

This chapter is a very close repeat of *materia* 8 from Chapter 6, except that it now contains personal reminiscences not found in the earlier and drier version. It sheds interesting light on Wey's process of compilation of *The Itineraries*. His earlier account of the 1458 journey is divided between three chapters, in each of which the treatment is different. Chapter 8 is a mere list of the places in Europe through which he passed on the way from England via Rome to Venice and, after the galley voyage to and from Jaffa which is not described there, from Venice back to England. Chapter 14 deals with Rome, but concentrates on churches and indulgences. *Materia* 8 of Chapter 6 shows a few signs of personal involvement and observation. In particular, in describing the arduous pilgrimage to the Jordan, Wey goes beyond simple descriptions and catalogues of sites. He offers advice about the food which pilgrims should carry with them and the precautions they should take when they bathe. Such pieces of advice are developed more fully in Chapter 7 when Wey takes the plunge, as it were, and, abandoning the very detached style of his earlier narrative, includes episodes like the Masses of the Earl of Worcester and the death of a French priest. These provide vivid glimpses of the journeys and add much to the interest of his writing.

NOTES

1   Bachelor of Sacred Theology: the modern equivalent of this degree is Bachelor of Divinity, but this term is seldom found in medieval usage. (Emden, *A Biographical Register of the University of Oxford to AD 1500*, Vol. 1, p. xlii.)

2   Perpetual Fellow of the Royal College of the Most Blessed Mary of Eton at Windsor. Eton College, founded by King Henry VI, was incorporated in 1442. Wey, while not one of the original four fellows, who were appointed together with the first provost, Henry Sever, on 11 October 1440,

was among the earliest to be elected. His name appears seventh in the list of fellows, the likely year of his appointment being 1441. He vacated his fellowship in about 1467 and entered the Augustinian Priory in Edington. Eton College still has the transcript of a letter from Henry VI in 1457 giving special permission to William Wey, notwithstanding the statutes, to absent himself from the College to go on pilgrimage "to Rome, to Jerusalem and to other Holy Places".

3 Cande, known today as Heraklion, lies halfway along the northern coast of Crete. It still has many remains of the Venetian occupation which lasted from 1204 until 1669. It was important as a port from which malmsey wine was exported.

4 Wey gives details of the major ports and distances between Venice and Jaffa on two occasions. The first, in English, is in Chapter 2 and the second, in Latin, is in Chapter 9.

5 St Nicholas. The monastery and church of San Nicolò al Lido, near the main entrance to the Venetian lagoon, were founded in 1044. The main entrance to the lagoon was always strongly defended; at one time it could be closed by chains to prevent the passage of enemy vessels. In the channel here, which was the "official" point of departure from Venice, the Doge performed the annual ceremony of the marriage with the sea.

6 Porenzo (Parense, Parentium, Poreč). Both in 1458 and 1462 Wey's pilgrim galley took about 36 hours to cover the 100 miles. Casola took a similar time in 1494 (Newett, *Canon Pietro Casola's Pilgrimage*, p. 162).

7 Ragusa (Dubrovnik) was an important trading city in the Middle Ages, at times rivalling Venice itself. The word "argosy" is derived from the name of the city. St Blaise (Blaize, Blazey), its patron, was a physician who became bishop of Sebaste, (d.c.316). His symbol is an iron wool-comb, the instrument of his martyrdom, and he is, therefore, often regarded as the patron saint of wool workers, tuckers, fullers etc. His feast day is 3 February and his aid was invoked for infections of the throat.

8 Durrës (Duracio, Dyrrachium) was known to the Ancient Greeks as Epidamnus; its traditional date of foundation was 627 BC. Always an important place, in Roman times it was the starting point of the Via Egnatia which led from the Adriatic to Constantinople. It was given by the Crusaders to Venice in 1203 but was lost shortly after. In 1392 it was returned to the Venetians, who improved the harbour and city walls and based a naval force there, as Wey describes, to deter the pirates who infested this part of the Adriatic.

9 Negroponte was the name given by the Venetians to the island of Euboea. Under the Venetians it ranked as a kingdom. Conquered by the Turks in 1470 it became part of the Ottoman Empire.

10 Casope (Kassiópi) is on the north-east coast of Corfu facing Albania. It has the ruins of an Angevin castle, and the church may occupy the site of the temple of Zeus visited by Nero. It is possible that Wey's story of the crocodile is the folk memory of an episode when animals destined for Roman arenas escaped from the ships carrying them to Italy.

11 Minos was the legendary king of Crete who kept the Minotaur, a monster, half-bull and half-man, eventually slain by Theseus, in the Labyrinth whose traditional site is in the Palace of Knossos, east of Heraklion.

12 "The Cretans are always liars, evil beasts"; Wey quotes the Vulgate, *Cretenses semper mendaces, malae bestiae*; Titus 1.12.

13 The Knights of St John. The origins of "The Knights of the Order of the Hospital of St John of Jerusalem", usually known as the Knights Hospitaller, are shrouded in legend. They appear in

the eleventh century and hold a firm place in history, together with the Templars, as valiant opponents of the Mohammedans. After the fall of Acre in 1291 they escaped to Cyprus and then moved to Rhodes where they stayed for over 200 years (1309 to 1523). Homeless for seven years, they then received the sovereignty of Malta in 1530 and remained there until 1798.

14 The crown of thorns was one of the instruments of Christ's Passion (John 19:2). There are many legends connected with this relic, or portions thereof. In the thirteenth century St Louis IX, King of France, built the Sainte-Chapelle in Paris to house it. (Newett, *Canon Pietro Casola's Pilgrimage*, p. 382, n71).

15 Paphos. St Paul visited Paphos on his first missionary journey with St Barnabas and there converted the Roman governor, Sergius Paulus, to Christianity (Acts 13:6–12).

16 Gourds. The reading in Roxburghe, *cucumeres*, means "cucumbers", an unlikely container for wine. Gourds, *cucurbitae*, on the other hand, which are bottle-shaped, were one of the traditional items carried by pilgrims, whether to Compostella or to Jerusalem, and are frequently shown in art attached to the pilgrim's staff. They are still sold to tourists.

17 Marcus and Marcellinus (Mark and Marcellian) were twin brothers and deacons who were martyred in about 287 at Rome under Maximian Herculeus.

18 Compline: the last of the canonical hours, said at about 8.00 or 9.00 p.m.

19 Warden of the Franciscans. The Prior or Guardian of Mount Syon was the prior of the Franciscan Friary there, as well as superior-general of all the houses belonging to that order in the Holy Land, and papal vicar and legate for all the countries in the East (Newett, *Canon Pietro Casola's Pilgrimage*, p. 384, n75). In this chapter Wey mentions the various functions he performed in relation to pilgrims during their stay in the Holy Land.

20 Caves. These caves, where all pilgrims had to spend at least one night, were notorious for filth and lack of amenities. (Prescott, *Jerusalem Journey*, p. 105; Mitchell, *Spring Voyage*, p. 91). Indulgences, however, were obtained by any pilgrim who endured the discomfort in the right spirit.

21 Two galleys. In the fifteenth century Venetian galleys undertaking long voyages, like those to Bruges, London, Alexandria and the Black Sea, normally travelled in pairs for extra security. Wey's *patronus* in 1462 was Andrea Morosini and his galley was therefore probably the *Morosina*. It is not known if this was the galley Wey used in 1458. The name of the other galley in 1458, the *Loredana*, is known from accounts written by other pilgrims in that year (Mitchell, *Spring Voyage*, p. 55).

22 St Sylvester was Bishop of Rome from 314 to 335. According to legend he cleansed Constantine the Great from leprosy and baptised him on his deathbed. In fact Constantine was baptised after the death of Sylvester.

23 Constantine the Great (c.274–337) was proclaimed Emperor at York in 306. He defeated his rival, Maxentius, at the Battle of the Milvian Bridge in 312. He established his capital at Byzantium, which he renamed Constantinople, in 330. He shares a feast day, 21 May, with his mother St Helena.

24 The sons of Noah were Shem, Ham and Japhet (Genesis 10:1). Jaffa has also been known as Japho and Joppa.

25 Tabitha, also known as Dorcas, was raised from the dead by St Peter (Acts 9: 36–41).

26 Jonah 1:3. Jonah was in fact fleeing to Tarshish. Roxburghe has a Tarsis – "from Tarshish".

27 Rama. The hospice here was run by the Franciscans from Mount Syon. Paid for by Philip the Good, Duke of Burgundy, it was built in 1420 (Prescott, *Jerusalem Journey*, p. 110). Casola

describes the spartan furnishings and sleeping arrangements there (Newett, *Canon Pietro Casola's Pilgrimage*, pp. 237–8).

28   Welsh miles. For the length of various "miles", see notes to Chapter 8.

29   St George. Many legends have grown up about St George. The traditional site of his martyrdom, Lydda (the modern Lod) is close to Ben Gurion Airport. The Tomb of St George is shown in the basement of the ruins of the twelfth-century Crusader church. In the Greek legend Perseus slew the sea monster at Jaffa and that story might have become interwoven with the story of St George and the Dragon. Wey was familiar with *The Golden Legend*, which deals with St George at some length.

30   Acts 9:32–35 describes how St Peter healed Aeneas, "sick of the palsy", in Lydda.

31   Nova Porta. Wey sites this place halfway between Ramla and Jerusalem, 12 miles from each, and describes the second half of the road as rough, rocky and steep. It is tempting to identify Wey's Nova Porta with the twelfth-century Crusader fortress Le Toron des Chevaliers, since in his account of his second Jerusalem pilgrimage Wey says that they rode from Ramys to Jerusalem by way of Betanobel Castle and New Castle, *per castellum Betanobel et Novum Castrum*.

32   Emaus Castle (Emmaus): Luke 24:13 gives the distance from Jerusalem as 60 furlongs – i.e. 7½ miles. Wey used Luke 24:18 as the text for his sermon in Jerusalem on 30 June 1458.

33   Judith and Holophernes. The Apocryphal Old Testament Book of Judith tells how the Assyrian king Nebuchadnezzar sent an army under his general Holophernes against the Jews. He besieged their city of Bethulia. Judith, a young and beautiful widow, saved her people by going to Holophernes in his camp where, after captivating him and making him drunk, she cut off his head and returned with it to Bethulia. The Israelites were thus encouraged to sally forth and the Assyrians fled.

34   Amatoth and Jeremiah. Anathoth is given as the home of the prophet Jeremiah in Jeremiah 1:1. It is mentioned again in Jeremiah 11:21–23.

35   The account of Eli and Samuel at Sylo (Shiloh) is to be found in 1 Samuel 1:3 and 1:24. The burial of Samuel at Ramah is mentioned in 1 Samuel 25.

36   Cleophas: Luke 24:18. For Mary Cleophas, his wife, see John 19:25.

37   Joseph of Aramathea: Matthew 27:57; Mark 15:43; Luke 23:50; John 19:38.

38   Mount Syon (Zion). More information about the Franciscans and their house in Jerusalem is given by the two slightly later pilgrims Friar Felix Fabri and Canon Casola. Casola (Newett, *Canon Pietro Casola's Pilgrimage*, p. 254) writes, "The Mount of Syon is the highest in Jerusalem and in ancient times it was called the rock or city of David … Now the observant Friars of St Francis live there, and they have a very well kept convent … The friars' church is very beautiful … At the time of Our Lord this church was the large room in which he ate the last supper …" "The friars were installed there by Robert, King of Sicily, in 1333. In addition to the 24 brothers in the convent on Mount Zion, two were always stationed in the Church of the Holy Sepulchre to tend the lamps and serve the altars there. There were another six at Bethlehem who performed similar functions there" (Prescott, *Jerusalem Journey*, p. 119).

39   The Church of the Holy Sepulchre was built over the rock cave where, according to tradition, Christ was buried and rose from the dead. The tomb was said to have been discovered by St Helena and the first church was dedicated there *c.*335. Enlarged on several occasions over the centuries, the present church dates mainly from 1810. It contains many chapels and shrines.

40   The stone: see p. 47.

41   Nestorius (d.c.451) was a native of Syria. In 428 he became Bishop of Constantinople. He gave his name to the heresy of Nestorianism, the doctrine which holds that there were two separate persons in the Incarnate Christ, one Divine and the other Human, (see *Oxford Dictionary of the Christian Church*, s.v. Nestorianism). Wey would have been unsympathetic to the Nestorian attitude to contemporary devotion to the Virgin as the Mother of God. Apart from the mention of Nestorians in Chapter 6, which is probably the first draft of Chapter 7, Wey mentions the Nestorians again in this chapter. He simplifies the relationship between the Nestorians and Islam. The Prophet Muhammed, founder of Islam, was born about 570 and died in 629.

42   Another example of the restrictions placed upon Christians visiting the Holy Land. Pilgrims were only admitted to the Church of the Holy Sepulchre at nightfall.

43   The sites of the Stations. Nowadays the Stations of the Cross are usually a series of fourteen images arranged around the walls of a church depicting incidents in the last journey of Christ from Pilate's house to His entombment. As an act of devotion worshippers visit them in order, thus re-enacting and commemorating Jesus' journey along the Via Dolorosa, the route followed by pilgrims in Jerusalem. For centuries the Franciscans acted as guides to the route – as Wey says here, *Fratres ducunt peregrinos*.

The fourteen incidents which now form the Stations are:

1.   Christ is condemned to death.
2.   Christ receives the cross.
3.   His first fall.
4.   He meets His Mother.
5.   Simon of Cyrene is made to carry the cross.
6.   Christ's face is wiped by Veronica.
7.   His second fall.
8.   He meets the women of Jerusalem.
9.   His third fall.
10. He is stripped of His garments.
11. He is nailed to the cross.
12. Christ dies on the cross.
13. His body is taken down from the cross.
14. His body is laid in the tomb.

While Wey mentions several of these incidents, it is apparent that his Franciscan guide gave a great deal more information about the sites and buildings which the group passed on their walk through the city.

44   The parable of the rich man and Lazarus is in Luke 16:19–31.

45   Simon of Cyrene: Matthew 27:32; Mark 15:21; Luke 23:26.

46   *Filiae Jerusalem, nolite flere super me*: "Daughters of Jerusalem, weep not for me." Here Wey again quotes verbatim from the Vulgate (Luke 23:28).

47   The legendary incident now occupies a position in the Stations of the Cross. A portrait professing to be the original imprint of Christ's features on Veronica's headcloth was translated by Boniface VIII to St Peter's in 1297. This relic was greatly venerated in Rome in the Middle

Ages. Wey mentions the vernicle and the indulgences it conferred in Chapter 14, which deals with relics in Rome.

48 Bethesda: John 5:2–4.

49 Two stones: cf. p. 37, line 121.

50 The school of the Blessed Virgin Mary. In art she is often shown seated beside St Anne and learning to read.

51 The House of Pilate: Mark 15:1–15; Luke 23; John 19.

52 The House of Herod: Luke 23:7–11.

53 Christ clad in a garment by Herod: Luke 23:11

54 Mary's sins forgiven: Luke 7:36–48.

55 The house of St Anne. The Gospels do not give the names of the parents of the BVM. They are traditionally known as Joachim and Anne (or Anna). In art St Anne is usually depicted either teaching her little daughter to read the Bible or greeting her husband, St Joachim, at the Golden Gate. She is commemorated on 26 July.

56 St Scholastica c.480–c.543. Regarded, traditionally, as the first nun of the Benedictine order, she was the sister of St Benedict. Her relics were kept at Montecassino. Her feast day is 10 February.

57 Christ and the doctors: Luke 2:46

58 St James the Less, the son of Alphaeus, was one of the Twelve. Some traditions identify him with the St James, the Lord's brother, who became first Bishop of Jerusalem and was martyred in 62 by being thrown from a pinnacle of the Temple and then stoned to death. He is represented also as the author of the apocryphal Book of James, the Protoevangelion, from which Wey obtained the stories of Joachim and Anna and some of the legends about the BVM.

59 In the accounts of both of his Jerusalem pilgrimages, 1458 and 1462, Wey mentions that the final resting place of Simeon's uncorrupted body is Jarra, in Dalmatia. Simeon was the aged and devout Jew "who held Christ in his arms". Luke 2:25–35 describes the event and gives the words of the Nunc dimittis: - "Lord, now lettest thou thy servant depart in peace", which Simeon spoke.

60 Palm Sunday: John 12:13.

61 Heraclius (575–641) was the Byzantine Emperor who, on 21 March 629, solemnly brought back to Golgotha the Cross, which the Persians had removed from Jerusalem in 614. The Feast, called the Exaltation of the Cross, observed on Holy Cross Day, 14 September, commemorates this recovery. Wey refers to the victory of Heraclius in Chapter 11.

62 The stoning of Stephen is described in Acts 7:58–60.

63 Sheba's visit to Solomon is described in 1 Kings 10:1–13 and 2 Chronicles, 9:1–12. The story of the Invention and Exaltation of the True Cross is to be found in The Golden Legend. The best-known cycle of paintings illustrating it is that by Piero della Francesca in the church of San Francesco, Arezzo, which was painted between 1452 and 1459. William Wey could have seen it, therefore, during his travels through Italy in late spring 1458.

According to tradition the tree grew from a seed from the Tree of Sin, planted in the dead Adam's mouth by his son Seth. The tree grew until the time of Solomon, who cut it down to build his Temple. The craftsmen rejected it and used it as a bridge over the stream, Siloam.

When she visited Solomon, the Queen of Sheba had a vision about the bridge which foretold that it would be used for Christ's Cross. She declined to cross it and Solomon had it buried deep in the earth. Wey's description of the episode of the Queen of Sheba and the bridge could be based on Piero's depiction of it.

64 Tomb of BVM: see p. 37, line 134.

65 Luke 22:44.

66 The betrayal by Judas and Christ's arrest are described in Matthew 26:47–49; Mark 14:43–46 and Luke 22:47.

67 Matthew 26:51; Mark 14:47; Luke 22:51; John 18:10.

68 The agony in the garden: both Matthew 26:41 and Mark 14:38 contain the words *Vigilate et orate*, i.e. "Watch and pray", repeated here by Wey.

69 Assumption of BVM. The belief in the bodily assumption of the Blessed Virgin is first met with in late-fourth-century New Testament Apocrypha. In 1950 Pope Pius XII declared the Corporal Assumption a dogma of the Church. The scene of Mary on her deathbed surrounded by the Apostles is often depicted in art. In the Eastern Church it is called the "Koimesis". Many legends grew up about the events that occurred at the time of the Virgin's death. One tells how the Apostles were miraculously reunited, some from very far afield, to be present at Mary's death. Thomas arrived late and expressed incredulity at what the others told him. To convince him the Virgin dropped her girdle to him from Heaven.

Wey refers to this important relic in his Chapter 11. His detailed description suggests that he saw it himself on his way from Bologna to Rome. *Cingulum beatissime Mariae, quod miserat sancto Thome Indie, in monte Oliveti est, in castello Prati, decem miliaria a Florentia, et est de filo lino, et habet in medio filum aureum et nescitur cujus coloris est, et habet in finibus pendicula per quae potest cingi.* "The girdle of the Most Blessed Mary, which she gave to St Thomas of India, is on Mount Olivet, in the castle of Pratus, 10 miles from Florence. It is made of linen thread and has a golden thread in the centre. Its colour is unknown; it has tassels at the end by which it can be tied." The girdle is now kept in the late-fourteenth-century Chapel of the Holy Girdle in Prato Cathedral. Agnolo Gaddi (d.1396) covered the walls of this chapel with frescoes illustrating the legend and, probably in the 1430s, Donatello and Michelozzo created the outdoor pulpit of the Holy Girdle from which it is displayed to the faithful five times a year. If Wey did visit Prato en route to Rome in 1458 he would have seen these masterpieces while they were still new.

70 "If thou hadst known: Christ wept over Jerusalem:" Luke 19:42.

71 "I will go before you into Galilee": Matthew 26:32; Matthew 28:7 and 10.

72 The Ascension. Wey echoes the words of the Vulgate (Acts 1:9–11), *Duo viri ... in vestibus albis ... Viri Galilei quid ...*

73 Wey wished to satisfy himself about the imprint of Christ's foot since there is a stone in Westminster Abbey which also is said to bear the mark. There used to be an interesting, mid-fifteenth-century Nottingham alabaster panel in Wells Cathedral which depicted the Ascension and the imprint of Christ's feet.

74 According to legend, St Pelagia the Penitent was an actress who was converted at Antioch. Dressing as a man she then travelled to Jerusalem where she lived a life of penance.

75 Bethfage: Matthew 21:1; Mark 11:1 and 2; Luke 19:29 and 30.

76 The Apostles' Creed. Although, traditionally, the formula was composed by the Apostles, the title is first found *c*.390. Its present wording probably evolved over a considerable time.

77 The Lord's Prayer: Matthew 6:9–13; Luke 11:2–4.

78 The Beatitudes: Matthew 5:3–11 The words of the Vulgate, *Beati pauperes spiritu*, are echoed by Wey.

79 The stone of the BVM: see p. 40, lines 229–30.

80 Death of Judas: Matthew 27:5.

81 Zacharias. According to the Protoevangelion (16:9–16), Zacharias, husband of Elizabeth and father of St John the Baptist, was murdered in the Temple at the command of Herod during the Massacre of the Innocents when the whereabouts of his infant son John were not revealed.

82 Hiding places: Matthew 26:56.

83 The Well of the BVM: see p. 41.

84 The blind man and the pool of Syloe (Siloam): John 9:7.

85 The martyrdom of Isaiah, by being cut in two by a wood-saw, is described in the second-century composite Jewish–Christian work *The Ascension of Isaiah*. There may be a reference to this episode in Hebrews 11:37.

86 Field of Acheldemach: Matthew 27:7–10; Acts 1:18–19.

87 The House of Evil Counsel and the Betrayal: Matthew 26:1; Mark 14:10; Luke 22:4.

88 *The Golden Legend* describes various events connected with the death of the Virgin. She was warned of her death by Gabriel, who brought her a palm, not, as at the Annunciation, a lily. Wey gives the location of this episode on his *Mappa Terrae Sanctae* with the notes, in Chapter 12, *Palma ad Virginem* and *Palma adducta ad beatissimam Virginem per angelum in monte Oliveti*. At her death her soul, in the form of a child, was received by Christ himself. While her body was being taken for burial a certain Hebrew, named Jephonias, tried to seize it. His hands stuck to the bier (or were cut off) until he repented and St Peter freed him. Wey includes the location of this episode also on his map with the words *Locus ubi Judaei voluerunt rapuisse corpus beatissimae Virginis*. On the third day the archangel Michael accompanied her body to Paradise where it was reunited with her soul. She left behind an empty tomb, later found by the Apostles to be filled with roses and lilies. At this point, according to one version, St Thomas, who had arrived too late to witness the Assumption himself in company with the other Apostles, typically refused to believe in the miracles which had occurred. Thereupon the Virgin appeared to him in a vision and herself dropped her girdle from Heaven into his hands.

There are several famous representations of this story, which Wey might have seen himself, in particular the Porta della Mandorla of Florence Cathedral by Nanni di Banco, (1414–21) and the Maestà by Duccio (1308–11) in Siena.

89 St Peter "wept bitterly". The words *flevit amare* are an echo of Matthew 26:75 and Luke 22:62. The episode also appears in Mark 14:72.

90 St Angelus of Jerusalem, 1145–1220, was born in Jerusalem of convert Jewish parents. One of the early friar hermits of Mount Carmel, he was killed in Sicily.

91 House of Annas: John 18:22 tells how Christ was slapped by one of the officers in the house of the high priest; cf. Matthew 26:67; Mark 14:65 and Luke 22:64. The high priest was Annas, father-in-law of Caiaphas.

92 The Last Supper: Matthew 26:26–28; Mark 14:22–24; Luke 22:19–20; 1 Corinthians 11:24–26.

93 The washing of the Disciples' feet: John 13:5–12.

94 Day of Pentecost: Acts 2:1–4.

95 Doubting Thomas: John 20:26–28.

96 Mary's prayers: see p. 42, line 294.

97 Today the Tomb of King David on Mount Zion is beneath the Hall of the Last Supper, on the lower floor of the large church built by the Crusaders to commemorate Mary's Dormition.

98 Paschal Lamb: Mark 14:12.

99 Nicodemus was the Jew, learned in the Law, and a member of the Sanhedrin (John 3:1–10), who sympathized with Christ (John 7:50–51) and assisted Joseph of Aramathea in giving Christ burial (John 19:39–40). Gamaliel, a Pharisee and a doctor of the law, spoke against the execution of Peter and other Apostles (Acts 6:35). St Paul was taught by him (Acts 22:3).

100 This event is known as the Dormition.

101 The selection of St Matthias is described in Acts 1:26.

102 All the sites described by Wey as "in the great church which was called Sancta Maria de Scala ad celos" were in the Church usually called St Mary on Mount Zion. This church was originally built in the late fourth or early fifth century. It was damaged by the Persians in 614. After repairs it then fell again into ruin. It was rebuilt by the Franks in the twelfth century. Also known as "Mother of the Churches", it had a flight of about thirty steps (or sixty-one in another account) at the end of the apse leading to the upper chamber where the table of the Last Supper could be seen.

103 Mark's words (Vulgate, Mark 15:46) about the great stone which was rolled to the mouth of the tomb, *advolvit lapidem ad ostium monumenti*, are echoed by Wey, *lapis ille qui erat advolutus ad [h]ostium monumenti*.

104 The events in the House of Caiaphas are described in Matthew 27:57–75; Mark 14:53–72; Luke 22:54–71 and John 18:12–27.

105 The death of St James the Greater: Acts 12:2.

106 The Three Marys: Matthew 28:1–6; Mark 16:1–7; Luke 24:1–10.

107 The view of Calvary: p. 43, line 308.

108 Another example of the tight control exercised by the Saracens over Christian pilgrims.

109 Pilate's flogging of Christ: Matthew 27:26; Mark 15:15; John 19:1. The column is often shown on the Symbols of the Passion.

110 Miracle of the Invention of the Cross. According to legend, St Helena found the crosses of Christ and the two thieves on Golgotha. The true one was identified by the miracle described by Wey. The Veneration of the Cross at Jerusalem is first described in the fourth-century pilgrimage of Etheria. Until 1960 a church festival commemorating the discovery was held on 3 May.

111 Christ's being mistaken for a gardener, *hortulanus*, and the *Noli me tangere* are recorded in John 20:15–17.

112 The stone with two holes: see p. 35, line 60.

113 Here Wey uses the exact words of the Vulgate, John 19:23, *tunica inconsutili*, to describe the seamless tunic.

114 These relics, and their whereabouts, interested Wey very much. Elsewhere he mentions the thorns kept by the Knights Hospitaller on Rhodes and the point of the lance, guarded by twenty-four knights at Nuremburg.

115 *Petrae scissae sunt*: "The rocks were rent". Matthew 27:51 is another exact verbal echo of the Vulgate.

116 The head of Adam. In Chapter 6 Wey gives more detail. There is a hole for the cross in white marble, tinged with red flecks. Adam's head was found in that hole after the flood as a sign that therein lay redemption. On that stone is written, "Here God achieved salvation in the centre of the earth." A tradition, first found in Origen, placed Adam's tomb on Calvary so that at the Crucifixion the blood of the Second Adam was poured over the head of the First. (See Cross, *Oxford Dictionary of the Christian Church*, s.v. Adam, p. 15.)

117 Godfrey of Bouillon (*c.*1060–1100) was a French noble and one of the leaders of the First Crusade, taking a prominent part in the capture of Jerusalem in 1099. He was chosen ruler of Jerusalem with the title "Advocate of the Holy Sepulchre". He died in 1100 and was succeeded by his brother Baldwin I as king.

118 Baldwin, brother of Godfrey of Bouillon, was the first King of Jerusalem (1100–1118)

119 Linen cloths: Matthew 27:59; Mark 15:46; Luke 23:53; John 19:39–40.

120 "Do not be afraid": Matthew 28:5; Mark 16:6.

121 A lion is the emblem of the tribe of Judah: Christ was called "the Lion of the tribe of Judah" (Genesis 49:9). In his eleventh-century hymn, "Chorus novae Ierusalem", St Fulbert of Chartres writes, *Christus invictus leo, dracone surgens obruto, dum voce viva personat, a morte functos excitat.* This hymn appears in translation as No. 139, "Ye choirs of New Jerusalem", in *The English Hymnal*.

122 The prior (warden, guardian) of Mount Zion had authority to admit to the Military Order of the Knights of the Holy Sepulchre pilgrims who were eligible through birth or military distinction. Mitchell (*John Tiptoft*, pp. 109–11) uses the account by Roberto da Sanseverino to describe the ceremony in detail. On this occasion, during Wey's visit, John Tiptoft represented the warden in dubbing knight two Milanese.

123 The centre of the world. Wey refers to this belief again in Chapters 6 and 9. In most medieval *mappae mundi* Jerusalem was placed in the centre as *omphalos*, or navel, of the earth. Wey was interested in cartography, and this tradition would have had a special appeal to him. His large *Mappa Terrae Sanctae*, with, as he says, "Jerusalem in the myddys", is now in the Bodleian (MS Douce 389). Sadly, the whereabouts of his *mappa mundi* which, on a flyleaf at the beginning of *The Itineraries*, he says he wishes to leave to the monastery at Edington are unknown. One of the origins of this tradition is to be found in Ezekiel 5:5.

124 Sir John Tiptoft, Earl of Worcester, was born in about 1427, the son of Sir John Tiptoft, member of Parliament for Huntingdon and a descendant of an old Norman family. He was educated at Oxford University, having rooms in University College (Emden, *A Biographical Register*, p. 1877) and inherited his father's estate in January 1443. Six years later he married the Earl of Warwick's sister, Cecily Neville, and was created Earl of Worcester on 1 July 1449. He served as Treasurer of England under Henry VI (1452–54). In May 1458 he sailed from Venice to Jaffa on the *Loredana*, engaging the *patronus* of the galley, Antonio Loredan, as his personal courier and guide. The contract for this, dated 14 May 1458, still exists. After his pilgrimage to the Holy Land he spent two years studying at Padua (1459–61), where he was well known as a scholar. During this time he was sent as a royal envoy to Pope Pius II, making a speech in Latin which moved the Pope to tears. On his death he left many of his books to Oxford University, some of

which are still in the Bodleian. Under Edward IV he held a succession of high offices, including those of Constable of the Tower of London, Constable of England, Treasurer of England and Chancellor of Ireland. He became notorious for his cruelty as a judge, adding impalement to the punishments imposed on those found guilty of high treason. Perhaps his experiences in Rhodes and the scenes recounted by Wey gave him the idea for this barbarity. He became known as the "Butcher of England" (Weir, *Lancaster and York*, pp. 363, 378). After Edward IV fled the country Tiptoft was captured by the Lancastrians and condemned to death on 15 October 1471. He was executed three days later on 18 October. (A full account of this remarkable man is to be found in Mitchell, *John Tiptoft*.) His effigy, together with those of two of his wives, can be seen in Ely Cathedral in the south chancel aisle.

125 The Magi: Wey quotes Matthew 2.10 verbatim from the Vulgate: *videntes stellam gavisi sunt gaudio magno valde*.

126 1 Kings 19:6 describes how Elijah, "under a juniper tree", found "a cake baken on the coals". Wey uses the Vulgate's words, *subcinericius panis*.

127 Elijah fled from the fury of Queen Jezebel: 1 Kings 19:2.

128 Jacob's ladder: Genesis 28:12.

129 Tomb of Rachel: Genesis 36:19–20.

130 Elijah (Elias is the Greek form) is described in 1 Kings 17:1 as "the Tishbite, who was of the inhabitants of Gilead".

131 Where the BVM dismounted: see p. 43, line 322.

132 Caesar's taxation: Luke 2:1–7.

133 St Jerome (*c.*342–420): one of the four traditional "Fathers of the Church". His Latin translation of the Bible is known as the Vulgate. Wey was very familiar with St Jerome's Letters. He quotes verbatim from Jerome's Letter to Desiderius in which Paula is mentioned.

134 Wey mentions this in Chapter 14, *Indulgenciae in curia Romana*. One of the five *integra corpora* seen by Wey in 1458 in the Church *ad sanctam Mariam majorem* in Rome was that *sancti Jeronimi*.

135 Matthew 2:16.

136 Matthew 2:11.

137 The manger: Luke 2:7. The ox and ass are not mentioned in the Gospels. They probably come from Isaiah's words "The ox knoweth his owner and the ass his master's crib" (Isaiah 1:3).

138 One of the timbers of the Cross. In one tradition the Cross was made of four varieties of wood, one from each quarter of the world.

139 Christ's circumcision: Luke 2:21.

140 The transformation of the Star of Bethlehem. Matthew 2:1–11 recounts how the star, seen by the wise men in the east, "went before them till it came and stood over where the young child was" (i.e. at Bethlehem). Wey refers to the descent to earth of this star again in Chapter 11, *Stella, que ducebat reges ad Bethleem, inter parietes ante speluncam in qua Christus fuit natus se demersit*.

141 The asp and the great cleft. The six Brothers, who were seconded from the Franciscan monastery on Mount Syon to tend the church at Bethlehem and to act as guides to pilgrims, had a fund of anecdotes about the events which, according to legend, had occurred in and around the Church of the Nativity. Some of the stories which Wey heard – e.g. those about the

grave of the Innocents and St Jerome's study – were also told to Felix Fabri in 1483 and Canon Casola in 1494 when they visited Bethlehem. (Prescott, *Jerusalem Journey*, pp. 146, 147; Newett, *Canon Pietro Casola's Pilgrimage*, pp. 262, 263).

142 Matthew 2:13.

143 Luke 2:8–14.

144 St Eustochium (370–419), a Roman virgin of noble family, was the third daughter of St Paula, who followed St Jerome to Palestine. Jerome's letter, Ep. xx, on the subject of virginity, is addressed to her. They left Rome and eventually settled in Bethlehem where they built four monasteries. Eustochium collated manuscripts for St Jerome's translation of the Bible.

145 Amos and Thene Castle. Amos, the earliest of the canonical prophets of the Old Testament, was "a herdman of Tekoa" who exercised his ministry between 760 and 750 BC (Amos 1:1).

146 Mambre (Mamre): Genesis 24:19, "Abraham buried Sarah his wife in the cave of the field of Machpelah before Mamre: the same is Hebron in the land of Canaan." And Genesis 25:9, "His sons Isaac and Ishmael buried him in the cave of Machpelah… which is before Mamre".

147 Philip baptized the eunuch: Acts 8:38.

148 Magnificat: Luke 1:46–55.

149 The story of how John the Baptist, as an infant, was saved from Herod's men is to be found in the Protoevangelion 16:3–7: "And instantly the mountain was divided and received them".

150 Circumcision of St John: Luke 1:59.

151 Benedictus: Luke 1:68–79. For other references to Zacharias, see above and Chapter 14.

152 Birth of St John the Baptist: Luke 1:57.

153 Desert of the Forty Days. The temptation of Christ in the wilderness is described in Matthew 4:1–11; Mark 1:13 and Luke 4:1–13. The Greek Orthodox monastery of the Temptation on Mount Qarantal (from *Quarantena*) marks the site.

154 A modern guidebook gives the distance from Jerusalem to Jericho as 28 miles (45 km).

155 According to the Apocryphal Gospel of the Birth of Mary (1:11), St Joachim was despised by the high priest, Issachar, for his childlessness and, "confounded with the shame of such reproach, retired to the shepherds, who were with the cattle in their pastures".

156 The story of the angel who appeared to Joachim and announced the future birth of Mary is in the Gospel of the Birth of Mary, Chapter 2, and the Protoevangelion 4:4.

157 "If thou art": Matthew 4:3; Luke 4:3.

158 Elisha's miracle with salt is described in 2 Kings 2:20–22.

159 "All this will I give thee": Matthew 4:9; Luke 4:6.

160 Zachaeus, the publican who was "little of stature", received Christ in his house: Luke 19:1–6.

161 Blind Bartimaeus's sight was restored near Jericho: Mark 10:46–52; Luke 18:35–43.

162 Monastery of St John and the Baptism of Christ; Matthew 3:13; Mark 1:9; Luke 3:21; John 1:32.

163 Jordan and Pilgrims: see p. 40, line 212.

164 Lot's wife: Genesis 19:26.

165 Lazarus raised: John 11:43–44.

166 Martha's cry: John 11:21.

167 The house of Simon the leper: Matthew 26:6 and Mark 14:3.

168 Bathfage and Palm Sunday: Matthew 21:1–11; Mark 11:1–11; Luke 19:29–38. See also John 12:12–15.

169 The sermon from an English priest. *Peregrinus es in Jerusalem* is a quotation from the Vulgate, Luke 24:18. This is one of the four sermons which Wey preached during his pilgrimages and which he mentions. The others are: La Coruña, in the Franciscan church, on 27 May 1456; Jerusalem, "on Mt Calvary", 20 July 1462 and 22 (or 23) July 1462.

Wey left two volumes of his sermons to Syon Monastery. They are listed under his name in the fifteenth-century catalogue of Syon Monastery Library, which is now MS 141 in the Parker Library at Corpus Christi College, Cambridge. See also essay "William Wey's Own Books", p. 235.

170 The Earl of Worcester, Sir John Tiptoft.

171 The twelve sects. Several pilgrims visiting the Holy Land in the fifteenth century remarked on the number and variety of sects to be found there. In 1458 Wey says there were twelve. Francesco Suriano, writing in 1485, says there were ten (Newett, *Canon Pietro Casola's Pilgrimage*, p. 391). Canon Casola, in 1494, says there were nine. Comments were often derogatory (Prescott, *Jerusalem Journey*, p. 184). The number of churches represented in Jerusalem today is seventeen. The variety is due to a great many historical schisms – e.g. after the Council of Chalcedon in 451, and the split between Eastern and Western Christianity in 1054.

172 Salinis is not far from Larnaca. It takes its name from the salt lake which is 3 metres below sea level and has been exploited commercially from ancient times. The salt, which is produced there by evaporation, was a source of great wealth for Cyprus. In the sixteenth century it was exported to Venice.

173 The story of the Good Thief is in Luke 23:40–43. He was later known by the name of St Dismas. Apocryphal stories grew up around him and his name is variously given. His feast day is on 25 March. Wey mentions his miraculous cross three times. The chapel "on a high mountain" in which the cross hung was in the Monastery of Stavrovouni in Cyprus. This was on an isolated mountain called "Olympus" in classical times and later "Olympia". A church of the Holy Cross was built there by Helena. In about 327 she established a monastery on the ruins of an ancient temple of Aphrodite. Benedictines were brought here by the Lusignans in 1197. The Mamelukes largely destroyed the monastery in 1426. In 1480 Felix Fabri described the cross in terms similar to those used by William Wey.

174 The King of Cyprus from 1432 to 1458 was John who married Helena Palaiologina, a Byzantine princess. John's father, Janus, had been king for thirty-four years from 1398 to 1432. In 1426 he suffered a terrible defeat at the hands of the Mamelukes at Khirokitia. He was taken to Egypt as a prisoner and only released in return for a ruinous ransom, the promise of an annual tribute, which Wey mentions here, and acceptance of the sultan as overlord (Davey, *Northern Cyprus*, p. xxi).

175 Camlet: a rich material made of silk and camel's hair.

176 St Catherine of Alexandria has her feast day on 25 November. Wey refers to St Catherine and Famagusta again in Chapter 9 where he writes, "St Catherine was born in a city called Constantia (formerly called "Salamis") 2 miles from Famagusta. In the Franciscan church in Famagusta there is a chapel behind the high altar and the place where Catherine learnt her letters."

The ruined church of Saint Francis in Famagusta is almost all that now remains of the Franciscan friary, which was described by Martoni in 1394 as having a fair cloister, dormitory, many cells and other rooms, with a fine garden and a quantity of conduits and cisterns. It is possible that William Wey stayed in this friary during his visit to Cyprus in 1458, on the way back from the Holy Land, and that the information about Saint Catherine was given him by one of the friars minor who showed him round.

A burial chamber in the necropolis of Salamis in Cyprus, which dates from the eighth century BC, was sometimes called St Catherine's Prison. It is possible that a local woman, called Catherine, was imprisoned in this tomb, and, in time, she might have become identified with the saint.

177 There is a most vivid, and detailed, illustration of the tortures described by Wey, in the codex, *Obsidionis Rhodiae urbis descriptio*, by G. Caoursin, Vice-Chancellor of the Order of the Knights of Rhodes, Par. Lat. 6067 in the Bibliothèque Nationale, Paris, published in Kollias, *The Knights of Rhodes*, p. 47.

178 The Morea was the medieval name for the Peloponnese, the large peninsula of southern Greece connected with the mainland by the Isthmus of Corinth. In view of its peculiar shape ancient geographers compared it to the leaf of a plane tree. The medieval name, Morea, is said to have been taken from the mulberry (*Morus*). Wey refers to the area again, *Turcus adquisierat Lamoreiam, que est in Grecia*, in Chapter 9.

179 This is a reference to Mount Athos, a peninsula in north-east Greece. (It was only an island when Xerxes, King of Persia, cut a canal across the neck of the isthmus for his invasion of Greece in 480 BC.) The first monastic settlement of which there is reliable evidence was founded there in 962. The rule of Constantine Monomachus (1060) which forbids access to "every woman, every female animal, every child, eunuch and smooth-faced person" is still officially in force.

180 St Titus, who was a Gentile, was a disciple of St Paul. He was left by Paul to organize the Church in Crete. Paul's Epistle to Titus instructed him to ordain presbyters and govern the Cretans firmly. His body was buried at Gortyne, the capital of the island in the Roman period, but in 823 his head was taken to Venice and placed in St Mark's. The ruins of the basilica of Hagios Titos can still be seen at Gortyn.

181 Mallasetum. *Revised Medieval Latin Word-List* gives a range of words for the sweet, Cretan wine, commonly known as "Malmsey". These are *malvesia, malasetum, malesinum* and *malevesinum*. Wey adds two more, *mallasetum* and *malmasetum*. The word is derived from Monemvasia, a Greek town in the south-eastern Peloponnese. Wey mentions Malmsey twice in Chapter 11, *Ulterius in Grecia est regnum Crete. In regno isto crescit malmasetum*, and in the same chapter, *In regno Crete crescit malmasetum*.

A number of documents testify to the importance of the Malmsey wine trade; see *Calendar of Venetian State Papers 1202–1509*, ed. Rawdon Brown, Longman Green, 1864, for fiscal arrangements made by Venice to prevent unfair competition in carrying the wine. Page 175, section 544, and page 161, section 510, tell how 150 butts of Malmsey, captured from the Flanders galleys by pirates in 1486, were recovered.

George, Duke of Clarence, was, allegedly, put to death in the Tower of London in 1478 by being drowned in a butt of Malmsey.

182 Sugar. Madeira, discovered in about 1450, eventually produced such a great deal of sugar that the price collapsed at the end of the fifteenth century. In Wey's time the Venetian galleys carried sugar from Cyprus, Alexandria, Syria, Damietta, Sicily and Valencia as well as Crete.

Sicily produced both refined and brown sugar (*Calendar of Venetian State Papers 1202–1509*, p. cxxxix).

183 St Zoyolus. A St Zoilus is believed to have been martyred under Diocletian in *c.*301 in Córdoba. It is more likely that here Wey is referring to St Zöellus, who was probably martyred in Istria.

184 St Anastasia was martyred in about 304 at Sirmium. In the fifth century her relics were translated to Constantinople. In Rome she was commemorated in a church near the Circus Maximus, where the Pope sang the second Mass on Christmas Day. Wey mentions this church in Chapter 14.

The Cathedral of St Anastasia, the "Sveta Stosija", in Zadar, is a fine Romanesque basilica. It suffered badly in 1202 when the town was pillaged by the Crusaders. The restoration continued until 1324. In the tympanum above the central portal is the Virgin Mary, enthroned with St Zoilus and St Anastasia at her side. The shrine of St Anastasia is in an altar in the left-hand aisle of the three-aisled crypt under the main altar.

8

William Wey's Route in 1458

SYNOPSIS

This chapter consists of a simple list of places between (a) Calais and Rome, (b) Rome and Venice and (c) Venice and Calais, together with the distances between them. It should be read in conjunction with Chapter 7 (The 1458 Pilgrimage to Jerusalem) and Chapter 14 (Rome), since the three together form a description of Wey's travels in 1458, although each chapter has a different format.

TRANSLATION
(Roxburghe, pp. 79–81)

These are the Cities and Towns on the Way to the Great City of Rome

Translator's note. The first column below shows the name as given by William Wey. The second column offers the likely modern equivalent. The third column contains the distances between locations as given by Wey and the fourth Wey's side-notes.

Calisia	Calais		Which is in Picardy
Gravenynge	Gravelines	3 miles	The start of Flanders
Dumkyrke	Dunkirk	4 miles	
Newport	Nieuwpoort	5 miles	
Bruggis	Bruges	7 miles	
Gawnte	Ghent	8 miles	This is a place to change money
Dundermounde	Dendermonde	5 miles	

106

Makelyn	Mechelen	5 miles	
Aschot	Aarschot	5 miles	Brabant starts
Dyste	Diest	2 miles	
Askylle	Hasselt	3 miles	
Mastrek	Maastricht	3 miles	
Acon	Aachen	4 miles	Germany starts
Durene	Düren	4 miles	
Seuernake	Sievernich	4 miles	
Rymbake	Rheinbach	3 miles	
Cense	Sinzig	3 miles	
Andenak	Andernach	3 miles	
Conflense	Koblenz	3 miles	The Rhine starts
Bobard	Boppard	3 miles	
Bagarath	Bacharach	3 miles	
Byng	Bingen	2 miles	
Odername	Odernheim	4 miles	
Wermys	Worms	4 miles	
Spyre	Speyer	6 miles	
Brussell	Bruchsal	3 miles	
Bryten	Bretten	2 miles	
Burname	Durmen	2 miles	
Fayg'	Vaihingen	2 miles	
Eslyng'	Esslingen	4 miles	
Gyppyng'	Göppingen	3 miles	
Gasslyng'	Geislingen	2 miles	
Ulma	Ulm	3 miles	Swesia
Memmyng	Memingen	6 miles	Here the mountains start
Kempton	Kempten	4 miles	
Nesserwan	Nesselwang	3 miles	
Attrowang	Heiterwang	3 miles	
Mownt Nicholas	Finstermünz	3 miles	
Merane	Merano	6 miles	
VII Kyrkys	Siebeneuch	6 miles	
Mounte Vernarde		2 miles	
Nazare	Nassereith (?)	2 miles	
Tremyng	Tramin	6 miles	
Trent	Trento	4 miles	Here Lombardy starts

Roffered	Rovereto	2 miles	
Ala	Ala	8 miles	Italian miles start
Clausura	Chiusa	20 miles	
Verona	Verona	12 miles	
Scala	Isola de la Scala	12 miles	
Hostea	Ostiglia	20 miles	
Merandela	Mirandola	12 miles	
Rouporte	Buonporto	14 miles	
Castellum sancti Johannis	San Giovanni	11 miles	
Bononia	Bologna	10 miles	Here Italy begins; there is a university there
Plenore	Pianoro	8 miles	
Florenschole	Firenzuola	22 miles	
Montes Scarpore	Scarperia	10 miles	
Florencia	Florence	14 miles	There is a second money changing there
Donatum	San Donato	16 miles	
Sere	Siena	14 miles	
Monterone	Monteroni	10 miles	
Ad Clericum	San Quirico	13 miles	
Lakarone	Radicofani	13 miles	
Aqua pendente	Acqua pendente	11 miles	
Ad sanctum Laurentium	San Lorenzo Nuovo	5 miles	
Pulsene	Bolsena	3 miles	
Muntflaske	Montefiascoe	6 miles	
Viterve	Viterbo	8 miles	
Rusbeon	Ronciglione	9 miles	
Suterse	Sutri	3 miles	
Monterose	Monterosi	5 miles	
Turrebocona	Baccano	6 miles	
Ad Romam	Rome	14 miles	
Castello Novo	Castello Nuovo	14 miles	
Arriane	Rignano	6 miles	
Castelliane	Castellana	7 miles	
Burget	Borghetto	4 miles	

Trekyl	Otricoli	8 miles	
Nerne	Narni	6 miles	
Serne	Terni	8 miles	
Spolet	Spoleto	12 miles	Christina lies there
Follyng	Foligno	12 miles	
Cantymane		15 miles	
Calia		5 miles	
Fellyne	Foligno	12 miles	
Assyse	Assisi	8 miles	St Francis lies there, and Clare
Parwse	Perugia	10 miles	There is a university there
Castele	Citta di Castello	12 miles	
Burgo	Borgo San Sepolcro	8 miles	
Alapeve	Pieve San Stefano	8 miles	
Sampere		18 miles	
Galyad	Galeata	15 miles	
Furse	Forli	20 miles	
Revennam	Ravenna	20 miles	

On Mount Alvernie St Francis Received his Stigmata

From Ravenna to Venice by water:	30 miles
The total of miles from Rome to Venice:	258 miles
The number of miles from Calais to Rome:	1,300

These are the Cities and Towns from Venice to Calais

Venesia	Venice		Which is in Italy
Padway	Padua	25 miles	
Bassan	Bassano del Grappa	25 miles	
Alascala	Castello de la Scala	5 miles	
Gryne	Grigno	8 miles	
Hospital	Ospedaletto	5 miles	
Alaburgo	Borgo	5 miles	
Alene		7 miles	

Trent	Trento	10 miles
Tremyng	Tramin	4 miles
Merane	Merano	6 miles
VII Kyrkys	Siebeneuch	6 miles
Mount Nycholas	Finstermünz	3 miles
Nazare	Nassereith [?]	8 miles
Mount Vernerd		2 miles
Karamath		4 miles
Esselnang'	Nesselwang	6 miles
Kempton	Kempten	4 miles
Memmyng	Memingen	4 miles
Olma	Ulm	6 miles
Gasselyng'	Geislingen	3 miles
Gyppyng'	Göppingen	2 miles
Esselyng'	Esslingen	3 miles
Fayg'	Vaihingen	4 miles
Burnam	Durmen	2 miles
Brytyn	Bretten	2 miles
Brussel	Bruchsal	2 miles
Spyre	Speyer	3 miles
Wermys	Worms	6 miles
Odername	Odernheim	4 miles
Byng	Bingen	4 miles
Bakarath	Bacharach	2 miles
Bobard	Boppard	4 miles
Coualense	Koblenz	3 miles
Andernake	Andernach	3 miles
Cense	Sinzig	3 miles
Rymbak	Rheinbach	3 miles
Sauernak	Sieverenich	3 miles
Durane	Düren	2 miles
Acon	Aachen	4 miles
Masteryke	Maastricht	4 miles
Assyse	Hasselt	3 miles
Dyste	Diest	3 miles
Astot	Aarschot	2 miles
Makalyne	Mechelen	4 miles

Dendermounde	Dendermonde	5 miles
Gaunte	Ghent	5 miles
Bruggis	Bruges	8 miles
Newport	Nieuwpoort	7 miles
Dunkyrke	Dunkirk	5 miles
Greueninge	Gravelines	4 miles
Calyse	Calais	3 miles

The total mileage from Venice to Calais: 1,056 miles.

COMMENTARY

Tantalisingly, Wey's description in Chapter 8 of his progress through the Low Countries, Germany and Italy is little more than a catalogue of the towns and cities through which he passed: in particular there is no mention of his mode of transport or the accommodation he used. Of the other two chapters which deal with his 1458 journey, Chapter 7 describes in scant detail Wey's voyage from Venice to Jaffa, in much greater detail his pilgrimage in the Holy Land, and then, again in very brief terms, his voyage back to Venice. Chapter 14, which is called "Indulgences in the Roman Curia", while not a day-by-day account of his visit to Rome, is more than a mere tariff of indulgences, since it contains some account of the churches in Rome which are visited by pilgrims, their history and the relics which can be seen therein.

The manuscript of Wey's *Itineraries* in the Bodleian is not a finely polished account of his three journeys; there are repetitions – for example, the mnemonic hexameters of Chapter 4 are repeated in Chapter 6; descriptions of holy sites given in Chapter 6 are repeated in Chapter 7; the Venetian "shopping list", given in English in Chapter 2, is repeated, in Latin, in Chapter 9; and the mainly topographical questions which Wey pondered in Jerusalem in 1462 occur both in Chapter 11 and in Chapter 9. This is not to criticize Wey as a poor craftsman; rather it adds to the interest of the book that one can almost see him at work in his room at Edington, using the notes which he made on his journeys years before and incorporating extracts from them and other sources as the basis for the more finely honed versions of his travels which give his work its traditional name. Chapter 15, which he wrote after his retirement to Edington in 1467, is possibly the tidiest of his three accounts, but even that shows some duplication.

In Chapter 8 there are some very brief marginal notes in which Wey indicates, for example, places where one can change money (Ghent and Florence), cities where there are universities (Bologna and Perugia), or where saints lie (St Christina in Spoleto, and St Francis and St Clare in Assisi). The remaining notes indicate border crossings, viz. Picardy, Flanders, Brabant, Germany, Swesia (Suebia), Lombardy and Italy, or natural features – for example, "The Rhine starts" and "Here the mountains start".

Possibly Wey intended these notes as aides-memoires for when he was writing up these sections of his pilgrimage in more detail, in the same way that a landscape painter will make notes on his preliminary outdoor sketches to remind him of the colours he should use in his final composition. Examples of this intention, perhaps, are the notes about St Francis, St Clare and Mount Alvernia. In Chapter 8 one of these notes, inserted in the list of places after Ravenna, reads "St Francis received his stigmata on Mount Alvernia"; another, beside Assisi, states "St Francis lies there and Clare". When Wey came to write up a fuller account of his travels and the reasons for pilgrimage, in Chapters 5 and 6, he discusses relics and shrines "along the road from the Holy Land". Those to be seen in Italy are grouped under Venice, Padua, Viterbo, Assisi, Mount Alvernia, Spoleto and Loretto. In Chapter 6 he writes, "At Assisi there lie the body of St Francis and St Clare. In that place also is the statue of the Cross which told St Francis to build a house for St Clare and the other nuns in Assisi. On Mount Alvernia St Francis received the stigmata on his hands, feet and heart." This elaboration might indicate that Wey was using the list of Chapter 8 as the basis for Chapter 6. Chapters 5 and 6 in turn formed the basis for a further recension in Chapter 7 and Chapter 9, where some material was added and some deleted. His note about Spoleto and St Christina is particularly significant. The St Christina who "lies in Spoleto" was not a saint of the front rank. It is a little odd that Wey singles her out in the same way as St Francis and St Clare. This Christina died in February 1458. Wey was passing through Spoleto on his route from Rome to Ravenna in April or May of that year, so her death would have been very recent and that may be the reason for his mention of her. The marginal note beside Ala, which reads "Italian miles start", highlights one of the problems facing anyone who tries to follow the routes described in *The Itineraries*. While the sequence of places Wey visited on his journeys across Europe between England and Venice in 1458 and 1462 can be followed, almost in its entirety, on a modern road map of Europe, the distances he gives between towns and cities appear to be different from those on a modern map and the differences are not consistent. The reason for this is that there was a variety of "miles" in Europe in the Middle Ages.

In Chapter 7, when Wey is describing the pilgrims' ride from Jaffa to Rama on 22 June 1458 he writes: "We took our donkeys to ride to Rama, which is 10 Welsh miles (*decem miliaria Wallica*) from Jaffa." Wey was well aware of the differing lengths of a mile in different countries and at different times.

The Roman mile, *mille passus* (literally, 1,000 paces) consisted of 2,000 steps, (one *passus* being in modern terms two steps), and is usually reckoned as 1,680 yards. While the English mile is 1,760 yards, the old Scottish mile was 1,980 yards and the Irish one 2,240 yards. On a map printed as late as 1650, the *Theatrum Orbis Terrarum sive Atlas Novus* (Pegli Naval Museum, Genoa) the scale in the margin is given in both Italian and German miles and shows that 24 Milliaria Italica were the equivalent of 6 Milliaria Germanica. If an Italian mile was the same as the ancient Roman mile, then a German mile comes out at 6,720 yards – that is, 3.8 modern English miles (6.1 km).

Further information on the length of various "miles" in the fifteenth century has recently come to light in an account of his pilgrimage to the Holy Land written by Richard of Lincoln, in 1454. Richard says explicitly that 1 Flemish mile is 3 English miles; 1 German mile is equivalent to 4 English miles and 3 Lombardy miles make 2 English miles. If one applies these factors to Wey's distances, the resulting mileages are much closer to those shown on modern road maps. The figures given by Richard, for those portions of his route which were also traversed by William Wey, bear out Wey's distances exactly. Both men give Nieuwpoort to Bruges as 7 miles, and Aarschot to Dyste as 2 miles, while along the Rhine each gives Andernach to Koblenz as 3 miles and Boppard to Bacharach as 3 miles.

In 1458, Wey did not follow the more usual route across Flanders to join the Rhine at Cologne, but left it at Aachen. Then, going via Düren, he picked it up near Koblenz, and followed it along the Rhine as far as Speyer. From Ulm his route can easily be followed on the map as far as Nesselwang. It then becomes rather more difficult. If the Roxburghe editor is correct in identifying Mount Nicholas with Finstermunz, it would appear that Wey was following the Via Claudia Augusta, as he did in 1462, but Nazare (if it is the same as Nassereith) is misplaced as it comes before Merano. From Merano the places named, Tramin, Trento, and so on, appear in the correct sequence along the Via Claudia Augusta. The difficulty might be resolved if the two places Wey names, VII Kyrkys and Mount Vernard, could be positively identified. The problem is made the more difficult as Wey's return route from Venice to Ulm, which should be the mirror-image of his outward one, is inconsistent with it and leads one to suspect that his Nazare is in fact Nassereith. This means that one cannot be completely certain which Alpine pass he used in 1458.

Another problem occurs on Wey's journey northwards from Rome to Venice. Foligno (Follyng and Fellyne) appears twice with the names of Cantymane and Calia in between. These two places have not been identified and it must remain open as to whether Wey made a detour to visit an important shrine.

9

The 1462 Pilgrimage to Jerusalem

SYNOPSIS

In Chapter 9, one of the most important in *The Itineraries*, William Wey describes his route from Eton to Venice and back to Eton in considerable detail. More than half of the chapter is devoted to Venice.

TRANSLATION
(Roxburghe, pp. 82–102)

The Second Journey of Master + William Wey to The Holy Land

In the Name of God, Amen. In the Year of Our Lord's Incarnation 1462, I, William Wey, Bachelor of Sacred Theology, Fellow of the College of the Most Blessed Mary and Saint Nicholas of Eton by Windsor,[1] inspired by God's Grace, in the fifty-fifth year of my life, consecrated in the manner of pilgrims,[2] began my journey to the Holy Sepulchre of Jesus Christ, starting from Eton aforesaid on the 26th day of February. Reaching Gravesend[3] on the 5th day of March,[4] we set sail on the 13th day of March and arrived on the 15th day of that month at Ermewthe [Annemuiden?] in Zeeland. From there we went to Antwerp by sea.

From Antwerp to Westerlo 8 Italian miles,[5] then to Maastricht 7 miles, then to Aquisgravis, commonly called Aachen. On the advice of some well-informed men we then took another road, because there was a war on the Rhine between two bishops.[6] Thus we travelled from Aachen to Cornelismunster 1 mile, to Raeren half a great mile, to Rotgen 2 miles, to Kalterherberg half a mile, to Büllingen 2 miles, to Zave [St Vith] 2 miles, to Prüm 4 miles, to Seffern 2 miles, to Bitburg 2 miles, to Hospytle [Helenenberg] 2 miles, to Trier 2 miles. St Mathias[7] lies in this place, which is on the River Moselle.

There too is a well where St Athanasius sat when he composed his Creed, namely *Quicunque vult* ["Whosoever will be saved"].[8] There also is the knife with which St Peter cut off Malchus's ear.[9] In the church and abbey of St Mathias there are as many saints' bodies as there are days in a year. The bishop of this city is one of those who elects the emperor of Germany,[10] who will be chosen in the city of Aachen. From Trier to Kirf 2 miles, to Sierck 3 miles; there one should get the coins called Rappis.[11] From there to Metz 6 miles, and 10 miles to St Nicholas in Gaul [St Nicholas-de-Port], where there is an arm of St Nicholas.[12] Many miracles are performed there. Here is also the largest collection of chains and fetters[13] which I have ever seen in any church. Then to Epinal ten miles, to Remiremont nine miles, to St Theobald [Thann] 7 miles and to Basel 5 miles. There we heard that there was a war between Pope Pius and the Duke of Austria[14] and that the Pope would excommunicate those who crossed his territory. We therefore sought a different, and longer, road to Venice. Accordingly we went from Basel to Rheinfelden, 2 miles, to Laufenburg 2 miles, to Schaffhausen 4 miles, to Konstanz 3 miles, to Arbon 3 miles, to Rheineck 1 mile, to Blüdenz 2 miles, to Klösterle 2 miles, to Arlberg 1 mile, to Prutz 2 miles, to Landeck 3 miles, to Tösens 2 miles, to Nauders 1 mile, to Mals 3 miles, to Latsch 3 miles, to Meran 3 miles, to Terlan 2 miles, then to Hoch Eppan 1 mile, to Numered 2 miles, Saladon 1 mile, Sanarel 1 mile, Tramin 2 miles, Salorno 3 miles, Trento 3 miles, Pergine[15] 2 miles. There we stayed from Good Friday until Easter Monday.

We attended a service in that place [Pergine] on Good Friday. After the service a reliquary was placed in the nave of the church and on the reliquary an image of the Holy Cross, veiled. Wax candles were set around the reliquary and the image. A little before dawn on Easter Day we three pilgrims, each called "William",[16] came to the church and greeted the secular priest[17] of the church. When we arrived he said, "Because you are priests you can stay with us in the church". Then he told all his parishioners to leave the church and when they left he closed the doors behind them. After their departure from the church he put on a surplice and a blue hood over his head, with the point of the hood wrapped around his neck. He went to the reliquary in the middle of the church and took in his arms the cross which had been veiled. Then, with a private chant, he went to the sacristy and after that opened the church doors. In his exhortation to the people on Good Friday [sic: an error for Easter Day] he made the ordinary folk sing in Italian:

"Tell us Mary, what did you see on the way?"

"I saw the tomb of the living Christ and the glory of His Resurrection."
He did the very same thing at Mass and at Vespers on that day, getting the girls
to sing these words in a higher voice after he had given them the lead.

Then we went 1 mile to Levico, 1½ miles to Borgo, 1½ miles to Ospedaletto,
1 mile to Grigno, 1 mile to Castello de la Scala, 15 miles to Bassano and 25 short
miles to Padua.[18]

We arrived at the large and noble city of Venice on the 22nd day of April.
On the Eve of St Mark we saw twelve gold crowns full of precious jewels on
St Mark's altar together with twelve pectorals equally full of precious stones.
There was a very tall and extremely rich chalice, two large, valuable thuribles,
either made of gold or gilded, and four gilded candlesticks. The high altar was
of gilded silver. The church of St Mark is built like the Temple of the Christians
in Jerusalem.

When the Most Illustrious Doge of this city entered St Mark's church at
the first Vespers on St Mark's Day, nine very long, silver trumpets bearing his
coat of arms and three smaller ones were carried before him. Ahead of him in
the procession[19] there were eight banners with eight gilded crosses in a circle. In
front were borne eight very tall candlesticks with eight white ceremonial candles.
On one side in front of him a man carried a large cushion of cloth of gold, while
another carried a gilded stool. Behind him a man carried a canopy of cloth of
gold and another a sword with a gilded sheath covered with precious stones,
and behind him a long, unlit, candle made of white wax. In the procession with
the venerable Doge went the Patriarch of Venice and the Premissory of Saint
Mark in episcopal vestments; the Patriarch had a cross and the Premissory
a crucifer of great worth. Ahead of him there were twenty canons robed in
amices together with many priests and clergy. Behind him came the lords of the
city and a large throng of ordinary people. On St Mark's Day the Fraternities[20]
of the various saints came in large numbers wearing white habits like monks.
They held wax candles in one hand and scourges in the other. Ahead of them
there were carried crosses and processional candles. Five hundred members of
the Fraternity of Saint Mark were in attendance.

At that time the name of the Most Illustrious Doge of Venice was Lord
Pascale Malopero.[21] He had the help of six "Councillors", some of whom
are changed each year. He also has under him six "Proctors of Saint Mark",
who hold office for life. Their titles are the "Three Within" and the "Three
Without". In the city ten of the leading citizens are called the "Ten Councillors".

In addition there are three "Advocates", who, in conjunction with the Doge, are able to execute all the city's business. There is one man, called the Podesta, who is the city judge. On any occasion when all those mentioned above are in disagreement they summon the 150 nobles, who are called the Precati. These have the power to carry out whatever they decide. Then there is another Great Council which all the nobles can attend. In this Council they choose the officers whose duties appertain to the city and to other places outside the city. Each year they appoint 800 officers for tasks inside and outside Venice, some of whom hold office for two years and some for one year. There are eight officers, however, who retain their office for life; these consist of the six "Proctors of St Mark", along with one who is charge of the Mint and one who is in charge of the Ropeworks.

In the city they have a very large area where they build the galleys to defend our Faith.[22] I saw eighty galleys there, either completed or still under construction. Below that place they have huge buildings for stores of all types. These are full of the various kinds of equipment needed to defend our Faith.

On the third of May, in the year aforesaid, Lord Pascale Malopero, the Most Illustrious Doge of Venice, departed from this mortal life. He lay in state in his palace for three days and his body was taken out for burial on the third day. In his funeral procession all the Schools went in front wearing monastic dress, carrying candles and scourges. In front of them were crosses and processional candles, behind them ordinary citizens, priests, clergy and members of the religious orders. Finally came the canons of St Mark with a cross and candles. They were followed by two men carrying his arms and then, behind his arms, his body was borne arranged as follows. On his head he wore the cap, the biricula,[23] his face being uncovered. Under his head there was a cushion of cloth of gold. His body was dressed in the Doge's robe of gold trimmed with fur. He had shoes on his feet with golden spurs beside them. On the other side of his body was his sword with its gilded sheath. He was buried with all this finery high up in the wall in the House of the Dominicans in the city of Venice.[24]

After his death and burial the Venetians assembled for the appointment of a new Doge. They were summoned for this election by the Councillors. All nobles of good birth were invited to this election, being sworn to select Lords from among the nobility who were loyal to the Catholic faith. These Lords would then swear, under pain of forfeiting their worldly goods, to select one wiser, better in status, truer to the Catholic faith and more able in worldly business to serve that city and its dominions. These nobles, to the number of one hundred, shall then be shut up, together with certain notaries, in a building which they may not leave until they have selected forty from those of nobler rank for that office. These shall then receive Our Lord's Body, undertaking to select the man whom they believe the most orthodox in our Faith and the most profitable for the city of Venice. They will accept as their Doge the man whom they recognize as having the larger number of votes. They will not disclose under pain of death the name of the one who receives the smaller number. Then the man who secures the majority of votes and is chosen as Doge shall be escorted to his home.

As he is led there the sailors will come and say,
"Your goods are ours."

He will reply,
"I know it well, but I ask you to accept these hundred ducats among yourselves and be satisfied."

He then gives them the money, and, as he goes along the street to his house, he scatters coins to secure a passage back home. Then, after making domestic arrangements, he will be escorted by the Lords of the city to the Doge's palace. They will make him a knight and then dress him in the robes of his office, placing the cap full of precious jewels on his head. The following Sunday he comes to the church of St Mark. All the "Schools" will appear before him there, and one of them will preach a sermon. Then will come the religious orders in a procession with their relics, candles, crosses and canopies. Among them they will have many boys, dressed as angels, who will be carried on high poles and sing various songs in front of the Lord Doge. The secular priests sing *Te Deum laudamus* ["We praise thee, O God"]; *Sermone blando angelus*, ["With sweet words the angel"]; *Ad cenam agni providi* ["Made ready for the feast of the Lamb"].[25] Thus he will depart from St Mark's church with a great procession and large numbers of people. He will then come to the Doge's palace and, standing in the entrance to his palace, turn his face to the people. Then all his Lords will pass before him doing him reverence. After that he will go in to dine in his palace where he will live for the rest of his days. After his election the ambassadors from the various provinces call on him, bringing him presents and offering him their congratulations on his elevation to that office.

The name of the Doge elected in this year was Christophero Mauro, a truly orthodox and devout man.[26] Immediately after his election he sent his delegates to make peace between Pope Pius and the Duke of Austria. I will describe in this book what I heard and what I saw on my journey to this most holy place. I will do it for the praise and honour of God, with the intention that what was well done may be an example for those who come after and so that they in their turn may do the same or better. For the honour of the city, I will describe in this account what I saw in the palace of the Most Illustrious Doge of Venice and in the palace of his Council later.

It is said that Pope Alexander the Third fled from Rome, disguised as a Franciscan monk,[27] in fear of the Emperor Frederick.[28] He came to Venice to the monastery called "Charity", a name it still bears.[29] He worked in the kitchen in this monastery and nobody knew who he was. As it happened, a certain pilgrim arrived at the monastery where Pope Alexander was working in the kitchen and saw him there. He recognized him because he had seen him earlier at Rome in his church of Saint Peter. Accordingly he went to one of the Lords of the city and informed him that Pope Alexander was in Venice. This Lord took the pilgrim to the Doge, whose name was Gayne Zia.[30] The Doge went to the House of Charity with the Lords of the city and asked the Prior to bring all the monks and servants in front of him.

When they had all appeared before him he said to the pilgrim,
"Which of these is the Pope?"

The pilgrim replied that he was not there.
Then the Doge said to the Prior,
"Do you have any other men in this monastery?"

The Prior replied,
"There are no others in the monastery except for one man who came here lately and works in the kitchen, but let him be called."

When this man came before them the pilgrim said to the Doge,
"This is definitely Pope Alexander."

Then the Doge and all the rest fell at his feet and immediately gave orders for robes befitting his office. They then escorted him to the Doge's palace

promising that they would be surety for his life. The Doge at once issued
instructions that many galleys be fitted out for a war against the Emperor.
Because this was a matter of the Faith the Doge himself offered to go to war
with the others. He appeared before the Pope in armour and begged for his
blessing and a full indulgence for himself and his forces.

The Pope first handed him a sword with the words,
"I give you the power to execute justice."

The Doge then advanced with his people against the Emperor. He captured
the Emperor's son and brought him to the Pope.[31] The son was next sent, under
parole, to his father to bring him to the Pope. This was done. The Emperor fell
at the feet of the Pope in Saint Mark's church with the words,[32]

"I am doing this for Peter."

The Pope replied,
"For Peter and for me."

Then the Pope placed his foot on the Emperor's neck, saying as he did so,
"Thou shalt walk upon the asp and the basilisk and thou shalt trample upon
the lion and the dragon."[33]

Thus they were reconciled.

Then the Pope said to the Doge,
"Behold, I appoint thee Lord of the Salt Sea, and as a sign of this I give thee
a ring with which thou shalt be married to the sea."[34]

He still does this, with great ceremony, once a year on the Day of Our
Lord's Ascension. The Pope also gave the Doge a candle of white wax to be
carried in front of him at important ceremonies. This white candle was given
by the Pope to the Doge of Venice because neither in France nor in England
nor in any other kingdoms were found men to champion our Faith but only in
Venice. It was his wish that a white wax candle should be carried in front of the
Doge, when he crossed to St Mark's church on Feast Days, for ever, as a mark
of honour to them and for the continuance of the Faith. He also presented him

with a canopy of cloth of gold, eight banners with golden crosses in a circle and eight silver trumpets. He is attended by these when he goes to St Mark's church for important ceremonies.[35] He also gave the Doge permission to use a seal of lead.

The city of Venice was built by fisherfolk in the year 200 AD.[36] Initially it was called Realti and later the "Province of Venice". St Magnus, the martyr, was the first Bishop of Venice, and his uncorrupted body lies in the Church of St Jeremiah in Venice.[37] This Saint had a vision that he should build seven churches in Venice. These are as follows: the first is the Church of St James on the Realto,[38] the second of St John,[39] the third of St Salvator,[40] the fourth is St Mary, the Beautiful[41] – this is the church attended by the Doge and Lords of Venice on the Eve of the Purification, and on the Day itself, for Mass, to make offerings to the Most Blessed Virgin for the miracles which were performed there; the fifth church is the Church of St Silvester,[42] the sixth of St Jerome; the seventh, of St Peter, is the cathedral church, where they have a Patriarch.[43]

Next follows an account of the relics which are in Venice and thereabouts. Chief of these are St Mark's ring and book, which are in St Mark's church. There is also the stone which Moses struck in the desert and which gave water in great abundance.[44] There is a picture of the Most Blessed Virgin on that stone which is fixed on the wall near the palace entrance. Above the door of St Mark's is a picture of Jesus Christ done in mosaic. It is very like Jesus Christ when He was carrying His cross towards Calvary. In the same church can be found a picture on linen cloth of Christ crucified. This picture once dripped blood when it was stabbed by a Jew with a dagger. There is a phial full of this blood in the church. Those who see the blood at the second hour of the night on Easter Eve will have full remission of their sins and permission to eat meat in the night.[45]

In the same city there is the body of Isidore, martyr; the bodies of St Sergius and Bacchus; the body of St Chrisostom, almoner; the body of St Zacharias, St John the Baptist's father;[46] the body of St Theodore, confessor; the body of St Chorax, hermit; the body of St Lierius, martyr; the body of St Ligorius; the body of St Barbarus, martyr; the bodies of the three saints, Nichomedes, Gamaliel and Abibon; the body of St Plato, martyr; the uncorrupted body of St Marina, virgin; the body of St Theodore, martyr; the bodies of the holy martyrs, Gordian and Epimachus; the body of St Florian; the body of St Paul, the first hermit; the uncorrupted body of St Maximus, bishop; the body of St Barbara, virgin and martyr; the body of St Magnus, martyr; the uncorrupted body of St Lucy, virgin;[47] the body of St Nicetas, martyr; the body of St Crisogonus, martyr; the body of St Constantius, confessor; the body of St Jonas, prophet; the body of St Hermolaus, martyr; the body of St Nicholas "on the shore"; the body of St Theodore, bishop of Giara; the uncorrupted body of St Helena;[48] the bodies of the two saints Cosmas and Damian; the body of St Cosmas, confessor; the uncorrupted body of St Paul, martyr, which has a coronet on his head because he was once Duke of Burgundy; the body of St Leo, confessor; the body of St Anianus, bishop of Alexandria;[49] the body of St Donatus, bishop.

On Murano: the body of St Gerard, bishop and martyr; the body of St Urcus, martyr; the body of St Dominicus, hermit; the body of St Cleodonius, bishop; the body of St Frucia, virgin and martyr; the body of St Antoninus, martyr; the bodies of the two saints, Hermacherus and Fortunatus, martyrs.

On Marianus: the bodies and bones of many of the Innocents; the body of St John, the almoner; the body of St Secundus, the martyr; the right hand of St Ciprian, the martyr – and on his hand there is the blood which fell from his neck when he was beheaded. In St George's church there is St Christopher's leg bone, which is very long. There is also part of Christ's sponge and a piece of His seamless tunic.

In Venice there are "Schools" of all the "Tongues". The doctors who teach in them receive their stipends from the city government.

Next follow the arrangements we must make before we leave Venice.[50] First you should agree a price for a berth in his galley and for your food with a "patron"[51] who is going there. Choose a place where you will be able to have light and air. If possible put the agreements made between you and the "patron" in writing and lay them before the lords of the city because then the "patron" will keep his side of the bargain with you. Your agreement should include the following:

That the "patron" will take you to the Holy Land and bring you back to Venice;

That, on the way, he will take you to certain ports for your benefit, and there obtain fresh water, meat and bread;

That he will not delay at a port more than three days without the agreement of the pilgrims;

That he will not load cargo either on the outward or on the return passage which will diminish your place in the galley or create problems for your sea voyage;

That he will convey you by these ports: Pula, 100 miles from Venice by sea: from Pula to Corfu, 600 miles: then to Motys (Methóni), 300 miles: then to

Candea (Heraklion) in Crete, 300 miles: then to Paphos in Cyprus, 400 miles: then to the port of Jaffa in the Holy Land, 300 miles. Make an agreement also that your "patron" will not take you to Famagusta in Cyprus because the air there is very poisonous for English people;[52]

That the "patron" will give you hot food twice a day, that the wine shall be good and the water fresh;

Finally that when he reaches the port of Jaffa he will guarantee to protect your property in his galley.

Next, the things which you must buy for your own assistance.

First, you must obtain for yourself and your companions three barrels, called "quarts", each holding ten gallons – two for wine and the third for water.

Put red wine in one barrel and keep it until you return from the Holy Land because it is good for the flux. Once you have left Venice, even if you were prepared to pay twenty ducats for a barrel, you would not get one. You can drink from the other barrel and refill it at a port on the way.

Third, you must buy a chest to place your belongings in under seal. In this way you will be able to protect the things which belong to you, like bread, cheese, spices, fruit and other essentials.

Fourth, you should buy biscuit for six months, pork, cheese, eggs and fruit to make meals after noon and in the evening, because what you get from the "patron" will be insufficient and you will often be very hungry. I also advise that you take with you from Venice medical confections, confortatives, like the powder called "powder duke"[53] [i.e. *poudre douce*] in a sachet, laxatives and restrictives, rice, figs, raisins, plums, damsons, pepper, saffron, cloves and other spices. You should also buy a small frying pan, large and small plates – both of pot and wood – glasses, mixing bowls, baskets for the eggs, vegetables, cheese, fish and meat which you will buy at various ports, when you should purchase your own supplies. You should also buy in Venice a small chamber pot because if you become ill and are unable to climb up to the upper parts of the galley you will be able to do what you have to in it. Provide yourself as well with a lantern and candles.

Fifth, you can buy a set of bedclothes in Venice near St Mark's. For three ducats you will get a feather bed, a mattress, two pillows, two pairs of small linen sheets and a small quilt. When you return to the seller in Venice he will take them back and give you one and a half ducats for the set of bedding.

Sixth, in Venice change ten or twelve ducats into new Venetian grotes. There you will get twenty-nine for a ducat but in other places you will only get twenty-six or twenty-four to the ducat. Take with you in addition three ducats in Venetian shillings (*soldi*). Take also two ducats in torneys; you will get eight [*torneys*] for a shilling, but on the way you will not get as many for a shilling. They will serve you well on the journey because you will buy food with them.

You must also buy a mat and a little cord to wrap up your bedding.

Seventh, when you come to a port it is good to be among the first to go ashore for you will thereby purchase what you want to eat at a better price, for example vegetables, chicken, meat, fish, fruit and eggs, which are very necessary.[54]

When you arrive at the various ports be very careful of the fruits because they very often loosen the bowels and, in those parts, lead to death for Englishmen.

Eighth, when you arrive at the port of Jaffa take with you from the galley bread, cheese and a gourd to carry wine. You will not get any food at Jaffa and the wine will be very expensive at Rama and Jerusalem. Have an eye to your knives and the things hanging from your belt because the Saracens want to steal what hangs from your belt, if they can. When you come to get donkeys at Jaffa arrive there in good time and then you will be able to select a better donkey. You will not pay any more for a better donkey than for a poorer one. Do not be too far ahead, nor too far behind, in case of evil men.

When you ride to the River Jordan take with you bread, wine, water, hard-boiled eggs, cheese and other food, enough for the two days to Jerusalem, because neither there nor on the way will you have a chance to buy. Keep one bottle of wine when you come from the River Jordan. If you want to climb Mount Quarantena, where Christ fasted for forty days and nights, take care when you come down from the mountain to the glade in the valley not to drink the water running there while you are hot. If you do, it will produce fevers or the flux. While you are hot, if you must drink, drink only a little undiluted wine, and then, later on, some diluted with the water which runs there.

These things and those stated above are what persons who propose to visit the holy places in Jerusalem and thereabouts must observe and do.

Thirdly I will write about our departure from Venice describing the cities by which we went, together with what we heard, what we saw and what we did. We departed from Venice on the 26th May for the "Towers of Venice" outside the city. We stayed there until the 1st June. We raised sail about midnight sailing, in God's name, for the Holy Land. We reached Parense [Poreč] in the land of Istria, approximately 100 miles from Venice, at about 1.00 p.m. on 3 June. Then we went on to Rovinj, ten miles from Poreč in the same country, where lies St Eufemia, virgin and martyr.[55] We stayed in that place on the Day of Pentecost and said our Masses there. After noon we sailed on to the city of Jarra [Zadar] in the land of Slavonia, where lies the uncorrupted body of St Simeon, who held Christ in his arms in the Temple at Jerusalem. We were there on 8 June. We next sailed, on 11 June, to the port of Sesule in Dalmatia.[56] Next we came by Cursula Castle [Korčula] in the land of Lysme:[57] one can get more strong wine there for one grosset than one can buy for eight in Venice. Next we sailed by Dalmatia, arriving at the city of Ragusa [Dubrovnik] on 16 June. In Dubrovnik there is an arm of St Blaise, and the silver there is very good. On 21 June we reached Corfu, an island in Greece, where St Arsenius is buried.[58] On 27 June we came to Axtis [Methóni], whence comes the wine called "Romney". About two miles from there is the body of St Leo, martyr.[59] In that place I heard that 30,000 Turks had been killed in the County of Greater Wallachia in the Kingdom of Hungary on Corpus Christi Day.[60] I will describe fully how this came about later on. I also heard that the Turk had taken Morea, which is in Greece and belonged to the Greeks.

We passed by the island called Carkey [Khálki] where, so it is said, St Nicholas was born in the city of Lyddon.[61]

Then we arrived at Rhodes in Colosa on 3 July. Here there is a thorn which was on Christ's head. It blooms on Good Friday, when the "Passion" is read, from the third hour until noon, producing up to twenty flowers. When the "Passion" is finished and sung to the end, it absorbs its own flowers. When the priest starts to read the "Passion" the thorn is red in colour; from the middle until the end it is green, and as soon as it absorbs its white flowers it assumes its earlier colour. There is also a second of Christ's thorns there. At the time when the "Passion" is read this turns green but does not produce any flowers. The reason is thought to be that one thorn touched Christ's brain, but this other did not, and so, after the "Passion", it goes back to its earlier colour.

Seven islands belong to the island of Colosa on which Rhodes is situated. The first is called Lango [Kos]. I have heard that Hip[p]ocrates' daughter appears here in a hole beneath the ground in the form of a serpent and she will be restored to her true shape when a knight who is chaste gives her a kiss. This island is very fertile in corn, fruit, animals and flour.[62] The second island is called Semys [Sími]. There is a governor there who arrived bare-legged at Rhodes along with his followers. He captured a large number of Turks, and guards that island well and faithfully against all foes. If it happened that that governor were foolish and unwilling to fight the Turks they would kill him and appoint another in his place.[63] The third island, called Carkey [Khálki], is where St Nicholas was born in the city named Lyddon. Through his grace, iron tools last without need of repair for two generations, fathers to sons. Because of the number of stones they do not till the soil there with animals but use iron tools instead. The fourth island is called Episcopia [Tílos]; the fifth is Nysere [Nísiros], the sixth Calamo [Kálimnos] and the seventh Aron [Leros?].[64]

On Rhodes there is a hospital for the sick.[65] If anyone is ill or wounded, provided he be a Christian, he may come there and have everything necessary for his treatment provided by doctors and surgeons at the expense of the Knights of Rhodes – this being the reason for their foundation. The foundation started in Jerusalem, and the place where their order began is still there just in front of the Holy Temple of Christ in Jerusalem.[66] If anyone dies in the hospital and is buried in the cemetery nearby, he will obtain remission of his sins. His flesh and bones will decay within five days of his burial in that place.

The knights of Rhodes have a castle in Turkey, called "Sympere" [St Pierre].[67] Previously this was the site of the city of Tarsys, and the Three Kings of Cologne took ship in its harbour. After their departure Herod in his fury burned the ships of the people of Tarsys.[68] In this place too St Paul, who had come with his father from the town of Giscallus in the province of Galilee, was brought up as a young man. This is why he is called "Paul of Tarsus", because he was brought up there.[69]

In their castle the Knights of Rhodes have huge hounds which are let out at night to keep guard outside the castle and to seek out Turks. They are well able to distinguish Christian from Turk. If they do not find any Turks they return to the castle the next morning barking, but if they find any Turks they return without barking. If one of the dogs goes to sleep and does not come with them at night outside the castle, they will destroy it themselves; if, however, any of the dogs happen to be wounded by the Turks they have doctors to heal them.

From Rhodes we came to Paphos on 9 July. St Paul was imprisoned there in the place belonging to the Franciscans where there is "St Paul's Spring". St Catherine was born in a city called Constantia two miles from Famagusta. In the Franciscan church in Famagusta there is a chapel behind the high altar and the place where St Catherine learned her letters. In the city of Nicosia, which is one of the chief cities of Cyprus, in the Benedictine Abbey lies, uncorrupted, the body of Lord Mountford. Formerly an English knight, he is revered as a saint. It is a little over 200 years since he was buried there.[70] Outside Nicosia is the corpse of St Mamas,[71] whose body distils oil, together with the body of the Abbot Hilarion.[72] We did not visit Seleeucia[73] because there were 12,000 Mamelukes, Moors and Saracens there. There were 50,000 of these pagans with the bastard king[74] at Nicosia. Twenty miles from Seleeucia is the cross of the Good Thief, which hangs in a chapel on a mountain without visible attachment.

On 13 July we reached the port of Jaffa in the Holy Land, where, to glorify God, we sang *Urbs beata Jerusalem* ("Blessed City of Jerusalem"), in "faburden".[75] We waited at sea for three days until the Saracen officials came to our galley. On 16 July we came to Jaffa and, on our entry, we sang, kneeling, *Christus resurgens ex mortuis* ("Christ rising from the dead").[76] We reached the port of Jaffa from Venice in six weeks. We then waited at Jaffa for one night in a subterranean cave. On the morning of 17 July we reached Ramys by way of Jessara and Gazara. We spent that night in the Christians' hospice, lying on the ground. On the 18th to Lidda, where we entered what was once a Christian church but which is now in ruins. This is the place where St George was beheaded. There, in honour of God and St George, we sang, in "faburden", *Miles Christi gloriose* ("O Glorious Soldier of Christ").[77] We then came back to Ramys and spent that night there in the same way as the night before.

We rode to Jerusalem on 19 July by way of Betanobel Castle and New Castle, dismounting from our horses to eat what we had brought with us and buying water there. Then we rode by Emaus Castle and the mountains of Gelboa by Sylo and Aramatha arriving at the holy city of Jerusalem at about four o'clock in the afternoon. We visited the courtyard before the Temple entrance where there is a stone covered with crosses. This is the stone on which Christ fell when He was carrying His cross and we kissed it. We then crossed to the Christian hospice where we had dinner. After dinner we lay on our mats. At dawn the Brothers arrived summoning us to make our pilgrimage to the "Stations". These are the ones we visited on 20 July:

First, the stone with the crosses where Christ fell;
Second, the street where Christ carried His cross;
Third, the home of the rich man who was damned;
Fourth, the crossroads where Christ fell with His cross;
Fifth, the place where the women wept over Christ;

Sixth, where Veronica took Christ's face in her handkerchief;

Seventh, where the Most Blessed Virgin Mary fainted;

Eighth, the gate through which Christ was led to death;

Ninth, the pool where the sick were healed when the waters were disturbed;

Tenth, the two white stones in the wall above the heads of passers-by on which Jesus stood when he was condemned to death by Pilate;

Eleventh, the school of the Blessed Mary where she learned her letters. Along that street, on the other side, is Pilate's house, where Christ was flogged and condemned to death.

Then we visited the other places in Jerusalem, Jehoshophat, Mount Olivet, the valley of Syloe and Mount Syon, just as I have described in my earlier itinerary.[78] At nightfall on this day we went into the Temple of Jesus Christ, where, after a procession and a visit to the holy places in the Temple, we had a sermon from an Englishman, a Bachelor of Sacred Theology, on the Mount of Holy Calvary. His text was *Indulgenciam ejus fusis lacrymis postulemus* ("Let us beg his forgiveness with tears outpoured").[79]

We rode to Bethlehem on 21 July and on the 22nd to the Mountains of Judaea. Near the place where St Mary greeted Elizabeth, we sang the Magnificat in "faburden", in honour of God and the Blessed Mary.[80] In the house where John the Baptist was born we sang *Inter natos mulierum* ("Among the sons of women").[81] The following night we entered Jesus Christ's holy Temple and, in the chapel there where Christ appeared to His Most Blessed Mother, we sang *Beata Dei genetrix Maria* ("Mary, Blessed Mother of God"), in "faburden".[82] At the entrance to Jesus Christ's most holy Sepulchre we sang *Christus resurgens ex mortuis* ("Christ rising from the dead") and, on the Mount of Calvary, *Vexilla regis prodeunt* ("The king's standards forward go"), in "faburden".[83] Immediately after the hymn we had a sermon on the same Mount of Calvary from the Bachelor mentioned above, whose text was, *Heu me fili mi* ("Woe is me, O my son").

On the 24th we rode to Bethany, entering Christ's holy Temple the following night, where, in the chapel of St Mary mentioned above, we sang *Ave regina coelorum* ("Hail, Queen of Heaven"), and, at the entrance to Christ's Sepulchre, *Dum transisset Sabatum* ("When the Sabbath had passed"), and, on the Hill of Calvary, *Pange lingua gloriosi* ("Declare, my tongue, the mystery of his glorious body").[84]

We stayed in Jerusalem on the 25th, where I had certain questions[85] about things whose answers were found in this country.

The first question was about the inscription which is beside the hole of the Holy Cross. The inscription, in Greek, runs *O theos vasileos ymon proseonas ergase sothias emose tis gis*. In Latin this is *Hic Deus rex noster operatus est salutem in medio terrae* ("Here, in the centre of the earth, God, our King, wrought our salvation").

The second question. Was the column, to which Christ was tied, spattered with Christ's blood? The answer was that it is no longer, but the marks of the lashes are still there.[86]

The third question. Does the lamp above the Tomb, which used to put itself out at the time of Christ's death and light itself again at the time of the Resurrection, without human assistance, still do this? The answer was that it does not do it now because our Faith has now come to an end there. It is said, however, that on Easter Day a Saracen saw fire descending from heaven and falling on the Tomb.

The fourth question. Since the Valley of Jehoshophat takes its name from the burial there of King Jehoshophat, whereabouts was he buried? The answer is that it is thought that he was buried in the grave which is called the "Grave of Absolon" and then he was later moved from that grave and buried among his fathers. Although it is called the "Grave of Absolon", he was not buried there, but rather he was cast out into a field beneath a heap of stones in the Pass of Effraym, where he was killed far away from the Valley of Jehoshophat.[87]

The fifth question. How far is the Mount of Calvary from Solomon's Temple, because Christ's voice was heard at Solomon's Temple when He shouted, "Father, into thy hands"? The answer is that it is 2½ furlongs away.[88]

The sixth question. How far away is the cave, in which Christ sweated blood, from the house of Annas, to which He was led after His arrest? The answer is 6 furlongs.[89]

The seventh question. Where are David and Solomon buried? The answer is that they are buried under the Franciscan chapel on Mount Syon, on the left-hand side of the chapel.[90]

The eighth question. Where is Gyon in which Solomon was crowned? The answer is that it is 3½ furlongs outside Jerusalem. There is a tower there and it is also called the "House of Evil Counsel" because that is where Judas went to betray Christ, since that is where the chief priests were gathered to deliver Jesus to death.[91]

Ninth. Where is the stone on which Our Lord's body was laid after His death when He was wrapped in linen cloths? The answer is that it is in Constantinople.[92]

Tenth. Where was Joseph, the Most Blessed Mary's husband, buried? The answer is that he was buried in a cave on Mount Olivet.[93]

Eleventh. Are the prints, made by Christ's feet as He ascended into heaven, on Mount Olivet? The answer is that there are the prints of Christ's two feet on a hard rock, but the right print is easier to see. As Supplicius, the Bishop of Jerusalem, says, the place where the prints of Christ's feet were made at the time of His Ascension have never been able to be covered with paving. Indeed the marble slabs rebounded in the faces of the paviours. The earth still preserves the same appearance, as of footprints, as when Our Lord was taken away from their sight. Petrus Calo also states, "It is said to be so hallowed by the divine prints that it could never be covered with marble or anything else. Such things are always rejected. The soil itself spurns whatever a man's hand has tried to place on it by way of decoration. So it is that in the whole area of the basilica this spot alone stays green with the look of turf. As one worships the dust trodden by God, one sees the marks of the divine feet still preserved in the sand for those who come to worship. Thus it can be truly said, "We have worshipped in the place where his feet stood." In Jerusalem also there is a print of Christ's right foot in the former house of Simon the leper, where Mary Magdalene washed and kissed Christ's feet.

On 26 July we rode to Ramys and stayed there two days, because some Saracens were there to travel with us to be converted to our Faith. When these things had been done and no persons were found there they [sic] returned to Ramys. Then, on 28 July, we rode to the port of Jaffa and boarded our galley that evening. Thus we were in the Holy Land for thirteen days. We paid the Saracen chiefs fifteen ducats for our safe conduct over this period. A new chief, however, had been sent by the Sultan to govern the city of Jerusalem and my *patronus*, Andrea Morason, was delayed two days ashore at Jaffa until he paid the new lord of Jerusalem fifty ducats. In addition there was a war at that time between two Sultans, those of Babylon and Damascus, for control and power over the Holy Land and to settle which of them should be ruler there. At the same time the land was so full of Arabs that those people who lived in Jericho collected their goods and came to live in Jerusalem. The result was that pilgrims were not able at that time to go to the Jordan or to the Mount of the Forty Days where Christ fasted forty days and nights.

When everything was completed in the Holy Land we began our voyage. We came to the port of Paphos in the Kingdom of Cyprus on 7 August. The

"Bastard" had invaded this country with the help of the Sultan of Babylon and had made the real king and the queen flee.[94]

We reached Rhodes on 19 August. There I heard that there is a castle and a small village, called Fylerme [Philerimos], six miles from Rhodes. There there is a painting of the Most Blessed Mary which was sketched by St John the Evangelist when he was on the island of Patmos 150 miles from Rhodes. This was afterwards painted by others. It is the first picture which was made in honour of the Most Blessed Mary and many miracles occurred there.[95]

I also heard from a reliable informant at Rhodes that after the Turk had killed Baron de Mulda in the kingdom of Hungary, in the County of Greater Wallachia, which is within the borders of Hungary, he took the Baron's two sons and brought them up until they reached the years of discretion. The elder brother pleased the Turk in all things, and so the Turk gave him the barony of his father, whom he had killed, on condition that he would pay him a yearly tribute. This he did, but only for a few years. Then, on the advice of the lords of Hungary, he refused the Turk the tribute. Thereupon the Turk sent two ambassadors with a hundred men to collect the tribute. Baron Flak[96] killed the latter and after slitting the noses and lips of the ambassadors sent them back to the Turk in dishonour.

The Turk was furious. He collected 30,000 men under one of his lords to do battle with the Baron. When Lord Flak heard of their approach he collected all his people and all the animals which were in his barony for the distance of a three-day journey along the route by which the Turk would come. He left no food there except in small tents, where he left behind a few loaves of bread, as though they were fleeing in haste and terror of him. On the third day, when the Turks saw where Lord Flak was with his army, Flak immediately charged at them with his troops and killed 30,000 of them together with their commander. These events happened on Corpus Christi Day.

Next, that is after 26 July, the Turk advanced with a huge army a three days' march into Flak's territory and then pitched camp. At nightfall Flak and his men made a sudden attack on the Turks and killed 100,000 of them. The Turk fled. When he had ridden about twenty miles and had reached a certain stream, where the Turks who were with him drank water to refresh themselves, the Turk turned to them and said,

"Refresh yourselves and show yourselves warriors. Let us return against our enemies because we are a match for them. At this moment they are busy collecting our goods; they have put down their weapons thinking that we are not willing to turn back against them. Come then with all speed and we shall soon destroy them."

Flak, who was pursuing the Turk, thinking that he would do exactly this, charged at them and killed 20,000 of them. Thus the Turk fled a second time.

The Turk sent messengers to his great city of Aternopyl [Hadrianopol][97] with orders that, when he arrived, no one should speak or murmur against him on account of the death of parents, kinsmen or relatives. He himself entered the city by night to allay or avoid grumbling by the people. Nevertheless the people did rail against him so loudly that he could not stay there in peace because of the public outcry.

He moved to Constantinople and told those at his court what mischief Lord Flak had done him. When Flak's younger brother, who was with the Turk at that time among his retinue in the palace, heard this, he said to the Turk,

"If an argument or quarrel could come about between my brother and a captain of that country, he [sic] would seize him and I would bring him to you, because many of them love me more than him."

Lord Flak heard about this plan through the mediation of friends in the Turk's palace. He made an agreement with a captain, in whom he placed great trust, that they should have an open quarrel in the presence of the lords of his country, and that the captain should go away from him as if in anger and should muster a great force as though to wage war on him. When the younger brother, the one who was with the Turk, heard that this captain was preparing to join battle with his older brother, he asked the Turk that the captain should meet with him on the way. The captain greeted the younger brother and got him to go ahead with his Turkish soldiers so that he was between his older brother and the captain. In this way it was arranged that an assault was made from both directions against the Turks who were in the middle. In the fourth battle they slew 30,000 Turks. Flak himself took his brother and inserted a stake in his anus which he drove in as far as his throat. Then he had the stake on which his brother's body was impaled set out in the full sun. Thus between the Feast of Corpus Christi and the Nativity of the Blessed Virgin Mary 9,000 [sic] Turks were killed.

When the Knights of Rhodes heard the news they rang their bells for joy and sang the *Te Deum* in praise and honour of God. When he heard of this the Turk announced that he would sail with a large fleet of galleys against Rhodes and do battle with them. In reply the Lord Master of Rhodes[98] summoned his brother Knights and gave orders to stock the city with two years' supply of wheat and wine.[99] He also instructed the Knights to guard all quarters of the city.[100]

I also heard that the King of Hungary[101] sent Lord Flak gifts when he heard of his loyalty. Indeed at the time of the third battle the King himself gained the largest city in Hungary and seven other cities from the power of the Turks. Thus the Turk departed from Hungary in great disgrace. Thanks be to God.

On the 5th September we reached Candia [Heraklion] where a man coming from Constantinople reported that the Turk was at sea with 300 ships, galleys, grypis and fustis[102] and heading for Rhodes. We do not know, however, whether he got there.

We arrived at Methóni on 20 September, Lissa[103] on 24 September and Venice on 11 October. We left Venice for England on the 13th of that month, arriving at Dover on 1 December. Thus our return trip from England to the Holy Land back to England took thirty-seven weeks and three days.

COMMENTARY

On this final pilgrimage Wey sailed from Gravesend to Antwerp and, as in 1458, he then went via Maastricht to Aachen. He must have been disappointed not to visit Cologne, with its great shrine to the Magi, in either 1458 or 1462.

In 1458 Wey had cut south-east from Aachen to join the Rhine at Koblenz. In 1462 he was advised to avoid the Rhine route "because of a war between two bishops", and so he turned almost due south to Trier and from there followed the Moselle, via Metz and Epinal, to Basle. At least this route enabled him to visit "Zawe" (St Vith), with its shrine to St Vitus, as well as the relics of St Matthias in Trier and those of St Nicholas (St Nicholas in Gaul) and St Theobald (Thann). At Basle Wey followed the Rhine to Konstanz and then passed along the southern shore of the Bodensee. He travelled eastwards through the Vorarlberg and over the Arlberg Pass to Landeck. Here he joined an important Roman road, the Via Claudia Augusta, built 1,400 years earlier by the Emperor Claudius to join the Danube to the Adriatic. From Landeck he crossed the Reschenpass to Merano and then, following the wide valley of the Adige, he came to Trento. Another river valley, that of the Brenta, took him to Padua and so to Venice.

After the hardships of the previous eight weeks Wey would have been relieved to reach the comforts of that splendid city. His admiration is palpable as he fills the next seven pages with descriptions of three great ceremonies he witnessed during his five-week stay: the Doge's Procession on St Mark's Day, the funeral of Doge Pascale Malopero on 5 May and the coronation of his successor, Christoforo Moro. As well as vignettes from Venetian history, including the origin of the ceremony of the Doge's marriage to the sea, Wey describes the churches and the relics which the faithful may view. Then follows a section of useful advice on the sailing arrangements, both administrative and practical, which must be made to ensure a successful return passage from Venice to Jaffa. Much of this section also appears, in English, in Chapter 2, "A Prevision".

Eventually, more than halfway through this chapter, Wey reaches his departure from Venice on 26 May. His narrative continues with a concise account of the seven-week voyage by galley down the Adriatic along the coast of Istria, Dalmatia and Greece to Methóni. Rhodes also impressed Wey and he devotes an interesting page to the city and the Knights Hospitaller. His galley, the *Morosina*, reached Jaffa on 13 July. Since he had described in Chapter 7, in detail, the programme his group followed in 1458, he does not repeat that in Chapter 9. Instead he gives details of the hymns the pilgrims sang at significant points in their journey and then discusses his "Questions" and their answers. These "Questions" appear again, with one or two variations, at the end of Chapter 10. This fact and the appearance of other repetitions noted elsewhere reinforce the view that Wey's *Itineraries* did not receive a final editorial polish. The last three pages of this chapter describe the return home and include an account of the bloody conflict with the Turks.

NOTES

1   According to the Roxburghe editor, no trace of this twofold dedication is to be found in the charter, statutes or annals of Eton College. William Wey seems to have transferred the dedication from the sister foundation, King's College, at Cambridge to which it rightly belongs. In the 1458 Itinerary Wey gives the correct designation, "the Royal College of the Most Blessed Mary of Eton at Windsor".

2   In the manner of pilgrims... As early as the eleventh century pilgrims attended a service before setting out on their travels at which their scrips and staffs were blessed. The Worcester Pontifical indicates a short ceremony consisting of prayers and the bestowal of the scrip and staff, followed by further prayers. The Ely Pontifical describes a more complicated service (Birch, *Pilgrimage to Rome in the Middle Ages*, p. 77).

3   A fourteenth-century building, which Wey could have seen and which is now known as Milton Chantry, can be visited in Gravesend. It once housed the chapel of a leper hospital, later becoming a tavern and, in 1780, part of a fort.

4　　This was a leisurely pace. The distance from Eton to London Bridge by river is about 50 miles and by road approximately half of that distance. Whichever method Wey used he does not appear to have been in a hurry. On horseback the journey would be an easy two days' ride. From London Bridge to Gravesend the distance by water is 26.5 miles. The normal way to travel between London Bridge and Gravesend at this time was by boat known as the "Long Ferry". The boatmen of Gravesend guarded the privilege of providing this ferry very jealously for centuries. There is a reference to it in a Royal Grant of 1401 which shows that this right was old even then. With the help of an ebb tide the ferrymen could complete the journey in a day.

5　　In Chapter 8 of *The Itineraries* Wey gives the names of the cities and towns he passed through in 1458 on his route from Calais to Rome, from Rome to Venice and from Venice to Calais. In 1462 Wey avoided Bruges and Ghent and Mechelen, which he had visited four years earlier. On this later pilgrimage he was unable to use the Rhine barges which in 1458 had carried him from Sinzig to the Bingen Loch, where the river ceased to be navigable and pilgrims had to disembark and continue by land via Bad Odernheim to Worms.

6　　The "war on the Rhine between two bishops". This war in the Rhineland ended in November 1463. It has a special significance in the spread of printing because, when Archbishop Adolph of Cologne seized Mainz on 28 October 1462, he abolished the city's liberties, reduced it to its legal condition of obedience to his see and expelled 800 citizens. Mainz, the birthplace of Gutenberg, was the home of printing and the expulsion of so many of its citizens with their knowledge of printing meant that other cities were able to set up presses of their own. (For further information on the reasons for the quarrel between the bishops, see *Cambridge Medieval History*, Vol. VIII, pp. 142 ff and 149).

7　　St Matthias Abbey is about a mile west of the centre of Trier. The relics of St Matthias, removed from Jerusalem by St Helena, were brought here in the eleventh century.

8　　Wey was very interested in identifying not only the locations of events in the life of Christ and the Saints but also where well-known prayers and canticles were first composed. In Chapter 7, for example, he notes where the Apostles' Creed and the Lord's Prayer were composed and where the Magnificat was first sung. For a discussion of the authorship and place of composition of the Athanasian Creed, see *Oxford Dictionary of the Christian Church*, p. 98.

9　　John 18:10.

10　The seven members of the Electoral College which appointed the Holy Roman Emperor and which was regularized by the Golden Bull of 1356 consisted of the Archbishops of Mainz, Trier and Cologne together with the rulers of the Rhine Palatinate, Saxony, Brandenburg and Bohemia. Later, in the seventeenth and eighteenth centuries, the rulers of Bavaria and Hanover were also included. The college disappeared when the Holy Roman Empire was abolished in 1806.

11　Although Wey devotes the whole of his Chapter 1 to a description of the various coins pilgrims will use between England and the Holy Land, he does not mention rappis there.

12　St Nicholas in Gaul. A reference to St Nicolas-de-Port on the left bank of the Meurthe, about 8 miles from Nancy. The present church is one of the most important Flamboyant Gothic churches in Lorraine. The nave was completed in 1514, more than fifty years after Wey's visit. It is still a place of pilgrimage, especially on Whit Monday, its chief treasure being a finger joint of St Nicholas of Myra.

St Nicholas(d.*c*.350) was a bishop of Myra in Lycia. His relics, stolen by Italian merchants in 1087, are now venerated at Bari.

13 Chains and fetters were often presented to a church as ex-voto offerings by former prisoners in gratitude for their release. A similar collection may still be seen in the church of St Léonard-de-Noblat, in France.

14 "Pope Pius and the Duke of Austria". Aeneas Sylvius Piccolomini, who assumed the name "Pius", was Pope from 1458 until 1464. The Duke of Austria was Albert VI of Hapsburg, who declared war on the Western Emperor, Frederick III, in June 1461. He beseiged Frederick in Vienna until peace was made through Podebrady, King of Bohemia, in December 1462, when Frederick gave Austria to Albert for eight years. Albert died in December 1463 (*Cambridge Medieval History*, Vol. VIII).

15 At Klösterle the lower rooms of a small hospice built by the Knights Hospitaller in 1218 can still be seen in the present Johanniter-Stübe inn. At Landeck Wey joined the Via Claudia Augusta, the Roman road built by the Emperor Claudius to connect the Danube with the Adriatic. Some of the places he mentions, such as Nauders, had been the sites of Roman *mansiones* or *mutationes* and later became medieval staging posts. He has misplaced Prutz, which comes between Landeck and Tösens. At Terlan he crossed the Adige to the right bank, crossing back at Salorno. I have not been able to identify Numered, Saladon or Sanarel; the names of these three places might have been transposed from elsewhere. From Trento Wey followed the Brenta to Bassano and Padua.

16 The three "Williams". One of the very few personal references made by Wey. He does not give any other indications of these companions in his narrative, but in the list of his gifts to Edington, written on the flyleaf to *The Itineraries*, there is a reference to "a cloth stained with three Marys and three pilgrims". Perhaps Wey kept this painting as a souvenir of the visit he made to the Holy Land with his two fellow pilgrims. The other two priests called "William" might be identified with some confidence if, for instance, a papal licence for a portable altar or permission from a diocesan bishop for one of his priests to be away on pilgrimage revealed their names and destinations.

Sir Baldwin Fulford, a West Countryman known to Wey, was in Santiago de Compostela with him on Trinity Sunday in 1456. His brother, William Fulford, became a canon of Exeter Cathedral on 10 September 1446 and was described as a canon of Wells in a will dated 24 October 1449. He was granted permission for a portable altar by Pope Nicholas V on 17 June 1450. A contemporary of Wey, he died in 1475. Sir Baldwin, who fought for Henry VI at Towton, where the Lancastrians suffered a disastrous defeat, was captured and beheaded, together with the Earl of Devon, in York, probably on 3 April 1461. In the aftermath of all this it would not have been unreasonable for William Fulford to go on pilgrimage to Jerusalem with a fellow Lancastrian, William Wey, but, without further proof, this must remain merely an intriguing possibility.

17 "Secular priest" is a term, first used in the twelfth century, to describe a priest living "in the world" as opposed to a "regular priest", who was a member of a religious order and lived according to a "rule" (Latin *regula* monastic rule).

18 Padua's famous university was founded in 1222. Sir John Tiptoft, one of Wey's fellow pilgrims in 1458, studied there. Donatello's equestrian statue of Erasmo da Narni in front of the Basilica del Santo was finished in 1453, only nine years before Wey's visit.

19　The painting by Gentile Bellini in the Accademia in Venice entitled *Procession in Saint Mark's Square*, painted in 1496 but depicting events which took place on St Mark's Day in 1444, shows many of the officers and objects described by Wey in 1462.

20　The Fraternities or Scuole (Schools) were lay confraternities dedicated to charitable works, including help for the sick and visiting prisoners. Members were drawn from the middle class; no priest or patrician could hold a position of responsibility in them. The most important, known as the Scuole Grandi, were those of San Marco, San Rocco, Santa Maria della Carità, the Misericordia and San Giovanni Evangelista (San Teodoro became a Scuola Grande in the sixteenth century). There were probably about another hundred Scuole. The Fraternity of St Mark, founded in 1260, stands beside the church of Santi Giovanni e Paolo.

21　Pascale Malopero (Pasquale Malipiero) was Doge from 1457 to 1462.

22　The Arsenale was founded in 1104 and enlarged many times. Normally foreign visitors were not admitted – a restriction which still applies. It is noteworthy that Wey gained entry to this restricted area. Among the many anecdotes about the skill and industry of the *arsenalotti* is the story which recounts how tree trunks could be brought into the Arsenale in the morning to emerge by nightfall as a completed galley.

23　The biricula was the distinctive cap traditionally worn by the Doge of Venice.

24　The Dominican Church of Santi Giovanni e Paolo is one of the largest brick churches in Venice. Begun in 1333, it was consecrated in 1430. Twenty-five Doges are buried there. The funerary monument of Doge Pascale Malopero can still be seen in the north aisle. One of the earliest Renaissance monuments in Venice, it is a masterpiece of delicate carving.

25　The three Latin hymns:

(a) *Te Deum laudamus.* The famous thanksgiving hymn, "We praise Thee, O God…" which the Book of Common Prayer prescribed for use at Matins with the Benedicite as an alternative. At one stage its authorship was ascribed to St Ambrose and St Augustine, but it is now thought to be by Nicetas of Remesiana; see (c) below.

(b) *Sermone blando angelus.* "With sweet words the angel…" This fourth- or fifth-century hymn appears, in a translation by T.A. Lacey, as number 124 in *The English Hymnal*: "His cheering message from the grave/ An angel to the women gave…"

(c) *Ad cenam agni providi, Et stolis albis candidi.* This hymn, normally used at Easter, has been attributed to St Nicetas of Remesiana, a missionary bishop in Dacia, who died in about 410. Some scholars also consider him to be the author of the *Te Deum*. Neale's translation appears as number 128 in *Hymns Ancient and Modern*:

> "The Lamb's high banquet called to share,
> Arrayed in garments white and fair…"

26　Doge Christoforo Moro died in 1471. His tomb is in the church of San Giobbe in Venice, for the building of which he provided most of the money.

27　In this detail of the story Wey appears to have been misinformed. The events he narrates occurred in 1177 and St Francis was not born until 1182. The monk's habit worn by the Pope when he sought asylum must have been that of another order.

28　"The Emperor Frederick" refers to Frederick I (Barbarossa) of Hohenstaufen (*c.*1123–1190). He succeeded Conrad III as Emperor with the ambition of restoring the universal monarchy of Charlemagne. He was drowned whilst on the Third Crusade.

29 "The monastery called 'Charity'". The Church of Santa Maria della Carità, originally a small wooden building, was probably founded at the beginning of the twelfth century. In 1134 some Augustinian monks came from Ravenna to Venice and built their convent next to the church. According to the legend, repeated here by Wey, Pope Alexander III sought refuge from Frederick Barbarossa in 1177 by hiding in the convent for six months. He consecrated the church on 5 April and the anniversary of this was celebrated thenceforward every year until the end of the Republic, with the Doge's procession crossing the Grand Canal by a bridge of boats. Under Eugene IV, Pope from 1431 to 1447, the monks of La Carità prospered greatly. Work started on enlarging the church in 1441. In 1450 the apse chapels were built and in 1453, five years before Wey's first arrival in Venice, a Madonna was bought from Donatello and placed over the door to the sacristy. In 1807 the whole complex of the Carità, convent, church and school was chosen to be the site of an Academy of Fine Arts. Work began on the alterations in 1811 and today the building forms part of the Accademia.

30 Sebastiano Ziani was Doge from 1172 until 1178. In the former Sala dell' Albergo of the Scuola di Santa Maria della Carità hangs a sixteenth-century painting which shows Doge Ziani meeting Pope Alexander III.

31 On 29 May 1176 there was a crucial battle between Frederick and the Lombards at Legnano. The Germans were defeated with great slaughter. The Emperor's shield, banner, cross and lance were all captured.

   The eldest son of Frederick Barbarossa, Henry, succeeded his father as the Emperor Henry VI, when Barbarossa was drowned on 10 June 1190. Henry, the son of Frederick and Beatrice, was born in 1165, became King of Germany at the age of four and King of Italy on his marriage to Constance. He was knighted at Mainz in 1184. His next two brothers were Frederick of Swabia and Philip of Hohenstaufen. The records do not show that any of these were captured at Legnano and Wey's informant might have been thinking of various other noble hostages.

32 On the pavement in front of the great door of St Mark's a slab of red Verona marble with a white marble lozenge marks the spot where, according to tradition, Barbarossa knelt before Pope Alexander III in 1177.

33 The asp and the basilisk. The basilisk, also called a cockatrice, was allegedly hatched by a serpent from a cock's egg. It was the fabulous king of serpents, having the wings of a fowl, the tail of a dragon and the head of a cock. Isaiah 11:8 combines references to the asp and the cockatrice.

34 The Marriage with the Sea. This ceremony, later called the Sposalizio del Mar, grew out of an event on Ascension Day 1000 AD when the Doge led an expedition down the Dalmatian coast to subdue pirates. Success brought him the title Dux Dalmatiae. Thereafter the anniversary of this event was celebrated with a service of supplication and thanksgiving. Over the years the ceremony became more elaborate and included the casting of a propitiatory golden ring into the waters, which became identified with a mystic marriage to the sea.

35 *The Doge's Procession Crossing St Mark's Square*, by Bellini, shows a splendid canopy like that described by Wey.

36 Fisherfolk. In Chapter 11 of *The Itineraries* Wey gives a little more information, apparently obtained from the *patronus* of his galley, Andrea Morosini, stating that the earliest settlers were Hungarian refugees from Attila the Hun.

37 St Jeremiah, the second of the greater prophets, lived in the seventh century BC, and tradition says he was stoned to death at the age of fifty-five in Egypt. Some of his relics were believed to rest in his church in Venice. Originally founded in the eleventh century, the church was reconstructed in 1292 and later demolished. The present church of San Geremia dates from 1753 and houses the body of St Lucy, which was brought here in 1863.

38 The little church of San Giacometto, set in the heart of the market area, is said to be the oldest church in Venice. The present building dates back to the twelfth century.

39 San Giovanni Evangelista was founded, according to tradition, in 970.

40 San Salvatore was rebuilt in 1508. It contains the tomb of Caterina Cornaro, sometime queen of Cyprus, who died in 1510. She was the wife of James II, "the Bastard", mentioned by Wey later in this chapter.

41 Santa Maria Formosa. The present church, rebuilt in 1492, preserves the Greek-cross plan of the earlier church, which was founded by St Magnus in the seventh century after he had had a vision of the Virgin Mary as a splendid, buxom woman, who asked him to build a church just under a cloud.

42 San Silvestro. The original ninth-century church, rebuilt in the fourteenth, was demolished in 1837. All that remains of the original structure is a fragment of a column with a Veneto-Byzantine capital set in the wall.

43 San Pietro di Castello was the cathedral of Venice from the eleventh century until 1807 when St Mark's was designated a cathedral. The first church on the site was built in the seventh century and was dedicated to St Serge and St Bacchus. This was replaced in 841 by a church dedicated to St Peter. The present church dates from 1557. San Lorenzo Giustiniani became the first Patriarch of Venice in 1451, only seven years before Wey's first visit to the city.

44 Exodus 17:6.

45 The Jew and the Picture. For other examples of anti-Semitic stories, see Index.

46 The relics are preserved in the church of San Zaccaria. The original ninth-century church, rebuilt between the tenth and twelfth centuries, was restructured between 1444 and 1515.

47 The body of St Lucy, martyred in Syracuse in 304, was stolen from Constantinople by Venetian crusaders in 1204. It was placed in the church of Santa Lucia where Wey could have seen it. When that church was demolished in 1863 to build the railway station her body was moved to the church of San Geremia where it can be seen today.

48 The church of Sant'Elena, founded in the early thirteenth century and rebuilt in 1435 shortly before Wey's visit, was abandoned in 1807 but reopened in 1928. The body of Saint Helena, mother of Constantine the Great, used to be displayed in a glass case under the altar in a small chapel on the south side. At the time of writing (April 2007) it has been removed while repairs are carried out to the church. Wey had a special interest in the part played by St Helena in the discovery of the True Cross and other relics.

49 St Anianus (first century) was a disciple and immediate successor of St Mark in the see of Alexandria. He was said to have been a shoemaker.

50 One of the curiosities of The Itineraries is that these "Provisions" are given twice over, once in English, in Chapter 2, and once in Latin, here.

51 Patronus. Wey mentions the name of his patronus, Andrea Morosini, twice.

52 In this, Latin, version William Wey has accidentally omitted the stages from Candia (Heraklion) in Crete to Rhodes and from Rhodes to Paphos. These are named in Wey's English version

of the contract in Chapter 2. That the sea route did include Rhodes is shown by Wey's own narrative – *venimus ad Rhodys in Colosa iij die Julii.*

53 Powder duke, more usually spelled *poudre douce*, was a mixture of four spices: ginger, nutmeg, cinnamon and liquorice. (In Wey's time fennel was probably used instead of liquorice.) While *poudre douce* was used to flavour sweet dishes there was a parallel powder for savoury dishes, called *poudre forte*, which contained ginger, nutmeg, cloves and pepper. If a large amount of pepper was used it was given the name "gunpowder"!

54 Food. Although the contract with the *patronus*, which Wey describes here and in Chapter 2, stipulated that pilgrim passengers should be given two hot meals per day, they would be glad to take the opportunity of purchasing fresh food, especially fruit, vegetables, meat and fish, when their galley put into a port. Invitations to dine ashore were eagerly accepted (see Mitchell, *Spring Voyage*, pp. 63 and 81; Prescott, *Jerusalem Journey*, p. 50; and Newett, *Canon Pietro Casola's Pilgrimage*, p. 90).

55 Rovinum and St Euphemia. Rovinj, about 10 miles south of Poreč and 15 miles north of Pula still has a church of Sveta Eufemia, which uses the walls of a Romanesque predecessor. Her sarcophagus can be seen in the church. She was martyred under Diocletian in 304 AD, being thrown first to the lions in Chalcedon and then, when they refused to kill her, being broken on a wheel. Her body was taken to Constantinople where it disappeared after the sack of that city. It reappeared, miraculously, in 800 AD on the shore at Rovinj. The church became a place of pilgrimage, especially on the saint's day, 16 September.

Zadar and the neighbouring coastline had been sold in 1409, fifty-three years before Wey's visit, by the Hungarian king, Zsigmond, to the Venetian Republic for 100,000 ducats. Before this it had been one of the most bitter adversaries of Venice of all the Dalmatian towns. It became the seat of the Venetian Providetore (Governor) of Dalmatia and Albania.

Simeon is credited with composing the *Nunc Dimittis;* given William Wey's special interest in those sites where, according to tradition, other canticles and prayers (e.g. the Magnificat and the Benedictus) were composed, one may assume that he was eager to see the shrine and relics of Simeon. The present church of Sveti Simun in Zadar was once dedicated to St Stephen and was built on the site of an earlier, fifth- or sixth-century, church. In 1632 the relics of St Simeon were reinterred here. In front of the choir is the late Romanesque sarcophagus of St Simeon. It was created between 1377 and 1380 by Francesco da Sesto, a goldsmith from Milan, so Wey and his companions could have seen it on their visit.

56 The "port of Sesule in Dalmatia" is placed by Wey after Jarra (Zadar) and before Cursula (Korčula). His galley reached Sesule on 11 June and Dubrovnik on the 16th, but they could have spent a day or two at Sesule.

57 Cursula Castle may be identified with Korčula.

"The land of Lysme". Wey describes, in Chapter 11, the Venetian possessions in Dalmatia as follows: "Beyond ([stria is Jadra, Sybynica, Spolaton, Traon and Kataron, together with several islands, Lesyna and Cursula." If these two spellings refer to the same place it would appear that Lysme/Lesyna is somewhere between Split (Spolaton) and the island of Korčula (Cursula), and Hvar is a possibility. Confirmation comes from Canon Casola who says (Newett, *Canon Pietro Casola's Pilgrimage*, p. 171) that the city of Lesina is otherwise called Fara – i.e. Hvar (the Lighthouse, *pharos*). In a book of 1598, *Viaggio da Venetia a Constantinopoli*, two places are illustrated between Spalato (Split) and Ragusi (Dubrovnik) which reinforce this identification. They are "Liesena Isola" and "Cruzola".

Newett (*Canon Pietro Casola's Pilgrimage*, p. 397) adds that there was a Franciscan monastery in Lesina, one of those described so warmly by a pilgrim in 1480, Santo Brasca: "In the Levant there is no comfortable lodging to be found, whatever you would be willing to pay for it, except in the monasteries of the observant friars of St Francis." It is noteworthy how many of the places that Wey names, and probably stayed at, on his route from England to Jerusalem had a Franciscan house.

At one time Lesina was the permanent station for about thirty light galleys of the Venetian fleet, and there was an arsenal there.

58 St Arsenius was a native of Constantinople. Of Jewish ancestry, he became the first bishop of Corfu and died in 959.

59 Axtis and St Leo. The identification of Axtis presents a problem. It may be another name for Methóni or it may merely be a misprint. Wey's mention of Romney wine growing here recalls his phrase in Chapter 11 where he says Romney grows on the Greek island of Motys (Modyn, Methone, Modone). Methóni, being equidistant between Corfu and Candia, was an important stage point for Venetian galleys sailing to Jaffa. It is 300 miles from each of these ports. Wey is methodical in naming, in their correct order, the ports he visited, which means that "Axtis" is somewhere between Corfu and Carkey (Khálki).

The most significant clue to the identity of "Axtis", however, lies in Wey's mention of the body of the martyr St Leo, which he says lies about 2 miles from there. Richard of Lincoln, who went there in 1454, says, "There is a fair pilgrimage a mile from the town of Methóni to the body of St Leo, the holy hermit." When Canon Casola made his pilgrimage to the Holy Land in 1494 he called at Methóni, where he was shown the body of St Leo (Newett, *Canon Pietro Casola's Pilgrimage*, p. 193). About 2 miles from Methóni on the road to Pylos there is a small, apparently disused, Byzantine church in the middle of a smallholding which local people claim to be dedicated to St Leo.

Traces of the Venetian quay can still be seen just below the surface of the water in front of the great Venetian castle of Methóni.

60 Wallachia and Hungary. Wallachia, which occupied some of the area now covered by Romania, on the north bank of the Danube, was a vassal of Hungary.

61 Lyddon and St Nicholas. William Wey states four times that St Nicholas was born on the island of Carkey (modern Khálki), giving the name of the "city" where the saint was born as Lyddon. The normally accepted birthplace of St Nicholas, however, is Myra, in the diocese of Lycia, on the present Turkish mainland, not far from Bodrum. It seems that Wey's city of Lyddon is a reference to Lydia, which was adjacent to Caria where Bodrum (Halicarnassus) was situated. There is, however, a tradition that St Nicholas was the first to preach Christianity on the island of Khálki. This tradition, added to the fact that there is a Byzantine church, containing some frescoes probably of the fifteenth century, dedicated to the saint on the acropolis of the island, might have underlain the misinformation given to William Wey about the saint and the island. It does seem that Wey's informant for this portion of the voyage was not wholly reliable because there is much confusion also about Bodrum and Tarsus, as well as the fanciful tale about Hippocrates' daughter and Kos. Wey's comments about the difficulty of cultivating

the land on Khálki, however, are accurate. The island is extremely stony and ploughing with animals very difficult. The two crops Wey mentions in a later reference to the island, figs and barley, are still to be found on Khálki.

62 Kos. The medieval name for Kos was Lango, the name being derived from the elongated shape of the island. Wey's fantastic story about Hippocrates' daughter and her chances of transformation has its roots in several facts. There was a magnificent shrine of Asklepios, the god of medicine, on the island, which was the birthplace, in about 460 BC, of Hippocrates, the most famous doctor of antiquity and founder of a medical school there. This medical school, under the priests called the Asklepiadai, continued for many centuries. Today's visitor can see there a memorial dedicated by Gaius Stertinius Xenophon, doctor to the Roman emperors Tiberius, Claudius and Nero. The snake, a traditional symbol of medicine, was shown on the city's coinage. While other medical centres, notably Epidauros, had subterranean labyrinthine structures which might have housed sacred snakes, there does not appear to have been such a building on Kos. There is, however, near the western tip of the island, a large cave, the Cave of Asprípetra, where neolithic artefacts have been discovered, and where Pan and the nymphs were worshipped. This, together with the huge fossil bones found on the island, could have contributed to the story of the serpent waiting for a chaste knight.

Perhaps Wey's informant was not without a sense of humour in introducing such a figure into the tale, with the implication that such a knight was unlikely to be found. Their religious status did not protect the Knights of Rhodes from such scurrilous gibes worthy of Aristophanes. Rhodes, as a port, always had its quota of immoral and dishonest residents. In the previous century there had been a scandal involving Grand Master Foulques de Villaret, while in 1456, two years before Wey's first visit, Grand Master Jacques de Milly and his Chapter decided that the city's prostitutes should be confined to one quarter of the city and forbidden to live elsewhere. Perhaps it was one of these disgruntled ladies who made up the story in revenge! Wey's remarks about the fertility of Kos still apply. Its green slopes and productive plain impress today's visitor as strongly as they did the traveller in the fifteenth century.

63 Semys (Sími) was a very important island in the Knights' defensive planning. Situated 35 km north-west of Rhodes, it is only 6.5 km from the coast of Turkey at its nearest point. It was an early-warning post in the event of a Turkish attack on Rhodes and was always itself liable to attack by the Turks. It was occupied by the Knights in 1309, who built a castle there in Khorió. The garrison there repelled a Turkish assault in 1456, only two years before Wey arrived in Rhodes.

In conversation, Maria Kasdagli, a resident archaeologist on Rhodes, offered me an interesting and plausible explanation for Wey's story of the medieval sans-culottes who came to the island *nudis tibiis* – bare legged. She told me that from the late eleventh to the early sixteenth century there was a steady stream of refugees coming out of Asia Minor fleeing the Turkish expansion. One of the places the refugees made for was Sími, because of its proximity and because the Knights normally helped the resettlement of such displaced persons. In these circumstances it was quite likely that a social structure emerged where a "strong man" became leader and commander of the local community with a group of "elders" around him, who would conduct business with the Knights and make sure that he performed the military duties expected of him.

64   Episcopia is now called Télos. The Knights took control of it in 1373. The number of castles and watchtowers on the island led to its medieval name of Episkopí – "lookout". It lies to the west of Sími about halfway between Rhodes and Kos.

       Nísiros, Wey's Nysere, lies due south of Kos and about 20 km from the coast of Turkey. It was first taken by the Knights in 1312, and was attacked by the Turks in 1457. In the fifteenth century, according to Buondelmonti, there were five castles on the island. Because of its strategic importance the Knights always maintained one galley there ready for action.

       Kálimnos, which Wey calls Calamo, lies north of Kos and west of Bodrum. The Knights controlled the island from 1313 to 1522. There were castles there at Khrisokhería and Khorió.

       The identification of Aron is not certain. Of the Dodecanese not already mentioned by Wey, Kásos, Kárpathos and Astypalaia remained outside the jurisdiction of the Knights (Kollias, *The Knights of Rhodes*, p. 14). Leros is a possibility as it is the next island in the north-west sequence listed by Wey, running from Khálki, through Tílos and Nísiros to Kálimnos. Moreover, the Byzantine castle at Plátanos, near Kastro, on the island of Leros was rebuilt by the Knights.

65   The Hospital of the Knights on Rhodes was begun in 1440 and completed between 1481 and 1489. Their great Infirmary can still be seen at the end of Ippoton Street. This most evocative of buildings is now open to the public and houses the Archaeological Museum. The Infirmary Ward held thirty-two beds and the patients, who were regarded as "Our Lords the sick", ate from silver plates. Two surgeons were permanently on duty.

       Ms Kasdagli informs me that the cemetery mentioned by Wey was probably the cemetery of St Anthony on the site of the Orthodox Cathedral of the Annunciation. While some burials were made in the Catholic Cathedral (Panayía tou Kastrou) and the Conventual Church of St John, these were exceptional. It is much more likely that patients who died in the Infirmary were buried in St Anthony's cemetery. The story about the rapid decomposition of the corpses may indicate the use of quicklime.

66   The original home of the Knights of St John.

67   Sympere is the Hospitaller Castle of Saint Pierre or Petrounion at Bodrum. This modern resort is on the western coast of Turkey, opposite Kos, and near the ancient city of Halicarnassus. Wey shows some confusion in this section as he equates it with Tarsus, which is a considerable distance from Bodrum, being in Cilicia on the south-east coast of Turkey. In another reference to Sympere, in Chapter 11, Wey says that the island of Patmos "is 150 miles from Rhodes and about 40 miles from the castle of Sympere". The actual distances as the crow flies (120 miles and 50 miles) are not very different from Wey's figures. The name Bodrum is a corruption of the Greek Petrounion just as Saint Pierre has become Sympere. Following on from his misidentification of Sympere with Tarsus in Cilicia, Wey here introduces the story of the journey of the Magi to Cologne and the migration of the young St Paul.

68   "The Three Kings of Cologne". The Magi were venerated in the Middle Ages as the first gentile pilgrims. The Milanese claimed to possess their relics, which had been brought from Constantinople in the fifth century. In 1162 these relics were taken to Germany by Frederick Barbarossa and are now exhibited in Cologne cathedral.

69   "Paul of Tarsus". In Acts 23:2 St Paul says, "I am verily a man which am a Jew, born in Tarsus, a city in Cilicia." See also Acts 9:11 and 21:39.

70 The Blessed John de Montfort, a Knight Templar, was one of the most important Latin saints of Cyprus. Wounded in a battle against the Saracens, he was carried to Nicosia where he died in 1248. The Augustinian Church of St Mary, which housed his shrine, became a place of pilgrimage. His feast day was long celebrated in Cyprus on 25 May. "So great was his reputation, and so numerous the miracles attributed to his power, that pilgrims came from all over Europe to pray at his tomb, where his body lay unchanged and uncorrupted by time" (Gunnis, *Historic Cyprus*). The Latin Archbishop of Nicosia retired here in 1469 and had a hospice built near the church to accommodate poor pilgrims who were on their way to the Holy Land. The west door and a rose window survive from the original building, which was converted into the Omerye Mosque by Mustafa Pasha in 1571.

71 St Mamas, Ayios Mamas, is one of the most popular saints in Cyprus. His feast day is on 17 August. There are several versions of his life, but perhaps the best known is as follows. He refused to pay a poll tax and was arrested. While he was being taken under guard to Nicosia a lion was seen pursuing a lamb. Mamas held up his hand, the lion abandoned the chase, Mamas picked up the lamb, mounted the lion and so rode, with the lamb in his arms, to the Duke's palace in Nicosia. The astonished Duke exempted Mamas from taxes for the rest of his life. There is a monastery of Ayios Mamas in Morphou. The first church, Byzantine in style, was perhaps built on the site of a pagan temple. This church was replaced by one in the Gothic style, which was in turn rebuilt in 1725. A few Gothic features still remain. The sarcophagus containing his relics exudes a liquid which is believed to have the miraculous power to cure various ailments. It is still visited by those with rheumatic pains.

72 St Hilarion. The tradition is that an anchorite, named Hilarion, who was born in Gaza, came to Cyprus in the fourth century in search of solitude. A disciple of St Antony the Great, according to some, Hilarion founded a number of monasteries in Palestine and worked many miracles before fleeing from the crowds that followed him everywhere. He died at the age of eighty, and, on his death, an Orthodox monastery was built around his tomb to accommodate his relics and to provide shelter for pilgrims in the Kyrenia mountains. The Byzantines made the monastery into a castle, probably in the eleventh century. It was handed over to Richard I, King of England, by Isaac Comnenus in 1181. His feast day is on 21 October. (See Eileen Davey, *Northern Cyprus*, p. 85).

73 "Seleeucia", which is otherwise unknown, appears to be a misprint for Salinis. Here Wey writes: *Est eciam xx miliario a Seleeucia crux sancti latronis que pendet in capella super montem sine pendiculo visibili*; "Twenty miles from Seleeucia is the cross of the Good Thief which hangs in a chapel on a mountain without any visible fastening." In Chapter 6 he says that the cross of the Good Thief is 20 miles from the harbour of Salinis, and hangs, so it is said, in a chapel without the support of anything else – *viginti milliaria a portu Salinis est crux sancti latronis, que, ut dicitur, pendet in capella sine alicujus alterius adminiculo*.

74 King James, the "Bastard King", of Cyprus has received a "bad press" because of his relations with the Saracens. In 1458, on the death of his father John, the legitimate successor was John's daughter, Charlotte. She was backed by the island's nobility. Her illegitimate brother, James, went to Cairo to obtain support from the Sultan. With the help of an Egyptian fleet, James took the island and besieged Charlotte's supporters in Kyrenia Castle. She fled to Rome, and in 1460 James was crowned King. He recaptured Famagusta from the Genoese and married the

Venetian, Caterina Cornaro. In 1473, within a year of the marriage, both James and his infant son died, perhaps poisoned. From 1474 to 1489, when she abdicated, Caterina reigned as a Venetian puppet. So ended the Lusignan dynasty. She is buried in the south transept of the church of San Salvatore in Venice.

75 faburden; fauxburden: see Harrison, *Music in Medieval Britain*, p. 249.

76 *Christus resurgens ex mortuis*. This was a processional antiphon according to the customs of Salisbury Cathedral, forming part of the procession before the Mass of the Day on Easter Day. The processions of Salisbury Cathedral were especially elaborate and its liturgical customs and material were recognized as an independent rite. York, Hereford and Lincoln had their own "uses" or liturgies also. Earlier in this chapter Wey describes in detail three magnificent processions he saw in Venice, while in Chapter 15 he notes the processions which he witnessed in Spain in 1456, in Santiago cathedral and in La Coruña.

The words of the antiphon sung by the precentor were: *Christus resurgens ex mortuis iam non moritur, mors illi ultra non dominabitur: quod enim vivit, vivit. Deo alleluia, alleluia*; "Christ being raised from the dead dieth no more; death hath no more dominion over Him; for in that He liveth, He liveth unto God. Alleluia, Alleluia." This was followed by the verse: *Dicant nunc Judaei, quomodo milites custodientes sepulchrum perdiderunt regem ad lapidis positionem, quare non servabant petram justitiae; aut sepultum reddant, aut resurgentem adorent, nobiscum dicentes alleluia, alleluia*; "Now let the Jews declare how the soldiers who kept the sepulchre lost the King when the stone was rolled, wherefore kept they not the rock of righteousness; let them either produce the buried, or adore the risen One, saying with us, Alleluia, Alleluia."

The anti-Semitic attitude of the times, embodied in these lines, is similar to that shown in the story about the Jew who stabbed the picture of Christ in St Mark's, Venice. Other anti-Semitic stories appear in "Things of Note in Bethlehem" (Chapter 11), *Judei habuerunt locum illum in odio* ("the Jews detested that place") and the attempt to destroy Mary's body at the time of the Dormition. It is to Wey's credit, therefore, that he not only had a conversation with a Jew in La Coruña, during his Compostella pilgrimage in 1456, but that he expressly mentions it as one of the more significant features of his stay there.

77 The hymn, *Miles Christi gloriose*, which the pilgrims sang in honour of St George, is intriguing. While there might well have been several hymns which commenced with these words, the text of one has survived (Harrison, *Music in Medieval Britain*, p. 300):

Miles Christi gloriose,	Glorious knight of Christ,
Laus, spes, tutor Anglie,	Renown, hope and protector of England,
Fac discordes graciose	Graciously make those who are at variance
Reduci concordie,	To be led back to harmony,
Ne sternatur plebs clamose	So that our people may not be sadly laid low
Dire mortis vulnere.	By the wound of dread death.

This is an antiphon of Thomas of Lancaster, who was executed by Edward II in 1322. Thomas's brother Henry recovered the family titles and estates two years later, and in 1330 began the foundation of the St Mary Newarke Hospital and College. He encouraged the popular devotion to the memory of his brother and made efforts to have him canonized as the martyr of Pontefract. The canonization did not take place, but the devotion continued and this antiphon is part of a rhymed office in honour of "Saint" Thomas.

It is possible that this hymn, if it was the one used, had a poignant, contemporary political significance for Wey and his fellow pilgrims, who had endured so much *discordia* and *vulnera* at home in the Wars of the Roses.

78 The normal pilgrim itinerary in the Holy Land included Mount Quarantena but, as Wey explains below, those locations had to be omitted in 1462.

79 Wey preached two sermons during his stay in Jerusalem in 1462.

80 The meeting between the Blessed Virgin Mary and her cousin Elizabeth, described in Luke 1:39–56, is commemorated as the Visitation. The Magnificat is the Song of Praise sung by the Blessed Virgin Mary when Elizabeth had greeted her as the mother of the Lord. From very early times it was the canticle of Vespers and it appears in the Book of Common Prayer in Evensong.

81 *Inter natos mulierum* was a fourteenth-century hymn in honour of St John the Baptist. The full text is given in Mone, *Hymni Latini Medii Aevi*, Vol. III, pp. 38–9. The first line is derived from Matthew 11:11 where the Vulgate has *Amen dico vobis, non surrexit inter natos mulierum major Joanne Baptista*; "Verily I say unto you, among them that are born of women there hath not arisen a greater than John the Baptist."

82 *Beata Dei genetrix Maria.* "Mary, Blessed Mother of God." Two versions of this hymn are recorded. One (Arocena, *Los Himnos*, no. 205, p. 284) is said to be pre-1072 AD. The other version in Mone (*Hymni Latini Medii Aevi*, Vol. II, p. 424) is described as a hymn of the fifteenth century which is especially appropriate for a night service. Since Wey says that they entered the Church of the Holy Sepulchre at night, it is likely that they sang the version recorded by Mone.

83 *Vexilla regis prodeunt.* This hymn appears as number 96 in *Hymns Ancient and Modern*, "The Royal Banners Forward Go". The full text is given in Paris, folio 33 verso and 34 recto, which states that it is suitable for Passion Sunday and that the author was Theodulf (*c*.750–821), who was Bishop of Orléans. Arocena, however (*Los Himnos*, no. 101), and the *Oxford Dictionary of the Christian Church* attribute it to the Italian Venantius Fortunatus (530–600). See also below.

84 *Pange lingua gloriosi.* There are two hymns with these first words. The earlier, by Venantius Fortunatus, deals with Redemption. It appears as number 94 in *The English Hymnal* and as 102 in Arocena, *Los Himnos*. It continues with the words *Proelium certaminis*. The later, composed by St Thomas Aquinas (1227–1274), possibly on the orders of Pope Urban IV, continues with the words *corporis mysterium*. This celebrates the miracle of Transubstantiation. After the Miracle at Bolsena, which occurred in the church of St Christina, when a priest, Peter of Prague, was celebrating Mass, Pope Urban IV instituted the Feast of Corpus Christi. This version appears as number 326 in *The English Hymnal* and 134 in Arocena, *Los Himnos*.

85 Wey's "Questions" are written out again at the end of Chapter 11. This is one of the examples where Wey appears to have preserved draft notes which he later revised and incorporated in *The Itineraries*.

86 Accounts of the scourging of Christ are in Matthew 27:26; Mark 15:15; John 19:1.

The Column of Flagellation is regularly depicted in illustrations of the Instruments of the Passion, for example in bench-ends and stained glass as well as in paintings. A portion of the column was believed to be in the sacristy of the Franciscan Monastery on Mount Syon. Wey reverts to this again in Chapter 11.

87 On the basis of Joel 3:2 and 12, the Valley of Jehoshaphat was the traditional scene of the Lord's Coming Judgement. Wey reverts to the question of the burial place of Jehoshaphat in Chapter

11. For the death of Jehoshaphat, see 1 Kings 22:50; 2 Chronicles 21:1. For the death of Absalom, see 2 Samuel 18:14.

88 "Father, into thy hands": Luke 23:46.

89 "His sweat was as it were great drops of blood falling down to the ground": Luke 22:44. "They brought him to the high priest's house": Luke 22:54.

90 For the burial of David, see I Kings 2:10; for Solomon, see 1 Kings 12:43 and 2 Chronicles 9:31.

91 "Gyon" and the crowning of Solomon. According to 1 Kings 1:38, 39 Zadok anointed Solomon at Gihon.

92 The account of Christ's body being wrapped in linen cloths is in Matthew 27:59; Mark 15:46; Luke 23:53 and John 19:40.

93 In Chapter 11 Wey reveals that he discovered the whereabouts of Joseph's grave from Bede's *De Locis Sanctis Libellus.*

94 The "Bastard" was James and the "true queen" was James's half-sister Charlotte.

95 Wey's "Fylerme" is the ancient city of Ialyssos, 6 miles from the city of Rhodes. For the story of the icon, see essay "The Icon of Our Lady of Philerimos", p. 228.

96 Baron Flak is Vlad V, Count of Wallachia (1456–1476), known as Vlad the Impaler. He is supposed to have been the original of Bram Stoker's fictional Count Dracula.

97 Aternopyl is Hadrianople, whose present name is Edirne. This city, in Thrace, was the original capital of Turkey in Europe and is famous now for its beautiful mosque. Following the fall of Constantinople in 1453 the Knights felt under increasing threat and sent an embassy to Aternopyl in 1455 to discuss a peace treaty with Mehmet II. He demanded a tribute of 2,000 ducats a year. The Knights refused and a Turkish squadron attacked Kos and Sími the following year, 1456. Then, in 1457, they assaulted the islands of Telos, Misyros, Leros and Kalymnos and also made a surprise attack on Archangelos, a village on the east coast of the island of Rhodes, about 6 km north of Lindos. The Turks looted this village and carried off most of the inhabitants (Kollias, *The Medieval City of Rhodes*, p. 21.) It would appear that the dreadful punishment described by Wey in Chapter 7 was the Knights' retaliation for this attack.

98 The Grand Master at this time (1461–67) was Peter Zacosta.

99 Two years' supply of wheat and wine. On the north side of the Grand Master's Palace were huge underground rooms on three levels which served as storerooms and might be used as refuges by the non-combatant population of the city. (There is a plan in Kollias, *The Medieval City of Rhodes.*)

100 The Knights were organized into groups based on nationality, called "tongues". When the Order first came to Rhodes there were seven of these: Provence, Auvergne, France, Italy, Aragon, England and Germany. In 1461 the Chapter General, convened by Grand Master Zacosta, decided to split the tongue of Aragon into two parts. One of these retained the name "Aragon"; the other, which was given eighth place in the hierarchy, was called "Castile". Each "tongue" maintained its own "inn" in Rhodes where its members assembled and which offered hospitality to eminent visitors. In 1465 Zacosta divided the city's fortifications into battle stations, each assigned to one of the "tongues", whose duty was to defend them in the event of a siege.

101 Mátayás Hunyadi (Mátayás Corvinus) was king of Hungary from 1458 to 1490. He signed a truce with the Ottomans in 1465, which lasted until 1520. The *Cambridge Medieval History* (Vol. 7, p.

719) states: "Mátayás secured northern Bosnia by occupying the fortress of Jajce. The conquest of this citadel and its subsequent defence against the Ottomans' repeated attacks was an impressive military feat."

102 "Grypis" and "fustis" are two kinds of ship, appropriate to an invasion fleet. By the kindness of Ms Pamela Willis, curator of the Museum of the Order of St John, in Clerkenwell, I consulted the *Vocabolario Marino e Militare* by Alberto Guglielmotti, published in Rome in 1889, which gives the following information: "GRIPPO (masc.), (Grupos, ou, o in Greek). Sorta de Nave. Nome di grosso naviglio che, fin dal tempo dei Greci e dei Romani, dalle Indie all'Eretreo portava gli aromi ed i farmachi." The entry quotes as sources "Pomponio Mela" and "Plinio". An inserted translation continues: "Later writers, Ariosto, Bembo, Ceriffo, with simplest propriety called Grippo a ship specially constructed and assigned for the service of the sick. Hospital ship attached to the fleet, chiefly for the purpose of transhipment and treatment at a distance from the barbarians. It was constructed on the principle of greater stability and to contain the utmost number of beds and all other necessary comforts. Also known as 'gripo', 'grifo', 'griso', 'gribana', 'gripparia', 'gropparia' and 'gropperia'." William Wey's *grypi*, therefore, were probably hospital ships whose design originated in the large vessels used in the eastern spice trade.

The second entry runs: "FUSTA (fem.), (Kerkouros, ou, o in Greek). Crusca. Specie di navilio da remo, di basso bordo, e da corseggiare. Specie di piccola galera, più sottile, più fina, più veloce: armava da diciotto in ventidue remi per banda, un solo albero a calcese, et un polaccone a prua. Metteva fuori due o tre pezzetti d'artiglieria, otto tromboncini, e da cinquanta a cento tra soldati, et marinari, tutti scapoli, che al bisogno facevan pur da rematori." This second class of ship, the *fustae*, mentioned by Wey, were fast, narrow and handy boats; galleys carrying marines for boarding, and carrying two or three artillery pieces. They seem to have developed from the light vessels, with low freeboard, used by pirates for boarding their prey.

103 The modern identity of Lissa is uncertain.

10

Word Lists

SYNOPSIS

This chapter contains six sections:

1. A list of 132 words and phrases in English with their Greek equivalents, spelled phonetically.
2. The cardinal numerals from 1 to 20 written in Roman numerals. The numbers from 1 to 10 are written in English beneath the corresponding Roman numerals and the Greek numbers are then written beneath them, phonetically. From 20 to 100, in multiples of ten, the Roman numerals have only the Greek numbers written beneath phonetically. Then follows a selection of intermediate Greek numbers between 11 and 49, written phonetically, to provide a paradigm of the way William Wey believed Greek cardinal numbers were formed. It must be said that this section bears little relation either to the Ancient or to the Modern Greek system of numerals.
3. A long section containing 753 words or phrases in Greek, spelled phonetically and in alphabetical order, with their Latin equivalents.
4. A list of 64 Latin words with their Hebrew equivalents followed by 28 Hebrew words with their Latin equivalents. It is not clear why the order of presentation was changed part of the way through this section.
5. A list of Hebrew nouns with the Latin words followed by their Hebrew equivalents spelled phonetically.
6. The names of the letters in the Hebrew alphabet, spelled phonetically. Greek and Hebrew characters are not used. Wey's phonetic spelling uses ordinary English letters throughout.

Word Lists

COMMENTARY

In his Preface to the Roxburghe edition Bandinel says that Wey's "very curious Greek vocabulary clearly proves that our learned clerk was not quite at home in the Greek language" and "may exercise the ingenuity of the Modern Greek scholar, but would not repay the space requisite for minute criticism".

The present writer, while noting Bandinel's comment, feels that Wey's effort should not be dismissed too summarily. Chapters 10 and 13 were written in the fifteenth century by an Englishman who knew Latin but had not had the benefit of more recent methods of Greek teaching. It was more than sixty years after Wey's death, in May 1539, that an education bill was passed through both Houses of Parliament which provided, inter alia, that "readers of Greek, Hebrew and Latin should have a good stipend".

When Wey set sail for Corfu in 1458 Greek had already been spoken and written for two millennia, in a range of cities from Marseilles to the Black Sea. He experienced the difficulties facing anyone trying to converse in Greek in places as diverse as Corfu, Methóni, Crete, Rhodes and Cyprus, since, in a footnote in Chapter 10, he wrote, "Among the Greeks are these tongues, Attic, Aeolic, Ionic, Doric and Boetic. It is a wonder that Wey got as far as he did with the Greek language since he did not have the benefit of today's linguistic expertise built up over the past four centuries. In the 1450s and 1460s Wey was a pioneer and should be given credit for his efforts.

In his word lists in Chapters 10 and 13 Wey attempts a phonetic transcription of the Greek that he heard spoken between Venice and Jaffa. He was presented with a range of local dialects which he tried to record without the benefit of the phonetic alphabet used today. This was a formidable task. His notes, made presumably "in the field", were incorporated into the text of Bodleian MS 565. This manuscript, transliterated for the Roxburghe edition, was published in modern print in 1856. This protean process has left its mark.

The Greek language has been developing and changing from the time of Homer to the present day. The stems of some of the words in Wey's lists would be familiar to Pericles and Demosthenes; for example, *he chole*, ἡ χολή (bile, anger); *posos*, πόσος (how much?); *to melon*, τὸ μῆλον (apple); *ho tyros*, ὁ τυρός (cheese); *he thalassa*, ἡ Θάλασσα (sea); *he staphule*, ἡ σταφυλή (bunch of grapes); *ta zoa*, τὰ ζῷα (animals). It is of interest that Wey's lists straddle the change in pronunciation of the letter β, beta, from *B* in Classical Greek to *V* in Modern Greek. The list in Chapter 13 gives *basileos* for "king" but Chapter 10 offers *vasileos* as the phonetic equivalent. Similarly, while Chapter 13 gives *probaton*, πρόβατον as the word for "sheep", Chapter 10 gives it as *provatos* (*sic*).

During the next five centuries the form of Greek known as the *koine* developed. This is the language of the New Testament and it included some Hebrew words like *ho Messias* (the Messiah). Another development brought words like *to papousti* (shoe). The impact of the Turks after the fall of Constantinople in 1453 led to other changes. Wey's list includes *to neron* (water), *to psomi* (bread) and *to krasi* (wine), which are the normal words for those commodities in Modern Greek, but which were not used or which had a different meaning in Classical Greek.

Wey was breaking new ground. He was used to Latin, which has no definite article, "the", whereas Greek does, ὁ, ἡ, τὸ (*ho, he*, and *to*). In some places in Chapter 10 Wey makes the definite article an integral part of the next word; *tophos* instead of *to phos*, τὸ φῶς (light), and *otheos* appears instead of *ho theos*, ὁ θεός (god). Many of the words in the alphabetical list in Chapter 10 begin with *to*, τό, since Wey did not understand that this is really the neuter definite article "the".

Because Wey did not have the benefit of formal Greek grammar teaching and the advantage of a modern phonetic script, other misunderstandings arose. An example of another false division in Chapter 13 is *ferto do* where *to do* is really the Greek word *touto*, τοῦτο (this). Elsewhere Wey writes *d* for *t* – for example, *do nero* for *to nero*. The interrogative *ti*, τί (what?) in Chapter 13 appears as *the*.

Another source of error occurs when words are misplaced during one of the several stages of copying or transcription. An example from Chapter 13 is where *soter*, σωτήρ (saviour), has been moved from its place beside the Latin *salvator*. Nevertheless some of the words in Wey's Chapter 13 list could still be recognized in Greece today – for example, *kalhemera*, *kalenukta* and *kalespera* (Good morning, Good night and Good evening). More problematical would be Wey's version of *gregora*, γρήγορα ("Hurry up!"), which he gives as *Ligora, Latine statim*.

Wey realized that Greek was an inflected language, but perhaps did not realize the extent of Greek accidence and syntax revealed to students by Abbott and Mansfield in the once standard grammar book. In his footnote concerning Greek dialects, mentioned above, Wey continues: *Nomina Graeca desinencia in –ya producuntur* – "Greek nouns ending in 'ia' are lengthened." But Greek nouns are more complicated than that!

Despite these linguistic shortcomings Wey was trying in his Chapters 10 and 13 to produce something helpful to his successors. The general reader can relish the information he gives in them about the items of food and the situations which he considered sufficiently important to be included. Among such vital questions as "Where is the tavern?" and "Woman, have ye good wine?", Wey presents an appetizing list of comestibles, starting with butter, milk and cheese, going on to pork, mutton, goose and oysters, with onions, garlic and parsley included to add flavour, and closing with apples, pears, grapes, figs and cherries. This menu, of course, does not mean that Wey and his fellow pilgrims dined in such luxury every day, but it does show what he thought was worth asking for.

II

A Medley

SYNOPSIS

An interesting and varied collection of material, some of which Wey used in other chapters of *The Itineraries*.

TRANSLATION
(Roxburghe, pp. 117–28)

Concerning the City of Venice

The city of Venice used to be called Realti and later the "City of Venice". St Magnus the Martyr was the first bishop of Venice. His body lies, uncorrupted, in the church of St Jeremiah in Venice. This saint had a vision that he should build seven churches in Venice. These are they: the first is that of St James on the Rialto, the second is of St John on the Rialto, the third is of St Salvator, the fourth is of St Mary Formosa. This is the one to which the Doge and the government of Venice come on the Eve of the Purification and on the day itself to offer Mass. The fifth is the church of St Silvester, the sixth of St Jerome and the seventh of St Peter. This is the cathedral church and they have a patriarch at St Peter's.

Ravenna is the oldest city in Italy and was the first to be inhabited.[1] There is one cardinal there. Aquilegia was the second city to be inhabited and has a patriarch.[2] Once it was a papal see, and for that reason that province is called *Frulis*, which means "free" since it is free from all dues. Padua was the third city to be founded.[3] Its first name was *Pallude* because it was, and still is, situated among marshes (*palludes*). In 200 AD, when Atela,[4] the king of Hungary, had destroyed these cities together with many cities in Hungary,

Christian, Catholic, men came from these cities and from the kingdom of Hungary to the place on the sea where Venice is built and constructed a city there. Thus a large part of the nobility of Venice derives its origins from the Hungarians. Ser Andrew Morason, the *patronus* of my galley, traced his descent from them.

Concerning the Lands and Dominions of the Venetians from Venice to the Holy Land

Marona, where they make glass: four miles from Venice. Mazorbo. Lydo Major. The city of Jessulo, which is in the March of Trevysana. The whole of the March of Trevysana is under the control of the Venetians, and has three dioceses.[5]

Further along the route is Pyzeema, Kavrley, Maranus and the port of Gruaria. Gradun and Aquilegia. This city and others are in the province of Frulis. This province and everything in this country is under the control of the Venetians. There is one patriarch with sixteen bishops in that country.

Further along the route is Parense, 100 miles from Venice, Rumerna, the city of Pala and Justina. This land is called Istria. In it there are twelve dioceses under the control of the Venetians.[6]

Beyond that is Jadra, Sybynica, Spolaton, Traon and Kataron, together with several islands, Lesyna and Cursula. These are in the land of Dalmatia. In the whole of this territory, which is wholly under Venetian control, there are ten dioceses.[7]

Further again along the route are Bodowa, Antebery, Dulcynio and Duracio. These cities are in the land of Albania where there are nine dioceses of the Venetian empire.[8]

Beyond that, in Greece, there is the island of Corfu where there is an archbishop.[9] After that, still in Greece, there are Modyn and Coron in the territory of the Morea, where there are two bishops.[10] This area is under the control of Venice. Yet further, still in Greece, is the kingdom of Crete. Here there are Candia, Canea, Retimo, Citea, together with 14,000 towns and nine cities with nine bishops and one archbishop. Malmsey grows in this kingdom, which is under the control of Venice.[11]

Thus in the whole of the Venetian empire there are three patriarchs and sixty-two bishops and archbishops.

There Follows Concerning Other Places
on the Way to the Holy Land

The island of Patmos, where St John the Evangelist wrote the *Apocalypse*, is in Turkey, 150 miles from Rhodes and about 40 miles from the Castle of Sympere.[12] The Greeks have a house and a church there where fallen women cannot enter unless they are dying. In addition, on this island, robbers die immediately. The castle of St Pierre, where the Knights of St John live, used to be called *Tharsis*.[13] There are huge dogs there which keep watch outside the castle at night and distinguish Christian from Saracen. There too is the stone on which the Three Kings of Cologne stood when they took ship to their home countries.[14]

In Greece is the island called Carquy, where St Nicholas was born. There tools which are used among the stones are not worn away but last from father to son without renewal. This island belongs to the Master of Rhodes. They have no fruit there except figs and no grain except barley. They cultivate the soil with iron tools. St Nicholas was born in the city of Lydda on that island. The seat on which he sat when he was teaching the boys is there too.

Capadocia, where St George was born, is "in chief" to Dalmatia and in the territory of Albania. It is a large province and the city where he was born is called Alexo. St George's head is on the island called Archipelagus, in the castle in the city of Leiana.[15] His brain throbs in his head. Both Leiana and Archipelagus are under Venetian control. The city where St George was born is called Lesse and it is a great city.

At Cande in Crete I discovered among old accounts concerning the martyrdom of St George, at the end, the following: "These things were done in the city of Militena in the province of Capodocia under Dacian, whose wife was called Alexandria and who was martyred for our faith before St George."[16]

In the same source[17] it is stated that, "In answer to a prayer, St George, in Dacian's presence, brought 235 pagan corpses back to life. These had died 200 years before. He baptised them and immediately afterwards they turned into dust."

In the same source it says, "He drank poison three times in front of Dacian and was not harmed. Immediately the one who gave him the poison was converted and baptised."

In the *Stories of the Saints* it states that, "On one occasion St George came to a city in the province of Libya which is called Sylene. Near this city was a lake like the sea in which a deadly dragon lived."

In the city of Damascus there is a white column one cubit tall, on which St George set his foot when he mounted his horse to fight the dragon. One mile from Baruth, which is the port of Damascus, there is the cave where the dragon, which St George killed, lurked. In the church of St George in Rome there is the point of the lance with which he killed the dragon. In the Abbey of St George in Venice is his left arm with all the fingers and thick skin.

The Superscription on Saladin's Letter to the Grand Master of Rhodes

"To the Most Honourable Pillar of Baptism and Christianity, Friend of Kings and Princes, Grand Master of Rhodes, whom God preserve and hold in His hand."[18]

The Wording of Saladin's Letter

"On behalf of the Great Emperor, His Excellency the King, the Brave, Wise and Excellent Sword of Purity and of Justice, Emperor of the Moors and Mauretaura, Friend of the Good and Goodness, Protector against Wrong and Wrongdoers – just as Alexander in his time was the servant of two Holy Houses – Universal Emperor and Obedient Chalif of Abnysac and Jacmysac, whose rule God preserve and hold in his hand."

Here Are Noted Things Which Are in the Holy Land and in Other Places

Roses of Jericho grow along the entire road by which the Most Blessed Virgin Mary went to Egypt. Saracen women use them in childbirth.[19] In the city of Nazareth, in the chapel where he greeted the Virgin Mary, there is a likeness of Gabriel, pressed on the back of a stone column as though on a seal. When the rays of the evening sun touch the top of the angel's head, that is the hour when Christ was conceived by the Most Blessed Virgin Mary.[20] There also is a spring of water to which Christ used to come to get water for His Most Blessed Mother. One mile from Nazareth is the mountain called the Mountain of Our Lord's Leap where the Jews threw Christ headlong. On this mountain there is a great stone which received Christ as if He were thrown on to damp clay.[21]

Things of Note in Bethlehem

Concerning the hut of Our Lord in Bethlehem, where Christ was born, Ysay or Jesse, the father of King David, lived there. Later it was a royal palace. After David's death it was a stable for mules and camels which were for hire. Later they put wood there which was not sold in the market. They also kept donkeys in the same place. After that, when they sold loaves of bread in the market there, they put bread in that holy hut. That is the reason why Bethlehem was called the "House of Bread". At the time of Our Lord's birth this house had been so completely destroyed that absolutely nothing remained in that place except a small, mean hut. It was to this that Mary and Joseph came in the evening, because all the inns were full when they arrived in Bethlehem. They went round the city and no one was prepared to take them in. In particular, although people saw the young Mary on her donkey, weary with the journey, groaning, sighing and pregnant, near to giving birth, no one in the whole city was willing to take her into a proper house or an inn. That is why Joseph took Mary to that hut which nobody cared about.[22]

The place where the shepherds saw the angels is about half a mile from Bethlehem, in that country's measurement. It was the place where the patriarch, Jacob, and David also, kept watch. It was here that David snatched his sheep from the jaws of the bear and the lion.[23] At about the Feast of Our Lord's Nativity barley in the fields at Bethlehem starts to produce spikes. That time is called "time to go to grass" and, in those parts, that is when the animals are taken out to pasture.

In recent times St Helen discovered all these things among the rags in which Christ was wrapped – the straw and the shift of the Blessed Virgin, which she forgot and dropped in the manger when she fled from the hut with Jesus for fear of the Jews. She found them in the manger just as the Most Blessed Virgin had dropped them and forgotten them. All of these, apart from the manger, St Helen placed reverently in the church of St Sophia in Byzantium 234 years later.[24] All these objects were preserved because the Jews detested that spot and did not allow either animals or people to enter it for the whole of that time. They thought the place was accursed and unholy and held that all who entered it were contaminated.[25] The Most Blessed Virgin sat near the manger when the Kings came to make their offerings. She raised Christ's head with her right hand and the Kings placed their gifts in the manger. Some books assert that just as the Kings were the first Gentiles in the Christian faith so too were they the first to honour the Virgin, because, though Gentiles, they offered honour to the Virgin as well as to Our Lord.[26] There are seventy columns in the church at Bethlehem. When the Kings made their offerings to Christ they first kissed the ground in front of the manger, then the hand of Christ and then they offered their gifts. The star which led the Kings to Bethlehem plunged down between the walls in front of the cave in which Christ was born. It is notable also that the town near Bethlehem where the Greeks live is called Betisilla. The people who live there have the right or permission from the Sultan to convert Saracens to our faith.[27]

One mile from Bethlehem is the grave of Jacob's wife, Rachel, and a fine tomb it is. Emaus, where Christ was recognized by His disciples in the breaking of bread, is also called Nicopolis. It is situated in Palestine seven miles from Jerusalem. Ramatha, the city of Helkane and Samuel, is situated in the land of Canaan near Diaspolis.[28] In this land too is the city of Lydda where St George was beheaded. In the city of Damascus there is a window through which St Paul passed when the Jews were persecuting him. This window has never been able to be closed since.[29] There is a hill close to the city of Damascus where Cain killed his brother Abel.[30] From that time the hill has remained barren and grass has never grown on it. Noah's ark was built on the plain of Boarchus, which lies between Barioth and Damascus.[31] A vineyard was planted by Noah in a valley near that plain and from this he got drunk.[32] Near Barutus there is a very high tower of St Barbara.[33] The pagan Moors climb it to call their people to come to prayer. Through the power of St Barbara, those who call tumble from the tower and perish. For this reason no pagans dare to climb it any longer.

In the city of Alexandria, which is in the kingdom of Egypt, there are two columns on which rested the wheels between which St Katherine was placed. Under these columns there is the prison where St Katherine was put. Through the window of this prison, which has never been able to be closed by the pagans subsequently, and which is still there, came angels bringing food to St Katherine.[34] In the same city is the street along which the pagans dragged St Mark to his death.[35] There too is the church where St Mark was buried. Maxentius' wife, who was martyred there with St Catherine, was called Nichostrata.

Concerning the Location of Two Relics

The girdle of the Most Blessed Mary, which she handed to St Thomas of India, is on Mount Olivet in the Castle of Pratus ten miles from Florence. It is made of linen and has a golden thread in the middle. Its colour is unknown. It has tassels on the ends by which it can be tied.[36]

At Aachen, or *Aquae Granae*, there is a chemise, which belonged to the Most Blessed Mary, and one of St Joseph's stockings. This is saffron coloured and Christ was placed in it because of the cold when He was lying in the manger.[37]

In Constantinople the Greeks display a stone brought from Jerusalem on which they say the Blessed Virgin wept and lamented at Christ's Passion, collapsing through the strength of her grief. The story is that traces of her tears seem to appear on it as though they have just been shed.

On the pavement of the Chapel of Calvary, where Christ was crucified, there is written in Greek letters O *Theos*, that is, "Here God"; *basileon ymon*, that is, "Our King"; *pros eonas*, that is, "before Time"; *ergase*, that is, "wrought"; *sothias*, that is, "salvation"; *emose tis*, that is, "in the midst"; *gys*, that is, "of the Earth".

Beneath Calvary is Golgotha, which is the Nubians' chapel. They built it because their king, Melchior, was in darkness and cloud there when he came to make his offering to Our Lord when He was born in Bethlehem.[38]

The bridge over the river Danube, where Heraclius fought with Cosdroe, is near the Castle of Surene inside the boundaries of the Kingdom of Hungary.

Concerning Christ's Spear

In Nuremburg, a city in Germany on the River Danube beyond Regensburg, is the whole point of the spear with which Christ was wounded in the heart while He was hanging on the cross. The whole of that part of it which entered Christ's heart is the colour of blood; the rest is the same colour as other spears. It is like a spear used for hunting boars. It is guarded by twenty-four lords, each of whom has a key to the casket in which the spear is kept.[39]

Concerning Pepper

To know where pepper originates, grows and is kept one must know that pepper grows in a kingdom called Mynbar and nowhere else. The grove where it grows extends an eighteen days' journey. There are two cities in the grove, one called Flandrina and the other Gynglyn. In the city of Flandrina live both

Christians and Jews. They are at war and the Christians win. In this city the pepper is obtained in this way. In the first place it grows on leafy plants, which are planted next to large trees just like vines in Italy. These leaves produce fruit just as vines produce grapes. They grow in such abundance that the plant seems to break. When the pepper is ripe it is green. It is harvested like grapes, placed in the sun to dry and collected in jars. There are many snakes in this grove. At the head of this grove is a city called Polumbum where the finest ginger grows.

On the island of Jane grow cloves, cubeb pepper, guinea pepper, nuts and nutmegs and many other precious varieties. "Malmsey" grows in the kingdom of Crete while "Romney" grows on the island of Methoney in Greece.

Concerning the Names of Various Places in the Holy Land and Elsewhere

Salym is a town beyond Jordan.[40] Gazer, which is now called Gazera, is between Joppa and Ramatha.[41] Nabaioth is a valley in Ramatha. The Valley of Beerino, or Tophet, is next to the Field of Acheldemack. The Valley of Jehoshophat has three names: the Valley of Saba, the Royal Valley and the Valley of Jehoshophat, called after King Jehoshophat who is buried there. On one side of this valley is Mount Olivet and the Valley of Syloe. There are two places called Bethlehem: one is in the land of Judah, where Christ was born, the other is in the land of Zabulon.[42] Galilee is fourfold: one is beyond Mount Olivet where He went ahead of the Apostles on Easter Day, the second Galilee is in the tribe of Zabulon, the third is Galilee of the Gentiles in the tribe of Neptalym, the fourth is the province of Galilee and, so it is believed, the tetrarchy of Galilee.[43] In this is the city called Cana where Christ turned water into wine.[44] There are three ports in the Holy Land, Joppa, Acre and Baruth. Joppa is the port for Ramath and Jerusalem, Acre is the port for Nazareth and Baruth is the port for Damascus.[45]

Concerning the Christian Kings of the Holy Land[46]

After the year of Our Lord 1089, the first Christian king was Godfrey, Duke of Lataria, in the time of Pope Urban.[47] The second was Eustrachius, the brother of Baldwin, Count of Roiheise.[48] The third king was Baldwin.[49] The fourth king was Fulco, Count of Andagavencium, in the time of Pope Honorius.[50]

The fifth king was Guido – last king of the Christians in Jerusalem.[51] In his time, on Saturday, 3 October (Dominical Letter D), in the year of Our Lord 1187, Christ's Holy Cross and the Holy Land were captured by Saladin and delivered into the hands of the heathen.[52] Jerusalem had been captured by the Christians on Friday, 15 July, in the year of Our Lord 1099, when Godfrey, Duke of Lotoria, was elected king by the whole army. The siege of the Holy Land started on 1 May in the year of Our Lord 1187 and, in the same year, on 3 October, Jerusalem was captured by the Saracens. Thus it was in the hands of the Christians for eighty-nine years. During this time there was a Patriarch of Jerusalem,[53] and archbishops and bishops, as follows. The Archbishop of Tyre, the Archbishop of Nazareth, the Bishop of Lydda, where St George was beheaded, the Bishop of Acon, the Bishop of Sidon and many other bishops. There were also various Counts in the Holy Land: the Count of Joppa, the Count of Tripoli, the Master of the Hospital, the Master of the Templars and other dignitaries.[54] When the city of Jerusalem was taken by the Saracens, because of the division[55] among the Christians there over the election of a king, the anchorites, hermits and men-at-arms fought for the city of Jerusalem. At this time the King of Syria[56] said, "I have often heard from the wise men of Alpichini that Jerusalem cannot be cleansed unless it be washed with the blood of the Christians."

Concerning Other Places in the Holy Land

Dotaym is near Jerusalem and so is Joseph's cistern. Modyn also is near Jerusalem.[57] Silo is two miles from Jerusalem, Ernaldus' castle three miles, Emaus seven miles. Mount Gelboe is near Emaus. Mount Gazarim and Mount Ebal are in the mountains of Judaea.[58] It is thought that Maledoym is the mountain on the road where the man fell among thieves; it is on the common road between Jerusalem and Jericho.[59]

The Names of Pagan Nations

Turks, Cordini, Syrians, Arabs, Alans, Cacumanni, Caffeohaki, Idumaeans, Saracens, Egyptians, Liemanni, Turcomans and Bedouins. The last two live by plunder and use neither houses nor castles. The pagans' pope is called the Caliph of Baghdad,[60] which is a city built near Babylon the Great. In his letters

Saladin writes, "In the 584th year of the arrival of our Prophet Mahomet.[61] By the Grace of the One God." In the black city of the island Raboch de Catey dwells the Pope Catey who is called Babassy.[62]

Concerning Questions Raised of Matters in the [Holy] Land and Their Solutions, by Master William Wey[63]

First. What colour is the hole for the holy cross?
The answer is. It is white.[64]

The next question. Was the pillar to which Christ was bound in Pilate's house spattered with drops of Jesus Christ's blood?

Answer. No, but traces of the scorpions' stings with which Christ was flogged remain on the column.

There was a question about the lamp over Our Lord's holy tomb. This used to burn for a whole year until Good Friday. It went out of its own accord on that day and no one was able to light it again. When the hour of Our Lord's Resurrection arrived, it relit itself.

It does not do this now because at present our holy faith has been extinguished in that place. It is said, however, that on Easter Day fire comes down from heaven and falls on Our Lord's tomb.

The next question was about the Valley of Jehoshophat. The valley itself was called the Valley of Jehoshophat because King Jehoshophat was buried there. But this is contrary to Holy Scripture which says that he was buried in the tomb of his fathers or among his fathers. This is true.

The answer is immediately after his death he was buried in that valley and then, later, the valley took the name because of his burial there. In a book describing the land of Jerusalem it is written that King Jehoshophat was buried in the Valley of Jehoshophat under a sharp-pointed pyramid, but, after his burial there, he was moved to Mount Syon and laid near his fathers.

There was a question about the burial of St Joseph, Mary's husband.

The answer. He was buried in a cave on Mount Olivet – according to Bede on the site of the Holy Land. Saint Simeon, the old man, who held Christ in his arms, was buried there too. His body now lies, uncorrupted, in Jarra, a city of Dalmatia.

On the right-hand side of the room, where Christ sweated blood, a stone has been let into the wall on which are imprinted the marks of Christ's knees.

There was a question about the length and breadth of the Valley of Jehoshophat.

The answer. It was 3½ furlongs long. In the middle of it, parallel to its width, is the tomb of the Most Blessed Virgin Mary in a round church.

There was a question. How far was the cave, where Christ sweated blood, from the house of the Priest Annas? He was led to this house immediately after His arrest.

The answer. Six furlongs.

The next question. How far is Mount Calvary from Solomon's Temple, where the temple servants heard Christ's voice as He died, crying, "Into thy hands I commend my spirit"? (Luke 23:46)

The answer. It is a distance of 2½ furlongs from the Temple.

The next question. Remembering that part of the print of Christ's right foot is shown on Ascension Day at Westminster, are the footprints of Christ, as He ascended into heaven, on Mount Olivet?

The answer. Two prints of Christ's feet when He ascended into heaven are there on a marble stone lying on the ground; but the right print can be seen and perceived more clearly than the left print.

A further question. Where are King David and the other Jewish kings buried?

The answer. They were buried on Mount Syon in the left-hand part of the church called "The Church of Mary's Steps to Heaven", where the Franciscans celebrate divine worship every day.

Another question. Where is Mount Gyon on which Solomon was crowned?

The answer. It is half a mile outside Jerusalem. It is a small hill situated between Acheldemack and the road to Bethlehem. It is now called the "House of Evil Counsel", because it was there the Jews took counsel as to how they should betray Our Lord Jesus.

Another question. Where is that stone on which the dead body of Our Lord Jesus Christ lay, and on which He was wrapped in cloths before His burial?

The answer. It is in Constantinople.

The final question. Where are the pieces of the pillar to which He was bound in Pilate's house when He was flogged there?

The answer. One piece is in the Chapel of the Most Blessed Mary in the Temple in Jerusalem, below a wooden grating. A second piece is on Mount Syon and a third piece is in Constantinople.

A Medley

According to Jerome the length of the Promised Land runs from the Fountain of Dan to the city of Bersabe towards the south; a distance of 160 miles; its width is from Joppa to Jordan in the west, a distance of 60 miles.[65]

COMMENTARY

The topics are grouped under fifteen headings. The first two deal with Venice and her "lands and dominions" overseas en route to Jaffa. Then follows a description of other places, not all under Venetian control. Some of these – for example, Patmos and Bodrum – were not on the route taken by Wey's galley. This section closes with reminiscences about St George, triggered by an account Wey found in Crete, probably in the Franciscan library in Candia.

There follow two extracts from a letter allegedly written by Saladin to the Grand Master of the Hospitallers, probably shown to Wey during his visit to Rhodes. This letter, however, can be shown to be a forgery.

The next two sections deal with things of note in the Holy Land, especially Bethlehem, and contain an eloquent account of the Nativity which reads almost like a sermon. Wey then diverges into anecdotes, including stories from Damascus, Beirut and Alexandria, which were not on his route.

Mention of the Blessed Virgin Mary leads him to discuss Marian relics, in particular those at Aachen, Pratus and Constantinople.

Next there is a short but interesting botanical section on the source of various spices, notably pepper. Then Wey ranges more widely into geography, history and anthropology, closing with his "Questions and Their Solutions", which he, presumably later, incorporated into Chapter 9.

This chapter reminds one of Herodotus and his approach to history: "I must report what is told me, but I do not have to believe it all!" Both men were travellers with enquiring minds and a wide range of enthusiasms. Like Herodotus, Wey is not infallible. The Itineraries contain some errors – for example, in his accounts of St George, St Nicholas and St Paul – but since, like Herodotus, he was often at the mercy of his informants, his lapses may be forgiven.

NOTES

1   Ravenna became the capital of the Western Roman Empire when the Emperor Honorius moved his court there from Milan in about 402. Wey visited Ravenna en route from Rome to Venice in 1458.

2   Aquileia is 7 miles from the head of the Adriatic and controls roads across the Julian Alps. Rome founded a Latin colony there in 181 BC. Under the Empire it became one of the world's largest cities and was called Roma Secunda. It was the capital of the Regio Venetia et Istria, its amber trade being especially important. It was razed by Attila in 452. It is now a town of 3,500 people.

3   Padua was a Roman *municipium* from 45 BC. It suffered from barbarian attacks and the Lombard invasions but prosperity returned and it became a free commune in the twelfth century. The university was founded in 1221. Wey passed through the city en route from Venice to Calais in autumn 1458.

4   Atela, more usually known now as Attila, or Etzel, the Hun, died in 453.

5   Marona. Murano is an island about 1½ miles from Venice. It has been the centre of the Venetian glass industry since 1292, when it was moved here from Venice because of the danger of fire.

     Mazzorbo is a further 4 miles to the north, between Torcello and Burano.

     The Lido is the largest of the islands between the Lagoon and the Adriatic. At the far end of the Lido is the church of St Nicholas.

     Jesolo was formerly known as Equilium, since horses were bred on the marshes there.

6   Istria. Parense, later called Parenzo, is now known as Poreč. It has a splendid sixth-century basilica of Euphrasius whose mosaics are comparable with those of Ravenna.

     Pala. Pula is a few miles south of Poreč on the Istrian peninsula. It was once the chief naval base of the Austro-Hungarian Empire and has a huge and remarkably complete Roman amphitheatre. Other sights are the first-century Temple of Augustus and the thirteenth-century Franciscan church.

7   Dalmatia. Jadra (later Zadar and Jarra), with its reliquary of St Simeon, made a special impression on Wey.

     Sybynica, now Sibenik, is about halfway between Zadar and Split (Spalaton). Its cathedral was begun in 1431 and took many decades to be completed. It would have still been a building site when Wey passed by.

     Split grew out of Diocletian's palace and is now a city of a quarter of a million people. Venetian rule was established there in 1420.

     Kataron, now called Kotor, is in Montenegro. Lesyna, now Hvar, had a Venetian Arsenale. Cursula is probably the present Korčula.

8   Albania. The places named are now called Budva (Bodowa), Bar (Antibery), Ulcinj (Dulcynio) and Durrës (Duracio). The first three of these, like Kotor, are in the present-day Montenegro. Durrës, in the present Albania, was called Dyrrhachium in classical times. The Greek colony of Epidamnus was nearby. In 148 BC Dyrrhachium became the terminal point of the northern fork of the Via Egnatia, the main road from the Adriatic to Byzantium.

9   Corfu in classical times was called Corcyra. It is the name both of the island and of its main city. One of Wey's special interests was in "continuing miracles". One example of these was the miraculous lamp at Casope (Kassiópi) in the north of the island.

10   Modyn and Coron (Methóni and Coroni), called "the twin eyes of Venice", were important citadels at the ends of two of the promontories in the far south of the Peloponnese.

11   Crete. The remains of the Venetian Arsenale can still be seen at Heraklion (Candia). For Titus and the church in Crete, see Chapter 7. Canea is now sometimes spelled Chania. Retimo is now Rethymnon and Citea is Sitia. All three places still have interesting Venetian buildings.

12   Patmos: see Revelation 1:9. Visitors are shown a grotto where by tradition St John lived. Sympere: St Pierre at Bodrum.

13   Tharsis and Tarsus. Wey's confusion might have arisen because the name Cilicia was used for different areas of south Asia Minor at different times. The boundaries and names of the Roman provinces in that area, viz. Lycia, Caria, Pisidia, Pamphylia and Cilicia, were changed from time to time. St Paul's Tarsus was on the south-east coast of the modern Turkey, facing Cyprus, while Bodrum, later known as Halicarnassus, was on the west, the Aegean, coast.

14   The Three Kings of Cologne, the Magi. For their return "into their own country another way", see Matthew 2:12.

15   St George was one of Wey's favourite saints and is mentioned several times. Gibbon and others argued that St George was George of Cappadocia, the Arian bishop of Alexandria, but it is more generally accepted that he was a Roman officer martyred near Lydda during Diocletian's persecutions.

16   Dacian. Datianus was the "provost" under Diocletian who arrested and tortured St George because he had spoken out against the pagan gods. When the beatings and torture had no effect a magician prepared a deadly potion, which was equally ineffective. The magician was converted and martyred. After further torture, George prayed and a fire descended from heaven destroying the heathen temple, idols and priests. Datianus's wife was converted, but Datianus, after ordering George's decapitation, was himself consumed by fire from heaven. (See *Butler's Lives of the Saints*, Vol. 2, p. 149.)

17   It is possible that the place in Candia where Wey discovered these "old accounts" was the library of the Franciscan house where he might have stayed. For *The Golden Legend*, see Chapter 5 note 3 above.

18   Saladin (1138–1193), Sultan of Egypt and Syria and founder of the Ayubite dynasty, captured Jerusalem in 1187. Acre, recaptured by Richard the Lionheart in 1192, finally fell to the Saracens in May 1289. The Master of the Hospital, Jean de Villiers, gravely wounded in defending the city, was carried to his ships and sailed to Cyprus. The Hospitallers, led by Grand Master Foulques de Villaret, captured Philerimos towards the end of 1306 and the city of Rhodes, probably, in 1309. It was only after this that they took the title "Knights of Rhodes".

Saladin's letter. The above chronology means that the document copied by Wey, with its reference to the Domino de Rodys, cannot be genuine, since Saladin had died more than a century before there was any "Master of Rhodes". See below for more of Saladin's letters.

19   Roses of Jericho. *Anastatica hierochuntica* (see footnote at the end of this section).

20   Conception of Christ. Luke 1:26–31. The Church of the Annunciation in Nazareth was believed to have been built over the house of Mary. Wey does not appear to have visited Nazareth personally. Few pilgrims at this time did. (See Prescott, *Jerusalem Journey*, p. 202.)

21   These permanent records of Christ's time on earth were of special interest to Wey, but it is

not certain that Wey himself saw these marks since he might not have travelled as far as Nazareth.

22   This paragraph contains much that does not appear in St Luke's Gospel. The language is more highly coloured and emotional than Wey's normal style elsewhere in *The Itineraries*. One wonders, therefore, if Wey is quoting a Franciscan guide's account delivered to pilgrims as they visited the holy sites in Bethlehem. The descriptions of the Blessed Virgin groaning and sighing, raising Christ's head for the Magi with her right hand and finally dropping items of clothing as she fled from the hut, while vivid enough, rely on imagination not Scripture. Another part of the story, involving one of Joseph's stockings, appears below.

23   The shepherds and the angels: Luke 2:8–14. David slew the bear and the lion: 1 Samuel 17:36.

24   In one medieval tradition, found, for example, in Geoffrey of Monmouth, St Helena was by birth a British princess, being the daughter of Coel ("Old King Cole") of Colchester. This legend, like that of St George, led Wey to take a special interest in her.

25   The anti-Semitism shown in the mention of the alleged Jewish attitude to the site reappears in other places. In these cases Wey seems to be recording stories told by his guides, probably Franciscans. That his own attitude to Jews was rather different is shown by his defiant assertion in Chapter 15 that he had had conversation with a Jew in La Coruña.

26   The Magi as protopilgrims: Matthew 2:1–12.

27   The conversion of the Saracens to Christianity was a contentious issue. Wey mentions an episode when some Saracens who had been thinking of conversion did not appear at a rendezvous at Ramys: *ut converterentur ad nostram fidem*. In 1219 St Francis of Assisi landed at Acre and visited the holy places. At Damietta he entered the Saracen camp where he preached the Gospel and condemned the Koran. As Newett says, the audience probably did not understand what he was saying (*Canon Pietro Casola's Pilgrimage*, p. 6). In 1480 Santo Brasca went to the Holy Land. His account, published in 1481, gives a warning not to argue about the Faith with Saracens (ibid., p. 12).

    Emmaus is probably Colonia Amasia because of the distance of 60 stadia (7 miles) given in Luke 24:13 and also by Wey. Another possibility, however, also mentioned here by Wey, is Nicopolis, but that identification depends on a reading in Luke of 160 stadia (i.e. 20 miles) instead of 60 stadia. Wey's measurement is significantly in favour of Colonia Amasia.

28   Ramatha. Several places have a similar name, which could lead to confusion. Also, Wey's spelling is not always consistent. For the Franciscan hospice where pilgrims spent the night, see Chapter 7, "Rama", and Chapter 9, "Ramys". Wey says that it is 10 Welsh miles from Jaffa. The Ramah which was the home of Samuel (1 Samuel 1:19) was also called Ramathaim-zophim and, in New Testament times, Arimathea. The Ramah associated with Rachel (Jer. 31:15 and Matthew 2:18) was about 10 miles north of Jerusalem.

29   St Paul refers to his escape from Damascus by a window in 2 Cor. 11:33. The story of the window which cannot be closed is echoed again in the tradition about St Catherine. These are two of the "recurrent miracles" in which Wey was especially interested.

30   Cain and Abel: see Gen. 4:8 and 25 and 1 John 3:12.

31   Noah's Ark. The story is in Gen. 6–9, esp. Gen 6:13–22.

32   The vineyard and drunkenness of Noah are described in Gen. 9:20–27. The wines of Lebanon are still much appreciated.

33 St Barbara and St Catherine frequently appear together in paintings. Wey is following this tradition in placing them together here. St Barbara's symbol is a tower, since the legend has it that she was imprisoned in one by her father, Dioscorus. This story may derive elements from the myth of Danae, also imprisoned by her father in a tower. Barbara's father was killed by lightning and she became the patron of those liable to be killed by fire or explosion, e.g. gunners and miners.

34 St Catherine of Alexandria, persecuted for her Christianity by Maxentius, whose wife she converted, was broken on a wheel, which became her symbol. Her cult began in the ninth century on Mount Sinai, to which her body was said to have been transported by angels. Like Barbara, she was regarded as a Bride of Christ. In the Rhineland both were venerated as two of the Fourteen Holy Helpers.

35 St Mark. According to Eusebius, Mark was reckoned the first bishop of Alexandria. His martyrdom was placed in the "eighth year of Nero", who was Emperor from 54 to 68 AD. His body was taken to Venice in the ninth century and he became the city's patron saint. Nichostrata: Maxentius' wife.

36 In the Cappella del Sacro Cingolo in the Cathedral of Prato there are wall paintings by Agnolo Gaddo, which Wey could have seen, depicting this event.

37 Aachen (formerly Aix-la-Chapelle) was, and is still, a major place of pilgrimage. Apart from Charlemagne's shrine and throne, there is the Shrine of St Mary built to house the Great Aachen Relics. These are now said to consist of the swaddling clothes and loin cloth of Christ, the gown of the Virgin and the garb of St John the Baptist. They are displayed once every seven years.

38 Golgotha; the place of the skull; Matthew 27:33; Mark 15:22. One tradition held that it was Adam's skull. In two places Wey describes the ministers as Gorgians.

The Nubians and Melchior. Nubia is an area south of Ethiopia. The Magi are often represented in art as three kings from the three continents of Europe, Asia and Africa. They are shown as of three racial types, black, white and brown, and of varying ages, young, middle-aged and old. Their traditional names are Melchior, Gaspar and Balthasar, who brought respectively gold, frankincense and myrrh – typical products of their home countries.

39 The Spear of Longinus. The name of the soldier who pierced the side of Christ with his spear is given in the Apocryphal Acts of Nicodemus, formerly called the Acts of Pontius Pilate, Chapter 7:8 (see also John 19:34). It has been the subject of much superstition for two millennia, being connected with both the Arthurian legend and Charlemagne. Most recently it featured as part of Adolf Hitler's propaganda in the twentieth century. It is now accepted that the spear displayed as that of Longinus was not a Roman cavalry spear of the first century AD. See also Chapter 6.

40 Salym. John 3:23: "And John also was baptizing in Aenon near to Salim because there was much water there."

41 Gazer. Gazara is the Greek form of Gezer, the stronghold of Simon Maccabeus; 1 Macc. 4:15. It is about 4 miles south of Lydda. Topheth: 2 Kings 23:10; Jer. 7:31, 32; Jer. 9:6 and 11–14.

42 Bethlehem. For Bethlehem Judah, also called Bethlehem Ephratah, see Micah 5:2; Matthew 2:1 and Matthew 2:5–6. For Bethlehem of Zebulon, see Joshua 19:15–16; Judges 12:8, 10.

43 "I will go before you into Galilee": Matthew 26:32. "The land of Zabulon, and the land of Nephthalim, by the way of the sea, beyond Jordan, Galilee of the Gentiles": Matthew 4:13–15. The tetrarchy of Galilee: Perea, the territory beyond the Jordan, (from the Greek *peran* beyond), with Galilee formed the tetrarchy of Herod Antipas (4 BC–39 AD), one of the sons of Herod the Great.

44 Cana. For the miracle, see John 2:1–10.

45 Joppa (Jaffa): see Chapter 7; also Acts 10. Acre, also called Acco and Ptolemais: originally a Phoenecian city; see Judges 1:31. The Hellenistic name was Ptolemais; see Acts 21:7.

   Baruth: Beirut. Luxury goods were brought from the Far East by camel as far as Damascus. Beirut, as the port for Damascus, was so important for her trade that Venice maintained a consul there. Each year several galleys were equipped in the Venetian arsenal and put up for auction for the voyages to Beirut, Alexandria, the Black Sea and Flanders. See Newett, *Canon Pietro Casola's Pilgrimage*, p. 59; Mitchell, *The Spring Voyage*, pp. 126–7 and Prescott, *Jerusalem Journey*, p. 16.

46 "Concerning the Christian Kings of the Holy Land". There are some gaps in Wey's chronology in this section.

47 Godfrey of Bouillon led the knights from Lorraine, Germany and Belgium in the First Crusade. After the capture of Jerusalem, he was offered the crown but refused the title of "King", choosing to be "Advocate of the Holy Sepulchre". He died in the summer of 1100. His role was exaggerated by later writers.

   Urban II (*c*. 1042–1099) was Pope from 1088. He died in 1099, before the news of the capture of Jerusalem by the Crusaders could reach him (*ODCC* s.v. Urban II).

48 Eust[r]achius: Eustace, Count of Boulogne (1087–1126) was the eldest brother of Godfrey of Bouillon. He took part in the conquest of Jerusalem, returning home after the battle of Ascalon. His daughter Matilda married Stephen of Blois, King of England 1135–54.

49 Baldwin I, the brother of Godfrey, was elected by the nobility as the first king of the Latin Kingdom of Jerusalem, being crowned at Bethlehem on 25 December 1100. In 1118 he led an expedition to Egypt, penetrating into Sinai, when he fell ill and died. He was followed by Baldwin II, who does not appear in Wey's list.

50 Fulco. Fulk V (1095–1143) was Count of Anjou from 1109 to 1128 when he abdicated in favour of his son. He arrived in Jerusalem in 1129. When Baldwin II, a cousin of Baldwin who had followed him as King of Jerusalem from 1118 until 1131, died leaving no sons, the succession was in dispute. Fulk V married Melisande, the daughter of Baldwin II, and was proclaimed heir, becoming King of Jerusalem in 1131. He reigned until 1143.

   Honorius II was Pope from 1124 to 1130.

51 At this point Wey has omitted the names of several kings of Jerusalem. The gap between 1143 and 1186 was filled by: Baldwin III, son of Fulk V and Melisande, King of Jerusalem 1144–64. Amalric I, younger brother of Baldwin III, king 1164–74. Baldwin IV, the Leper, son of Amalric I, king 1174–85. His sister Sybil, who married Guy of Lusignan (see below), was previously married to William of Montferrat. Their son became the child-king Baldwin V in 1185, under a regency, and died, possibly poisoned, in 1186. Guido: Guy of Lusignan (1129–1194), who married Sybil in 1179, was "the last King of the Christians in Jerusalem", though not "the fifth". He was defeated by Saladin at the Battle of Hattin in 1187 and captured. He was forced to renounce his claim to the title by Richard I of England, who gave him the Kingdom of Cyprus where he reigned

1192–94. The Lusignan dynasty ruled there until the fifteenth century when Catherine Conaro gave up the throne to the Venetians.

52 Dominical Letter: i.e. the Sunday Letter. Explained in *ODCC* (p. 1305), as follows: "In ecclesiastical calendars that one of the letters A to G, allotted to the days of the year in rotation, which coincides with the Sundays in a given year." This system allows one to discover on what day of the week any calendar date in that year will fall. It is described in *The* Book of Common Prayer as the "Table to Find Easter Day". The days of the week given by Wey in this section, i.e. Saturday 3 October 1187 and Friday 15 July 1099, are correct and are testimony to his competence in this calculation.

53 Patriarch. At the Council of Constantinople in 381 four patriarchates were established, viz. Alexandria, Antioch, Constantinople and Rome. In the fifth century the see of Jerusalem was also elevated to this status.

54 The Templars, a religious–military order founded in 1119, were suppressed in the fourteenth century when Pope Clement V decreed that their possessions be transferred to the Hospitallers. The Hospitallers were the other great religious–military order. They grew from a hospital for pilgrims, founded in the church of St John the Baptist in Jerusalem by a group of Amalfi merchants in 1050. After the fall of Jerusalem they moved to Rhodes, where Wey visited them.

55 Wey is probably referring to the dispute between Guy of Lusignan and Reynald of Châtillon.

56 Syria was united by Nureddin in 1154. He was followed by Saladin, who reigned as King (Sultan) of Egypt and Syria from 1173 to 1193.

57 Modyn (Modin) was the home of Mattathias, father of the Maccabees. 1 Macc. 2:15, 23, 70: "He died in the hundred and forty sixth year and his sons buried him in the sepulchres of his fathers at Modin."

58 Mounts Gezirim and Ebal formed a pair of summits in the centre of Israelite territory which feature in Deut. 11:29 and Joshua 8:33.

59 Parable of the Good Samaritan: Luke 10:30–36.

60 Caliph was a title given to the successors of Muhammad.

61 The Muslim Calendar date which Wey gives here would be about 1188 AD, within Saladin's lifetime. From this one might assume the letter was genuine, unlike the one quoted above.

62 "In the black city of the island Raboch de Catey dwells the Pope Catey who is called Babassey." This is one of the most intriguing sentences in *The Itineraries*. Wey was seeking information about the most secret aspects of the Muslim faith and at the same time struggling against all the difficulties presented by differences in language and religion. Small wonder if the picture presented is obscure! However, the two references to "the black city" and "the island" might give a clue to what lay beneath Wey's research.

In Mecca the Ka'ba, the Cube, is the ancient stone building in the centre of the Great Mosque. It was first built by Ishmael and Abraham and incorporates the Black Stone kissed by the Prophet. Every hajji (pilgrim to Mecca) tries to do the same. It has been restored several times. It is covered with a black cloth embroidered in gold, the kiswah. Perhaps this feature lies behind Wey's phrase "the black city".

The Bodleian has a portable atlas (MS Marsh 294), drawn by Safakusi al-Maliki from Tunisia, which shows the compass rose with a representation of the Ka'ba as a black island in the centre. While this particular atlas dates from a century after Wey, one might hazard the guess that, with his interest in cartography, he had seen something similar on his travels. If so, his assumption that the Ka'ba was a "black city on an island" is entirely reasonable. (For illustration, see Barnes and Branfoot, eds, *Pilgrimage, the Sacred Journey*, p. 21.)

63   The questions appear in a slightly different form in Chapter 9, and the solutions are a little shorter.

64   This question does not appear in Chapter 9. Wey was very interested in the dimensions and colours of objects associated with the Crucifixion. Chapter 3, line 85 (p. 36) and Chapter 6 imply that Wey himself took measurements. His list of gifts to the chapel at Edington includes "A stone in which is the depth of the mortice of Our Lord's Cross" and a board with various measurements, including "the deepness of the mortice of the Cross and the roundness of the same".

65   These distances are repeated in Chapter 13.

ADDITIONAL NOTE

In William Turner's late-sixteenth-century *A New Herbal*, Rose of Jericho, also known as amomum, *Anastatica hierochuntica*, is described as follows:

Amomum is a small bush, about the quantity of a man's hand, like unto a cluster of grapes folden into himself, little sticks of wood going one beside and one over another, and partly it resembleth a net, and partly a round thick bush, or rather the head of a mace, if it were all made of little sticks or pieces of silver as big as straws in a round form; it hath little flowers as heart's ease hath, and leaves like unto briony. I saw about six years ago at Cologne a little shrub, something lesser than my hand, which was in all points like unto the shrub above described. A certain pilgrim, which had been at Jerusalem, brought it out of Jewry with him. The same is named of the herbaries *Rosa hierecuntis*, that is the Rose of Jericho. The saying is that it openeth every year about Christenmass; wherefore some call it a Christen mase rose. This same I would reckon to be the right amomum if it had that smell which Dioscorides requireth in amomo. In all other points the description doth wonderfully agree. If any man chance upon any that have a good savour with all these other properties above rehearsed let him take it for the true amomum. Silvius of Paris writeth in his Simples, that he had the true amomum. For the lack of the true amomum we may use the common *Calamus aromaticus* or *Carpesio*, called of some *cucuba*. Others judge that a man may use for *amomo*, *Asara bacca* or the right *Acorus*. But the seed that is commonly used for *amomo* is not of the strength that *amomum* is of.

The Virtues

Amomum hath power to heat, to bind and to dry. It provoketh to sleep, and laid to the forehead, it assuageth ache. It maketh ripe and driveth away inflamations and impostumes having matter in them like honey; it helpeth them that are bitten of scorpions laid to emplasterwise with basill and it is good for the gout. With raisins it healeth inflammations of the eyes. It is good for the diseases of the mother, either in a suppository taken before, or in a bath that women sit over. The broth of it drunk, is good for the liver, for the kidneys and for the gout. It is fit to be mixed with preservatives and precious ointments. (Turner, *A New Herbal*, p. 56)

12

Indices to the *Mappa Terrae Sanctae*

SYNOPSIS

The map of the Holy Land in the Bodleian (MS Douce 389) is possibly the one used by Wey, since there are apparent links between it and the two lists in Chapter 12. Introducing the first of these, containing 392 named places, Wey says, "In the following list are contained all the things in the map of the Holy Land." The second list, based on the first and with 394 names, consists of "the names in alphabetical order of the cities, towns, mountains, valleys, seas on my map of the Holy Land". While the two lists are not identical, since there are one or two omissions and one or two duplications, the differences are not numerous.

TRANSLATION
(Roxburghe, pp. 128–38)

In the Following List Are Contained All the Things in the Map of the Holy Land

The Chapel of St Mary in Sardinia
Mount Hermon
Baalgad; here Christ fed the five thousand
The Land of Amon
The Entrance to Emath; here Christ said,
    "Saul, why dost thou persecute me?"
Damascus
Siria of Damascus
The River Jordan
Obba
The Fountain of Dan
Belmas
Suba

The Tower of Libanus
Antelibanus
The Fountain of Jor
The River Eufrates
The River Farsan
The River Albana
Asor
Cananea
The Mount before Libanus
Sveta
The Tribe of Zabulon
The Place where St George killed the dragon
Baruch
The Port of Sydon

The Valley of Bechare
Great Sydon
Bosra
Ydumea
Mount Samyr
The Region of Trachonitis
The Fountain of Phalan
The Land of Hus, where Job lived
The Tomb of Job
The Sea called the Sea of Capharnaum,
   the chief city of that part
The Table where Christ fed four thousand
   people
Bethsayda
Cedna
Sopheth
The Tribe of Asser
The Tetrarchy of Galilee
The Tabernacle of Heber
Abelma
The Valley of Senyn
Cabul
Naason
Thooron, where St George fell and was
   blinded
Cana in Galilee
The River Euchetus
Tyrus
The Well of Living Waters
The River Balus
Sarepta of the Sydonians
Adalon
The Cottage of Lambertus
Cedar
Mount Galaad
Half of the Tribe of Manassah
Decapolis
Coroasym
Godora
Goroca
Ramathy of Galaad
Effrem
The Glade of Effrem
The Sea of Galilee
Pella (here Jesus walked; here Peter began
   to sink)
Neptalym

Magdalum Castle
The Castle of Tele
Belynder
Suna
Bethsay
Tyberias
Affech
Gyscallo, where Paul was born
Dotaym
Genereth
Caphersebe
The Valley of Sabaea
Jesrael
Mount Tabor
Naym
The Tomb of Jonah
The Mount of Our Lord's Leap
The Stone, on the Mount of the Leap, which
   received Christ
Mount Hermon the Greater
Mount Hermon the Less
The Tribe of Neptalym
Nazareth
Sephora
Endor
The Brook of Syson
Acris
Acron and Tholomeyda, where Helias slew
   the priests of Baal
The Chapel of St Margaret
The Castle of the Pilgrims
Caynar
The Home of Helias
The Cave of the Blessed Virgin
Mount Caym
Cayphas
Mount Carmelus
The Fount of Helias
The End of Finicia
The Mount of the Desert
Panicea
The Tribe of Gad
Anatoth Kyre
Esebon
Nasan
Manaym
Jabes of Galaad

The Tribe of Reuben

Helyale

Bochemath

Jaser

Socohoch

Ernon

The Ford of Jaboth; here Esau met his
    brother Jacob

Mount Garazym

Dan, formerly Lachys

The famous valley

Salym

Tersa

Bethel

Mount Ebal

Ernon

The Tribe of Ysacar

The Wood where the birds die for Christ on
    Passion Sunday

Half of the Tribe of Manassah

Samaria

Beryth

Mount Gelboe

In these mountains Galilee ends and Samaria
    begins

Sychym is in the centre of the Holy Land

The Fount of Jacob

Genyn

Cesaria

Magedo

Cato

The Pilgrim with a shield

Sarchan

Hay

Effeton

Arcopolis

The Angel appeared to Joachim

The Place of Christ's Ascension

The Chapel of Pellagia

Galgala

Fecolis

Docom

The Place of the Indulgences of Galilee

Bethfage

Rama

Beniamyn

Phasel

The Torrent of Berith

Betel

The Palm to the Virgin

The Creed

The Our Father

The Place where Christ wept

The Pool of Syloe

The Place where Christ preached

The Tomb of Isaya

Astaroth

Lebua

Betheron, where Mary handed her girdle to
    St Thomas, the Apostle

Here the Most Blessed Mary rested amid the
    Stations

Gabaa Savelis

The Place where Malchus' ear was cut off

The Mount of Olivet

The Cave of the Disciples

The Fountain of the Most Blessed Mary

The Place of Betrayal

The Place of the Apostles' first sleep

The Tomb of Zakarias, son of Barachias

The Place of the Apostles' second sleep

The Tomb of Absalon

The Room where Christ sweated

Neapelosa or Sekar

The Fount of Jacob

The hanging of the traitor Judas

The Castle of David

Taumascere

Archam

The Valley of Jehoshophat

The Brook Cedron

The Tomb of the Most Blessed Mary

The Place of the stoning of Stephen

Dora or Assur

The Tribe of Benjamin

The Tomb of Josua

Mount Effraym

Arran

Salym

Mount Phasga

Mount Abarym or Nebo

The Tomb of Moses

Setyr

The Place of Christ's baptism

The House of the Georgitae
The River Jordan
The Rod of Moses
The Place where the Devil showed Christ all the kingdoms of the world
The Mount of the Forty Days; there the Devil said, "Command that these stones become bread"
The Field of Acheldemack
The Caves of the Saints
The House of Evil Counsel
The Waters of Marath
Mount Syon, where Salomon was crowned
The Stones on which Christ stood when He was sentenced by Pilate
The House of Pilate
The House of Herod
The House of Symon
The Place where they wanted to seize the body of the Most Blessed Mary
The Gate through which Christ went to His Passion
The Room where Peter wept
The Temple of Christ
The House of Annas
Betania
The Place of the napkin
The Place where the women wept
The House of Dives
The Crossroads
The City of Jerusalem
The Holy Street along which Christ went to His Passion
The House of Cayphas
The Pool
The Place where the Most Blessed Mary fainted
The Temple of Our Lord
The Monastery of Syon
The Place of Mary's birth
The Temple of Salamon
The School of the Most Blessed Mary
The Place where Mathias was chosen
Mount Syon
The House of the Most Blessed Virgin
The Church of St James

Here the Most Blessed Virgin looked back at Calvary
The Golden Gate
Cariatharym
Aramatha
Sylo
Betulia
Maceda
Gabaon
Sarona
The Tribe of Effraym
The New Castle
The Plains of Moab
Newrym
Ornaym
Mount Phasga
Petra of the Desert
The Monastery of St Jeronimus
The Monastery of Carieth
The Monastery of Sebba
Mount Engadius, where David hid
The Sycamore tree which Zacheus climbed
The Chapel of St John the Baptist
The City of Jericho
The Fount of Engadius
The Place where the blind man was healed
The Place of St John the Baptist's birth
Thana, where the star appeared to the Kings, where the water bubbles at Epiphania
The Mountains of Judaea
The House of St Martha
The Church where the Blessed Mary greeted Elizabeth
The Tomb of Rachel
Where Martha met Christ
The House of Symon
The Tomb of Lazarus
The Stones hollowed beneath Christ's feet
The Fountain where Philip baptized the eunuch
The Tomb of the Machabees
Nabe
Geth
Saraha
Emaus
The Place where Christ's cross grew

Bethsames
Ramatha
Mount Modyn
The Valley of Nabaioth
Beroith
Lidda
The Port of Jaffa
The Port Janua
Tersa, where Peter raised Tabita
The Rock on which Peter stood to fish
The Statue of Salt
The River Amon
The Rivers of the Rock
Cades Barne
Bethsur
The Tribe of Juda
Segor
The Angel to the Shepherds
Magedo
Sodoma
The Dead Sea
Bethcar
The Mountain of Mabla
The City of Bethlehem
Ebron
Ygnapera
The Monastery of Bethlehem
Soboym
Here the Most Blessed Mary got off her
    donkey
The Valley of Mambra
The Fount of Etan
Sicheleth
The Tomb of the Patriarchs, Abraham, Isaac
    and Jacob
The Tribe of Dan
Sylo
The Tribe of Symeon
Eskabel
Oeschaol
The Plain of Damascus
Caperna [cave? for *caverna*?] Acharon
Azon
The Cave of Odella
Aschalon
The Mountain of Hor
The Mountain of Seyr

The Tomb of Aaron
The Land of Edom
Sodoma
Adama
Soboym
Segor
Gomorra
The Desert of Cades
The Mountains of Achilla
Assamar
Maon
Cariathsepher or Thabor
Mount Carmely
The Fount of Living …[water?]
The Tribe of Symeon
Bersabee
The Desert of Bersabee
The Mountains of Gaza
Gaza lugham
The Desert of Pharan
The Towers of Bozor
The River Rinoconoro
Mount Synai
Mount Oreb
Taurens Castle
The Monastery of Saint Katerine
The Burning Bush
The Garden of Saint Honoriferus
Macaria
The Land of Egypt
Agulia
The very tall vine of Balsamus
The Fig of Pharon
The Church of Saint Mary
New Babylon
Zacca
Galachia
Saris
Bilbes
Alariff
Catria
Alchamchi
The Cracks [?] of Butolus
Summuth the Accursed
The Twelve Ways in the Red Sea
Mecha, the city of Machamet
The Red Sea

The Place where the people of Israel
    worshipped the Calf
Helym, where there were twelve springs of
    water
Suachym
The Monastery of St Paul
Pevssayr
The City of Cayr
The Road leading to Ethiopia
The City of Choos
The Monastery of St Antony

The River Nyly
The Island of Gold
The Pyramids of the pagan lords of Babylon
The Flight
The Church in Arabia
Vruth
The very tall column in Alexandria
Salme the Great
Shericon
Rashero
The Mount in the City of Alexandria
The Ancient Port

The Names, in Alphabetical Order, of the Cities, Towns, Mountains, Valleys, Seas on My Map of the Holy Land

A
Aser
Abelma
Adalon
Affech
Acris or Athon
Aetholomeida
Anathot Kyre
Astaroth
Arcopolis
Archam
Ascol
Arran
Aramathia
Acharon
Ascalon
Azotus
Azon
Adama
Assamar
Alryff
Alchanchi
Alexandria the Great
Arabia
Antelibanus
The Angel appeared to Joachim
Acheldemach

The Angel appeared to the shepherds
Agulia the highest
The sycamore tree which Zacheus climbed

B
Baalgad
Belms
The port of Baruth
Bosra
Betsayda
Belynder
Basan
Bochemath
Bethel
Bethfage
Betel
Betheron
Betania
Betulia
Bethsames
Berioth
Bethsur
Betachar
Bersabe
Bilbes
Butole

The River Marath
The River which bubbles out on the day of the Epiphany
The River Rinoconora
The Fountain of Dan
The Fountain Jor
The Fountain Phalan
The Fountain of Elias
The Fountain of the Most Blessed Mary
The Fountain of Jacob
The Fountain of Engaddus
The Fountain where Phillip baptised the eunuch
The Fountain of Etau
The Fountain of living [water]
The Fertile Plain
The Fig of Pharon

G

George slew the dragon
Godora
Goroca
Giscallo where Paul was born
Genny
Of Saint George
Galgala
Gezer
Gabaon
Gabaa of Benjamin
Gylo
Gabaa of Saul
Gomorra
Galilea
Gaza

H

Hay
Helyale
Elijah slew the prophets of Baal
Here Christ preached
Here the Most Blessed Mary rested
Here the Most Blessed Mary looked back at Calvary
Here Martha met Christ
Here the Most Blessed Virgin got off her donkey

Hely where there were 12 fountains of water and 70 palm trees

J

Jesrael
Jabes of Galaad
The city of Jerusalem
Jerico
The port of Janua
The entry of Emath
In the pass of Effraym where there was the battle against Absalom
The Famous Valley begins
Galilea ends in these mountains
There "Order that the stones…"
The island of gold in Egypt

L

Lobua
Lidda or Diaspolis
The stone which received Christ on the mount of the Lord's Leap
The stones in the wall on which Christ stood when He was condemned to death
The place where Christ wept over Jerusalem
The place of indulgences on Mount Olivet
The place where Peter cut off Malchus's ear
The place where Christ was betrayed
The place of the first sleep of the Apostles
The place of the stoning of Saint Stephen
The place where the Jews wanted to seize the body of the Most Blessed Virgin
The place where Mathias was chosen
The place where Christ said "Hail" to the women
The place where Christ preached
The place where the women wept
The place where the woman had the kerchief
The place where the Most Blessed Virgin fainted
The birthplace of the Most Blessed Mary
The birthplace of Saint John the Baptist
The stones in Bethany hollowed out under Christ's feet
The place of Christ's Baptism

The place where the blind man was healed
   in Jericho
The place where the Holy Cross grew
The place where the children of Israel
   worshipped the golden calf

M
Magdalum castle
Elijah's house
Manaym or Macherenta
Maceda
Modyn
Magedo
Macedo
Maon
Mobe or Nobe
Mecha, the city of Mahomet
Mount Hermon
Mount Antilibanus
Mount Semyr
Mount Galaad
Mount Thabor
The Mount of the Lord's Leap
Mount Hermon the Greater
Mount Hermon the Less
Mount Cayn
Mount Carmel
The Mount of the desert
Mount Gazarim
Mount Ebal
Mount Gelboe
Mount Olivet
Mount Effraym
Mount Phasga
Mount Abarym or Nabe
Mount Quarentena, where Christ fasted 40
   days
Mount Syon where Solomon was crowned
Mount Syon
Mount Calvary
Mount Moria
Mount of Engaddius where David hid from
   Saul
The Mountains of Judaea
Mount Modyn
Mount Mable

Mount Hor where Aaron is buried
Mount Seyr
Mount Carmel
The mountains of Achille where David hid
   before Saul
Mount Gaza
Mount Synay
Mount Oreb
The mount in the city of Alexandria
Mount Maro near Damascus
The Sea of Galilee, Senereth or Genazereth
The Dead Sea
The Aegean Sea
The Tyrrenian Sea
The monastery of Syon
The monastery of Careth
The monastery of Selbe
The monastery of Bethlehem
The monastery of Katherine
The tomb of Lazarus
The monastery of Antony

N
Naason
Neptalym
Naym
Nazareth
Neapulosa
Newrym
Nebo
Neescol
New Babylon
The swimming pool of Syloe

O
Olba
Ornaym

P
Pella
Panicia
Phasel
Petra of the desert
Pevsavr
The old harbour
The well of living waters

The palm brought to the Most Blessed Virgin by the angel on Mount Olivet

The Our Father was taught by Christ on Mount Olivet

The pool in Jerusalem

The Golden Gate

Peter raised Tabitha from death

The port of Jaffa or Joppa

The rock in the Tyrrenian Sea on which Peter stood to fish

The pyramids of the lords of Babylon

R

The Region of Traconitis

Ramath Galaad

Rama of Benjamin

Ramatha

Rorcero

The Burning Bush

S

Sardinia, the chapel of the Most Blessed Mary

Syria of Damascus

Suba, the tower of Libanus

Sueca

Sydon

Sydon the Great

Sopheth

Sarepta of Sydon

Suna

Sephora

Sochoth

Salym

Samaria

Sychim

Sarcham

Sethyr

Silo

Sarona

Segor

Sodoma

Seboym

Sarraha

Sychelegh

Salachea

Sarys

Summit

Suachym

Salmochericon

The tomb of Job

The tomb of Jonah

The tomb of Josuah

The tomb of Jesus Christ

The tomb of Isaiah

The tomb of Zacharias

The tomb of Absolon

The tomb of the Most Blessed Mary

The tomb of the Machabees

The tomb of Rachel

The tomb of the Patriarchs

The tomb of Aaron

The tomb of Moses

Christ fed the four thousand

The wood where the birds die for Christ and rise again

The hanging of Judas

The caves of the Saints on Mount Syon

The caves of the Saints on Mount Olivet

The star appeared to the Kings [on] the way to Bethlehem

The road by which Christ went to His Passion

The school of the Most Blessed Mary

The statue of salt of Lot's wife

The cave of Odolla where Adam lamented the death of Abel for 100 years

T

Tyrus

Thoron

Tyberias

Tersa

Tampuascere

Tecua

Taperna

Taurus Castle

The land of Amon

The land of Hus

The land of Edom

The land of Egypt

The Tetrarchy of Galilee

The tabernacle of Heber
The table
The temple of Christ
The stream Syson
The stream Bereth
The stream Cedron
The stream Boser
The tribe of Zabulon
The tribe of Asser
Half of the tribe of Manasse
The tribe of Neptalim
The tribe of Gad
The tribe of Ruben
The tribe of Ysacar
The tribe of Benjamin
The tribe of Effraym
The tribe of Dan
The tribe of Symeon

V
Vruth
The valley of Bechara
The valley of Senyn

The valley of Saba
The valley of Achor
The valley of Nabaioth
The valley of Mambre
The valley of Jehoshophat
The ford of Jaboth
The Most Blessed Virgin sent her girdle to
    Saint Thomas on Mount Olivet
The rods of Moses grow near the Jordan
The glade below [Mount] Quarentena
The vineyard of balsam
The way leading to Ethiopia

X
Christ said to Saul, "Why dost thou persecute
    me?"

Y
Ydumea
Ygnpara

Z
Zalla

COMMENTARY

The first list appears to be rather haphazard, and if Wey is using a system it is hard to see what it is. One clue to the method Wey followed may lie in the fact that the first large place shown in the top left corner of the map (Douce 389) is Damascus, number 6 in Wey's first list. The city is represented as a tower with two flags surmounted by a bird. A little below it are the words "Mons Libani", number 21 in the list. Pella, at number 64, is below it; lower still and slightly to the left is Tiberias, number 71. Jericho is number 260; it is shown on the map to the left of Jerusalem, depicted with two towers, under the left hand of which flows a river. Emmaus, number 278, is slightly below and to the right of Jericho.

This sequence could be partly explained if Wey was working across his map, in columns, from left to right and from top to bottom. Perhaps he slid something like a ruler or straight edge across his map a little distance at a time and noted down the names in the order thus revealed. Nowadays the squares on an Ordnance Survey map are used in a similar fashion to produce a grid reference, giving eastings and westings before northings and southings.

Unfortunately for this theory, Jerusalem, which appears to the right of Jericho, predictably almost in the centre of the map, has a lower number, 224 in the list, compared with Jericho's 260. But on the above suggestion it should have a higher number than Jericho!

Many of the geographical locations in these two lists can be linked to passages in Wey's *Itineraries*. While a large number of the important sites which he indicates would be marked by any medieval cartographer on a *Mappa Terrae Sanctae*, some of the ones on the Bodleian map are so particular to Wey's narrative that they lead to the conclusion that this map may be the one which Wey describes as *Mappa mea de Terra Sancta*.

The most striking example of a connection with William Wey's narrative is the location of "The Wood Where the Birds Die for Christ and Rise Again". This appears on the first list as entry 127 and in the second list under letter "S". This phrase would be almost unintelligible if one did not have the story, taken from Robert Grosseteste (Lincolniensis), recounted in Chapter 6. Another indication of Wey's connection with Douce 389 is the "bubbling spring" which "appears at Epiphany". This location is joined to Thana, entry 264, in the first list and under letter "F" in the second. The story appears in the closing lines of Chapter 6.

Other indications are the interest in vestigia, the impressions on the ground made by Christ, which is one of Wey's most consuming passions. There are two examples of this in the lists. The first is "The stone, on the Mount of our Lord's Leap, which received Christ". Wey describes this, quoting from Bede, in the penultimate paragraph of Chapter 6. The second is "The footprints left by Christ at the time of the Ascension". There are references to these in Chapters 6, 7, 9 and 11.

Finally, Wey's use of the possessive adjective *mea*, "my", when describing the map, in the list of property he wishes to leave to Edington, shows ownership if not authorship.

13

Distances between Places in the Holy Land and Latin/Greek Vocabulary

SYNOPSIS

This chapter also contains two lists, but on different subjects. The first can be considered as a continuation of the gazetteer of place names just given in Chapter 12; the second is a Latin/Greek vocabulary of ninety words or phrases which is more akin to Chapter 10.

TRANSLATION
(Roxburghe, pp. 138–40)

Two miles from Damascus is the place where Christ appeared to Saul.

Four miles from Bethsayda [Bethsaida] is Coroazym [Chorazin].

Five miles from Coroazim [Chorazin] is Cedar.

Two miles from Capharnaum [Capernaum] is the way down from the mountain where Christ preached to the crowds.

Two miles from Genazaret [Gennesaret] is Magdalum [Magdala] Castle.

Two miles from Magdalum [Magdala] Castle is Tyberiadis [Tiberias].

Ten miles from Tyberiadis [Tiberias] is the city of Nazareth where Christ was conceived.

Two miles from Nazareth is Sephora [Sepphoris], the city which leads to Acon [Acco], Acris [Acre] or Tholomayda [Ptolemais].

Four miles from Nazareth, two miles from Sephora [Sepphoris], is Cana of Galilee.

One mile from Nazareth is the Mount of Our Lord's Leap.

Four miles from Nazareth, towards the east, is Mount Thabor [Tabor] where Christ was transfigured.

Two miles from Thabor [Tabor] is Naym [Nain]; above Naym [Nain] is Mount Endor at the foot of which is the stream Syson. On the descent from this mountain Melchisedech met Abraham. Two miles from Thabor [Tabor] is Mount Hermon.

Four miles from Naym [Nain] is the city of Jesrael [Jezreel].

One mile from Jesrael [Jezreel] are the Mountains of Gelboe [Gilboa] where Saul and Jonathan were slain.

Two miles from Gelboe [Gilboa] is the city of Neapolis which is called Bethsay.

Five miles from Jesrael [Jezreel] is the town of Geminum.

Ten miles from the town of Geminum is Samaria, which is now called Sebasta, where St John the Baptist was beheaded.

Four miles from Sebasta is Neapolis, which is also called Sychim [Shechem or Sichem], which Jacob bought from Emor [Hamor] and gave to his son, Joseph; and Jacob's spring is there.

One mile from Sychim [Shechem] is Dan where was the golden calf.

One mile from Sychim [Shechem] is Bethel where there was another calf. Twenty miles from Sychim [Shechem] and four from Jerusalem is the road which leads to Lydda or Dyaspolis; there is Mount Stylo which is near Aramathia [Arimathea].

Twenty-two miles from Lydda, twenty-four from Sychim [Shechem], sixteen from Ebron [Hebron], twenty-four from Jericho, six from Bethlehem, thirty-six from Bersheeba, twenty-four from Ascalon [Ashkelon], thirty-four from Joppa, twenty-four from Ramatha [Arimathea], is Jerusalem which is the most holy mother city of Judaea, which is also Syon [Zion].

Eighteen miles from Jerusalem is Modyn [Modin], and eight miles from Modyn [Modin] is Lydda.

Four miles from Jerusalem is the town in which the priest Zacharias dwelt.

Twenty-four miles from Jerusalem, going north, is Jericho.

Two miles from Jerusalem is Bethany and it is two miles from Bethany to Mount Olivet.

Twenty-eight miles from Jerusalem is Sebasta, which is called Samaria.

Five and a half miles from Jerusalem is Rama of Benjamin.

Three miles from Jerusalem is Anatoth [Anathoth], the town of Jeremiah.

Two miles from Jerusalem is Sylo [Shiloh].

One mile from Bethlehem the star shone on the shepherds.

Two miles from Bethlehem is the tomb of Rachel.

Three miles from Bethlehem, two miles from Tecua [Tekoa], is the place where most of the Innocents are buried.

Six miles from Bethlehem is the town of Tecua [Tekoa]; it abounds in pastures.

Twenty miles from Bethlehem is Ebron [Hebron].

Twenty miles from Ebron is Beersheba.

Ten miles from Ebron is the site of Aspaltus [Asphaltitis], which is the Dead Sea.

Eight miles from Nazareth is Mount Cayn.

Three miles from Cayn is Mount Carmel.

Sixteen miles from Nazareth towards the Sea of Galilee is Genazareth [Gennesaret], the village where Christ sent the legion of devils into the pigs.

Sixteen miles from Mount Carmel, towards the south, is Cesaria in Palestine.

Eight miles from Acon is Mount Carmel.

Fourteen miles from Carmel is the cave of the Most Blessed Mary.

Two miles from the cave is Cesarea of Palestine.

Twenty-one miles from Sebasta is Mount Thabor.

Twenty miles from Bethany is Quarentena.

Six miles from Quarentena is the River Jordan.

Two miles from Jericho is Galgal [Gilgal].

Seven miles from Jordan is Galgal [Gilgal].

Two miles from Jericho is Mount Quarentena.

According to St Jerome, the Holy Land stretches from the Fountain of Dan southwards to the city of Beersheba, and contains in its length 160 miles. Its width is from Joppa westwards [sic] to Jordan and contains in its width 60 miles.

LATIN/GREEK VOCABULARY
(Roxburghe, pp. 140–42)

William Wey gives a list of ninety Latin words or phrases with a phonetic Greek equivalent, in English letters, beside each one. This list offers the English translation in the first column, Wey's Latin in the second and his Greek transliteration in the third. Columns two and three are Bandinel's transcriptions from the Bodleian MS 565.

	Good morning	Bonum mane	Calomare
	Good night	Bona nox	Calonurte
	Welcome	Bene venisti	Calosertys
	Sit down	Sede	Catze
5.	Tell me the way	Dic mihi viam	Dixiximostrata
	With pleasure	Cum bona voluntate	Mitte caras

	English	Latin	Greek
	Come here	Veni istuc	Elado
	Give it to me	Da mihi istud	Doysime tutt
	Cross the road	Transi viam	Ame
10.	At once	Statim	Ligora
	Bring me	Fer michi	Ferine
	What do you say?	Quid dicis	The leys
	Do you understand?	Ne intelligis	Apopoukistis
	The Lord be with you	Dominus tecum	Otheos metasane
15.	My Lady	Mea domina	Kyrias me
	Where is the inn?	Ubi est taberna	Ecke canavte
	Where are you going?	Quo vadis	Popasy
	Would you like?	Vis tu	Thelisalo
	Bring it	Porta istud	Ferto do
20.	No	Non	Oche
	Yes	Ita	Nesche vel [or] Nee
	God preserve	Deus salva	Theos zasse
	Thanks	Grates	Spolate
	Take	Habete	Exe
25.	How much?	Quantum	Posso
	My Lady	Mea domina	Mo kyra
	Good Day	Bona dies	Caloporne
	Good evening	Bonum sero	Caloespera
	Good night	Bona nox	Canyzthera
30.	Give me bread	Da mihi panem	Doyso ipsomo
	Bring me bread	Porta mihi panem	Ferto do ipsomo
	Bring wine here	Porta istuc vinum	Ferto do crasse
	Bring water here	Porta istuc aquam	Ferto do nero
	God have mercy	Deus miserere	Kirieleyson
35.	Christ have mercy	Christe miserere	Christeleyson
	Lady preserve	Domina salva	Kiria chere
	Salt	Sal	Alasse
	Apple	Appyl [sic]	Mela
	Butter	Butirum	Sotir
40.	Meat	Carnes	Creas
	Milk	Lac	Gala
	Cheese	Casium	Tyri
	Eggs	Ova	Onaga
	Pork[?]	Portus [?porcus]	Grony [gourouni]
45.	Fish	Pisses	Ipsaria [psari]
	Mutton	Mutones	Provido
	Hen	Galline	Oryngha
	Goose/Duck	Anca [?anser]	Pappia
	Mussels	Musculis	Midea [mudi]
50.	Oysters	Ostria	Ostridea

	Vinegar	Vinum acre	Acide
	Pears	Pira	Pydea
	Candle	Candela	Kyri
	Cup	Ciphus	Cuppa
55.	Parsley	Petrocilium	Colomynde
	Garlic	Allium	Sorda
	Onions	Sepe	Cromidea
	Fire	Ignis	Fotya [photia]
	Grapes	Uve	Stephyle
60.	Shoes	Sotulares	Papasche [papoutsi]
	Stockings	Calige	Calche [kalsa]
	Shirt	Camisia	Camisa
	Hat	Caleptra	Talkia
	Fig	Ficus	Fige
65.	Broth	Potagium	Fayto
	Dish	Discus	Crucia
	Penny	Denarium	Cartesa
	All	Totum	Pan
	Moon	Luna	Mene
70.	Animals	Vivencia	Zoa
	Living	Animata	Sichea
	Four [quarter?]	Quatuor	Arbe
	City	Civitas	Cariath
	Town	Villa	Thas
75.	Saviour	Salvator	Pontificanech
	Exodus	Exodus	Elsomath
	King	Rex	Basileos
	Horse	Equs	Epos
	Swift horse	Equs velox	Ypodromos
80.	Lamb	Agnus	Agnon vel [or] Assidor
	The [Lord's] Anointed	Vnctus	Messias
	Sheep	Ovis	Probatos
	Guard	Servare	Philaxe
	Father	Pater	Pater
85.	Sea	Mare	Thalassa
	Black	Nigrum	Melam
	Bitterness	Fel	Colen
	Oh Mother	O mater	O thyso
	The Gods	Dei	Thera
90.	You may take	Habeas	Ethegis

COMMENTARY

The first list takes the usual form of early itineraries giving the distance between pairs of places. There are sixty-three pairs, eighteen of which feature Jerusalem.

The second list contains ninety words or phrases in Latin with their equivalent translations into Greek. The Greek translations, however, do not appear in Greek letters but are transliterated into English characters. The modern phonetic alphabet with its special symbols had not yet been invented. Two examples will show the complex situation thus produced:

1. Wey gives as a pair of questions, *Quid dicis* and *The leys*. The first two words are the normal Latin for "What are you saying?" The Classical Greek was τί λέγεις; probably pronounced *ti legeis*.

2. *Uve* is paired with *Stephyle*. The Classical Latin for "grapes" is *uvae*, written as *uve* in Medieval Latin. In Classical Greek *staphule* (σταφυλή) was a "bunch of grapes". In Modern Greek *staphule* is "a grape"; Wey's phonetic version is *stephyle*.

Other problems of translation and pronunciation (especially of the letter *beta*) have been considered above in the Commentary on Chapter 10. The word list in this chapter would be more at home in that one. Perhaps there was some economic or technical reason why it was combined in a folio with the list of distances which did not take up a whole folio. Seventy-five of the ninety words in this list appear in the English/Greek list in Chapter 10. The spelling of words which appear in both lists is not always consistent.

In Wey's Latin/Greek list in Chapter 13 *ovis* (Latin) is translated as *probatos* (Greek). But in Chapter 10 (in the English/Greek list) *schepe* (Middle English) is translated as *provatos* (Greek), yet in the Greek/Latin list in that same chapter *probatos* (Greek) is given as the equivalent of *ovis* (Latin). In fact, in both Classical and Modern Greek, the word for sheep is πρόβατον, *probaton*.

While not concurring with Bandinel's stern judgement on Wey's linguistic competence, the present writer agrees with him when he says that this area "may exercise the ingenuity of the Modern Greek scholar, but would not repay the space requisite for minute criticism".

14

Rome

SYNOPSIS

In 1458 William Wey visited both Rome and Jerusalem. His itinerary across Western Europe forms Chapter 8. Chapter 14 deals with Rome, concentrating on the churches and other places visited by pilgrims and the indulgences which could be earned thereby. It falls into two parts. The first deals with the Seven Great Pilgrimage Churches, the second with other churches, monasteries and hospitals.

TRANSLATION
(Roxburghe, pp. 142–52)

Indulgences in the Roman Curia[1]

St Silvester and St Gregory write in their chronicles[2] that at one time there were 1,505 churches in Rome, as is shown in this line of verse,

> Chapels there are in Rome one thousand five hundred and five.

The majority of these have decayed and have been destroyed by the pagans. There are, then, still 467 churches, or, according to some, 476. From all these churches the Holy Brothers have chosen seven principal ones.[3] These seven surpass the rest in prestige and indulgence and holiness. They are called "royal" because they were built by popes and emperors. They are as follows.

The first principal church is that of St John Lateran.[4] This is the supreme and chief of all the churches of the whole world. Here each day there are forty-eight years of indulgences, an equal number of Lents and remission of a third of all sins.

Pope Silvester and Pope Gregory consecrated this church, which had previously been the house and palace of the Emperor Constantine.[5]

Constantine said, "Holy Father, I bestow my house and palace to the honour of God and in praise of St John. Holy Father, confer on this house your grace and indulgence." The Pope[6] replied saying, "He who cleansed you from leprosy, the same cleanses all who visit this house with devotion and with the power of the Holy Apostles, Peter and Paul." Boniface[7] confirms this with his words, "If men knew the graces and indulgences of the church of St John Lateran, no one would go beyond the sea to Jerusalem and the tomb of Our Lord." On the anniversary of the dedication of the church there is remission of all sins from punishment and guilt. There is a step in the church and whoever goes up or down it has all his sins remitted. It has a chapel which is called the "Sacristy" in which is the altar on which the blessed John performed his final devotion in the desert.

There is also the Ark of the Old Testament there, together with the table at which Christ ate the Last Supper with His Disciples.[8] The rod of Moses and Aaron is there too.[9] On the high altar lie the heads of St Peter and St Paul.[10] When these are displayed there are great indulgences. No woman dares enter the chapel dedicated to the Holy of Holies.[11] In it there is the face of Christ as he was at the age of twelve. St Luke wished to paint the portrait but fell asleep.[12] When he awoke the portrait had been completed by the angels. This picture was not affected by the heat of the fire although the church was twice burned by the pagans.[13]

The head of Zacharias, John the Baptist's father, is there[14] and also the purple robe of Jesus Christ.[15] There is also Jesus Christ's handkerchief.[16] Titus and Vespasian bore the relics of the churches with them across the sea with their mercenaries.[17]

The second principal church is dedicated to St Peter and is situated on the mount called the Vatican.[18] In it there is a step and anyone who goes up or down it with wholehearted devotion receives from each step seven years' indulgence. There are 105 altars in this church. From these the Holy Fathers have selected seven chief altars which have been granted special graces and indulgences above the other altars. There too lie the bodily remains of saints. Every day there are forty-eight years of indulgence there, the same number of Lents and remissions of one third of sins. On the anniversary of the dedication of these altars there are forty-eight years of indulgences, doubled, as previously described and it lasts for eight days. At the Easter Festival and on the offertory days on the Day of Christ's Nativity and on All Saints' Day there are 1,000 years of indulgences.

The first capital altar is that of Simon and Jude who lie on the same altar.[19] The second altar is that of St George, in which his body lies.[20] The third is of Pope Leo.[21] The fourth is that of the Blessed Virgin where Mass is sung each day. The fifth is of St Andrew, the sixth of the Holy Cross and no woman dares enter it.[22] The seventh is to St Veronica.[23] Each of these altars has, every day, forty years of indulgences and as many Lents and remission of a third part of all sins. At the Lord's Supper and on the day of the Annunciation of the Blessed Virgin there are 1,000 years of indulgences and as many Lents and remission of a third part of all sins. At the tomb, every day, there are fourteen centuries of indulgences. In Rome lie eight bodies of Holy Apostles and a half of the bodies of the Holy Apostles Peter and Paul. The other half is in St Paul's church. In both cases they are on the high altars. St Boniface, St John Chrysostom, Processus and Martinianus lie there too.[24] There also are Petronella and 13,000 Holy Martyrs.[25] There are so many bodies of saints there, which are known only to God, that no man can number them. When the Vernicle is exhibited, the Romans have 3,000 years of indulgence, those who live nearby up to 6,000 years, but those who live beyond the mountains, the valleys and the sea have 12,000 years of indulgence and an equal number of Lents and remission of a third part of all their sin.[26]

In the entrance to this church there are six gates, one of which is closed. This is the true Golden Gate.[27]

The third principal church is dedicated to St Paul,[28] where there are forty-eight years of indulgence every day and the same number of Lents and remission of a third part of all sins. There are 1,000 years on the saint's day, 100 on the day of his conversion, another 100 on Holy Innocents' Day. On the anniversary of the church's dedication, the eighth day after Martinium [Martinmas?],[29] there are 1,000 years of indulgences, the same number of Lents and remission of a third part of all sins.

Anyone who visits this church each Sunday for a whole year gains as much grace as if he went to St James in Galicia.[30] Many have discovered that anyone who drinks from the three fountains is delivered from all his ailments. St Paul's staff is there together with the cross which spoke to St Bridget.[31] There too is the Bible which St Paul wrote, together with many other relics, a golden gate and many of the Innocents whose death Herod ordered.[32]

The fourth principal church is dedicated to St Lawrence.[33] There are forty-eight years of indulgence there each day with the same number of Lents and remission of a third part of all sins. Pope Pelagius consecrated this church.[34]

On the day when the Holy Martyrs, Lawrence and Stephen, were martyred there are eighty years of indulgences, the same number of Lents and remission of punishment and guilt for of a third part of all sins.[35] The above-mentioned martyrs lie on the high altar. There is the stone on which St Lawrence was roasted. Anyone who visits this church every Wednesday for a whole year delivers his soul from Purgatory. There is a tomb there and a golden gate and many other relics. Near the altar there lie also the bodies of the saints Sixtus and Hippolitus and forty other martyrs. Pope Pelagius doubled the aforementioned indulgences in Lent.

The fifth church is dedicated to St Mary the Greater, where there are forty-eight years of indulgences and an equal number of Lents and remission of a third part of all sins, doubled in Lent.[36] On the Festivals of the Blessed Virgin Mary 100 years were given by Pope Gregory.[37] In this basilica lie five uncorrupted bodies: that of St Matthew the Apostle, which is placed beneath a stone of porphyry; the body of St Luke the Evangelist; the body of St Jerome; and the bodies of the Holy Virgins, Romula and Redempta, beside the altar of St Agatha.[38] There too are the cloth of Jesus Christ, on which He was laid and some of the hay on which our Lord Jesus Christ was placed when He lay in the manger, and a piece of the wood of the Holy Cross on which Our Saviour Christ Jesus hung.[39] There are also relics of Cosmo and Damian.[40]

The sixth principal church is dedicated to St Sebastian, where an angel spoke to St Gregory in the Mass saying, "Here is true remission of all sins, light and splendour without end."[41] Here the Holy Martyr Sebastian gained merit with his martyrdom.[42] In this church every day there are 1,000 years of indulgences, an equal number of Lents and remission of a third part of all sins. In this church there is the same amount of grace as in that of St Peter because of the grace of Saints Peter and Paul, whose heads lay there for a long time, upwards of seventy years. Popes Silvester, Gregory, Alexander and Nicholas granted, each separately, 1,000 years of indulgences.[43] In this church lie forty-eight bishops and martyrs, each of whom separately bestows great indulgences. There is also a tomb called "The Cemetery of St Kalixtus".[44] Anyone who crosses it with devotion has all his sins forgiven. There are many saints' bodies there which no man can number, but only God. It is written in the ancient books of the Romans that on one Sunday in May there is there remission of all sins from punishment and guilt. There too is a footprint of Jesus Christ in a marble stone.[45]

The seventh principal church is dedicated to the Holy Cross.[46] Every day there are forty-eight years of indulgences there and an equal number of Lents and remission of a third part of all sins. On the high altar lie Anastasius and Rasius together with the daughter of the Emperor Constantine, who ordered this church in honour of the Holy Cross and in praise of Saint Helen.[47]

Pope Silvester consecrated this church and granted it 353 years of indulgences every Sunday. It contains two goblets, one full of Jesus Christ's blood and the other full of the Blessed Virgin Mary's milk. There too is the sponge by which vinegar and gall were stretched out to Jesus Christ on the cross. In addition there are twelve thorns from the crown of Our Lord Jesus Christ.[48] On the high altar is part of the Holy Cross and an arm of the thief crucified with Christ on his right.[49] No woman dares to enter the chapel which is called "The Jerusalem Chapel", except once a year. In it there is remission of all sins etc.

There Follow the Indulgences and Relics of the Other Churches of the City of Rome

At the Three Fountains there are 3,000 years of indulgences.[50] (Three springs broke forth at the place where St Paul was decapitated and they flow very copiously to the present day.) Nearby is the church of St Anastasius[51] which has the privilege of many relics and indulgences. Next to it is a chapel called Ladder to Heaven where are the bones of 10,000 Holy Knights.[52] That too has the privilege of great indulgences.

In the Church of the Annunciation of the Blessed Mary there are seventy-seven years of indulgence and, in the same church, there is remission of all sins.[53] All those who come in reverence to this church will never be hurt by lightning and thunder, or supercelestial flashes and fire.

In the church of the Blessed Mary Altar of Heaven, where was built the first altar beneath which lies St Helena, there are every day 1,000 years of indulgences.[54] In this church is a venerable portrait of the Blessed Virgin which St Luke painted and which is famous for many miracles.[55] In the church of Mary of the People there are 400 years of indulgence and an equal number of Lents. There too, together with many other relics and indulgences, is another portrait of the Blessed Virgin painted by the hand of St Luke, which St Gregory brought there.[56] In the Church of the Blessed Mary Rotunda there are, every day, 300 years of indulgences, and on All Saints' Day, which is when this church was consecrated, there is remission of all sins.[57]

In the Church of Mary Mona there are 200 years of indulgence. In this church there is a portrait of the Blessed Virgin Mary which was brought from Greece by a Roman and which, so the story goes, was painted by St Luke.[58]

In the Church of the Blessed Mary of the Fount of the Olive, where a spring of olive oil burst forth on the night of Christ's Nativity, there are indulgences from seven Popes, each one granting seven years of indulgence and seven [years *sic*] of Lent. There are 100 years of indulgence in the Church of St Mary, next to the Bridge of St Angelus,[59] where stand the pillars to which the Holy Apostles Peter and Paul were bound. In the Chapel of Mary, Free Us from the Pains of Hell, beneath which the dragon was bound by St Silvester, there are 9,000 years of indulgences. In the Church of the Blessed Mary of the Portico is a venerable picture of the Blessed Mary. This came from heaven in the presence of the Blessed Galla, daughter of the consul Sinachus, when the patroness of this monastery was dining here. She immediately decreed her house should be a church of the Blessed Mary and had this portrait set in sapphire and placed there, where it is seen up to this day.[60] There are many indulgences here. In the Church of St Bartholomew below the Bridges lie his body and those of St Paulinus, Albertus and Superacius, together with many other relics, above the high altar. These can be seen on the day itself and on Palm Sunday until Vespers and confer 7,000 years of indulgences. There too is the pit in which the bodies of Bartholomew and Paulinus lay for many years.[61]

In the Church of St Peter in Chains are the fetters with which St Peter was bound in Jerusalem on the first of August.[62] There is there remission of all sins from punishment and guilt. In the Church of St Silvester is the head of the Blessed John the Baptist together with many other relics.[63] Here there are 1,000 years of indulgences. In the Church of St Praxes the Virgin, where there is a portion of the column to which Our Lord Jesus was bound and where there are 2,000 years of indulgences, there are buried 300 martyrs and 22 holy priests together with many other relics which can be seen there every day.[64]

In the Church of St Potentia the Virgin there are 1,000 years of indulgences. In this church there is the bench on which Christ sat with his disciples at the Last Supper.[65] There is also a pit to which St Potentia carried the blood of 300 martyrs. In the Church of St Vivian the Virgin, where rest many thousands of the martyrs butchered by Domitian, there are 9,000 years of indulgences. In this church is the head of St Vivian. A herb grows there which she planted herself and which has power against the falling sickness.[66]

In the Church of Vitus and Modestus is a stone on which these martyrs were killed.[67] There are many other relics too and 100 years of indulgence. In the Church of St Martinus in the Mountains, where St Silvester lies on the altar, together with many other relics, there are 200 years of indulgence.[68] In the Church of St Lawrence in Chains there is the spring in which St Lawrence baptised the soldier Hipolitus and Lucilla: here there are 100 years of indulgence. There is another church, St Lawrence in Polisperna, which contains the oven where he was roasted and many other relics: here there are 100 years of indulgence. There is yet another church, St Lawrence in Lucina, where there is a large part of the gridiron and the fetters with which he was bound, together with many other relics. This church has the privilege of great indulgences.[69] Also there is another church, St Lawrence in Dammasus, which has the privilege of many relics and indulgences.

In the Church of St Nicholas in Prison, where the Tullianum Prison was and where there are several relics, there are 200 years of indulgence.[70] In the Church of St Alexius, where there still remains the staircase beneath which St Alexius lay for seventeen years without the knowledge of his parents or his wife, there are seventy-seven years of indulgence.[71] In the Church of St Saba, which St Gregory's mother built, there are 100 years of indulgence.[72] The bodies of Titus and Vespasian, who destroyed [Jerusalem] on account of Christ Jesus, still lie there.[73] In the Church of St Gregory, which he built for himself and where he became a monk, there are many relics and 1,000 years of indulgence. There is a hole there in which he lay for many years, where even more indulgences are conferred.[74] In the Church of St Peter in Chains, there is still the well from which the Apostles of God, Peter and Paul, drank and the stone on which they sat: here there is remission of a third part of all sins.[75]

In the Church of Cosmos and Damian, where they themselves lie with many other relics, there are 1,000 years of indulgence.[76] In the Church of St Gregory [George?], where there is his head and the spear with which he slew the dragon and his standard and some of his blood, there are seventy-seven years of indulgence.[77]

In the Church of the Twelve Apostles, where the bodies of St Philip and St James were hidden in the high altar, and the body of the virgin, Saint Euphemia, in another altar, and where can still be seen the foot of the Apostle Philip in the flesh and his bones together with many other relics, there are seventy-seven years of indulgences.[78]

In the Church of St John before the Latin Gate, where St John was placed in oil, there is deliverance of one year on that anniversary.[79] Likewise in the Church of St Agnes outside the Walls, where she herself lies and St Constancia, the daughter of Constantine, and many other relics.[80] There is another church of Agnes in Agony within the city, where she suffered and was placed in the arena [?]. Here there is the chemise which the angel of the Lord brought from heaven to cover her when she was naked.[81] This church is privileged with many indulgences. In the Church of St Cecilia, where she lies with her husband, Valerian, together with many other saints, there are 400 years of indulgence.

In the "Quo Vadis?" Chapel, where Our Lord met St Peter and where His footprints are still visible, there are 100 years of indulgence.[82] In the Church of St Matthew there is an arm of St Christopher and many other relics; here there are 1,000 years of indulgence.

There are four churches of St Saviour in Rome and four of the Holy Angels. There are several of the Blessed Virgin Mary, namely those of St Mary of the Well,[83] St Mary of the Greek School,[84] St Mary of the Hand, St Mary of Greece, St Mary of the Way,[85] St Mary in Molenini, St Mary in the Gruncta Piuncta, St Mary Minerva,[86] St Mary in the Field, St Mary Possibilia, and St Mary of the Salt Water, which are privileged with many relics and indulgences and tokens of the Blessed Virgin Mary. In addition there are many churches of the Apostles and Evangelists, namely St James across the Tiber and St James of Tigario, next to Mary of the People, and St James of Scossia in the borough of St Peter; the Church of St Peter on the Mount,[87] where he was crucified, and the Church of St Paul in Regula; the Church of St Thomas,[88] the Church of St Andrew[89] and the Church of St Mary, the Church of St Barnabas, and the Church of St Luke. All of these have the privilege of many relics and indulgences, etc.

There are many churches of the Holy Martyrs in Rome: three Churches of St Stephen;[90] the Church of St Eustachius,[91] where he lies with his wife and two sons; the Churches of St Adrian and Crisogonus[92] and Julian, Knights; the Church of St John and St Paul;[93] the Church of St Vitalis; the Church of Saints Peter and Marcellinus; the Church of St Nereus and Achilleus[94] and the Church of the Crowned Four;[95] the Church of St Sebastian; the Church of Saints Tyrus and Jer; the Church of St Saturninus and that of Saints Simplicius and Faustinus; the Church of St Pantaleon and that of St Pangracius Outside the Walls. These also are privileged with many relics and indulgences.

In addition there are many churches in Rome of the Holy Confessors, namely three of St Martin,[96] three of St Blaise and one each of St Apollinaris, St Anthony, St Eusebius and St Celsus. In this last there are a foot of Mary Magdalene and a finger of St Nicholas. Then there are individual churches of St Leonard, St Clement,[97] St Sixtus, St Ciriacus, and Saint Marcellus.[98] There is a church each to St Augustine, St Ambrose, St Jerome and one of St Benedict. All these also are privileged with many relics and indulgences.

Then, in Rome, there are many churches of the Holy Virgins; namely three churches of the Blessed Mary Magdalene,[99] three of St Katherine, two each of St Barbara and St Agatha, one of St Lucia and one of St Dorothy across the Tiber, where she herself lies. There are churches for St Vivian,[100] St Balbina,[101] St Prisca,[102] St Anastasia, St Susanna,[103] St Bergiata, St Felicity, St Elizabeth, St Petronella, St Clare and St Cristina, and many other churches where Masses are celebrated up to the present day. All these have the privilege of many relics and indulgences.

There are in Rome too various monasteries of the different Orders, both for monks and for nuns. There are also various hospitals of all nations, for example the Hospital of the Holy Spirit,[104] in which is the stone table on which Our Lord wrote the Ten Commandments with His own fingers. These have the privilege of many other relics and indulgences and miracles.

All the above indulgences are doubled in Lent. If the misfortune of death befall someone on the pilgrimage road, either coming or going, he is truly absolved from all his sins, both mortal and venial. Amen.[105]

COMMENTARY

With the exception of Venice, which made such an impression on him, Wey gives very little information about his travels in Italy. In Chapter 1 he talks about the coins encountered in Bologna, Florence and Siena. In Chapter 6 (*materia* 10) he writes of the saints or relics to be seen in Padua, Viterbo, Assisi and Spoleto and recounts the story of Loretto. His marginal notes in Chapter 8 mention the universities in Bologna and Perugia and the resting places of St Christina (Spoleto) and St Francis and St Clare (Assisi). Chapter 9 lists the places he passed through in the South Tyrol and Northern Italy, several of which were on the Via Claudia Augusta. There is a charming vignette of his three-day stay in Pergine over Easter and then, again, a bare list of places between there and Venice. As in Chapter 7 Wey gives no details at all of the return journey from Venice to England.

NOTES

1   The Roman Curia. Curia is the term now used for the papal court and its functionaries, particularly those who adminster the Roman Catholic Church. Here William Wey appears to use it in a geographical sense to describe the churches, monasteries and hospitals situated in Rome.

2   St Sylvester and St Gregory. St Sylvester was Bishop of Rome from 314 to 335. According to legend he baptized Constantine in the baptistery of the Lateran (see below) and cleansed him of leprosy. St Gregory the Great (c.540 to 604) became Pope in 590.

3   The Seven Great Pilgrimage Churches included the four Major Basilicas – St Peter's, St John Lateran, Santa Maria Maggiore and St Paul Outside the Walls – and three Patriarchal Basilicas – Santa Croce in Gerusalemme, San Lorenzo fuori le Mura and San Sebastiano fuori le Mura.

4   St John Lateran, San Giovanni in Laterano. Nikolas of Munkathvera travelled from Iceland to Jerusalem, probably in about 1150. His account of his pilgrimage, in Old Icelandic, is written in the form of a guide. He was excited by what he saw at the Lateran and among the relics he mentions are the blood of Christ, vestments of the Virgin and milk from her breast, a portion of the crown of thorns and many bones of John the Baptist (Birch, *Pilgrimages to Rome*, p. 111).

5   Constantine the Great (274 or 288 to 337) was proclaimed Emperor at York in 306. The Lateran Basilica stands on the site of an ancient palace on the Caelian hill which Constantine acquired as part of his wife's dowry. He gave it to the Church and it became the official residence of the popes for a thousand years. It has suffered from an earthquake and fires during the intervening period and has been rebuilt and restored several times.

6   The Pope. St Sylvester; see above.

7   Boniface. Wey does not clarify this reference. Perhaps the most likely candidate as this source is Boniface VIII (c.1234–1303) who became Pope in 1294. A great upholder of the power of the papacy, his writings include the *Sext*, the *Liber Sextus Decretalium*, a book of canon law, promulgated in 1298, which reflects the growing tendency to centralization in the later medieval church.

8   The table used for the Last Supper. The Franciscans on Mount Zion in Jerusalem claimed that the high altar in their church was where Christ and His Disciples celebrated the Last Supper (see Chapter 7).

9   The rod of Moses and Aaron: Exodus 4:4 and 4:20; Numbers 17:2 and 17:8.

10   The heads of St Peter and St Paul. Some bones from the heads of these two saints are kept at the top of the fourteenth-century baldaquin in silver reliquaries.

11   The chapel of the Holy of Holies. This term was used originally for the innermost part of the Jewish Temple in which the Ark of the Covenant was kept and which could only be entered by the High Priest and only on the Day of Atonement. Here the phrase is used as a metaphor for the most sacred shrine.

12   The miraculous portrait of Christ. For St Luke as a painter, see Chapter 9, and the essay "The Icon of Our Lady of Philerimos", pp. 228–32.

13   The church of St John Lateran was laid waste by the barbarians in the fifth century and damaged by an earth tremor in 896.

14   The head of Zacharias. In Chapter 9 Wey says the body is in Venice.

15 The clothing of Christ in a purple robe by the soldiers is described in Matthew 27:28 and John 19:2 (see also Luke 23:11).

16 The *sudarium*, Christ's handkerchief. According to legend, a woman, St Veronica, offered her headcloth to Christ to wipe away the blood and sweat from His face on the way to Calvary. He returned it with His features impressed on it. This cloth was known as the vernicle and Wey refers to it again in his description of St Peter's. A portrait, professing to be the original imprint, was translated by Pope Boniface VIII to St Peter's in 1297.

17 Titus and Vespasian. Vespasian was Emperor of Rome from 69 to 79 AD. Titus was his eldest son and succeeded him, ruling as Emperor from 79 to 81. When Vespasian returned from Palestine to become Emperor in 69, Titus remained there to finish the war, which he completed in 70 with the capture of Jerusalem. The reliefs under the vault of the Arch of Titus in the Roman Forum vividly depict the fall of Jerusalem, exhibiting the booty pillaged from the Temple there and including the seven-branched candlestick which Moses had made.

18 The Vatican lay outside the boundaries of ancient Rome. It was the site of a circus built by Caligula and used by Nero for the massacre of Christian martyrs, including, probably, St Peter. In 324 the Emperor Constantine built the church, over the site of St Peter's tomb, which is now St Peter's Basilica. By 1452 it was in a parlous state and Pope Nicholas V appointed B. Rossellino to restore it. The Pope died in 1455 and the project was abandoned for fifty years. At the time of Wey's visit in 1458 the building would have been rather less handsome than it is today.

19 St Simon and St Jude. Simon is called "the Zealot" by Luke; Jude is generally identified with Thaddaeus. In the West the two Apostles are commemorated together on 28 October.

20 St George: see Chapters 7 and 9.

21 Pope Leo. St Leo I, generally called "Leo the Great", was Pope from 440.

22 The Holy Cross: see Chapter 7.

23 St Veronica: see above.

24 St Boniface (680–754), "the Apostle of Germany", is also known as Winfrith. Tradition says that he was born in Devon, in Crediton, and martyred in Frisia.

   St John Chrysostom (347–407) was consecrated archbishop of Constantinople in 398 and was banished in 404. Thirty-one years after his death his body was taken back to Constantinople and reburied. With Athanasius, Basil and Gregory of Nazianus, he is regarded as one of the four Greek Doctors.

   Processus and Martinianus were early Roman martyrs, venerated from at least the fourth century. Tradition makes them the warders of St Peter and St Paul in the Mamertine Prison (see below), who were converted and baptized by Peter. Their relics were translated to St Peter's in the ninth century. Their altar is in the south transept.

25 Petronella (Petronilla) was an early Roman martyr whose dates and details are unknown. Some accounts describe her as a daughter of St Peter who refused marriage to a Count Flaccus and died after three days' fasting. Her sarcophagus was moved to St Peter's in the eighth century and her chapel there became that of the kings of France, who embellished it greatly. Her feast day is 31 May.

26 The vernicle: see above; also Chapters 7 and 9.

27 The Golden Gate. See also Chapter 7. Wey inserts the word "true" because, as he says below, there were several other "golden gates", for example in San Paolo and in San Lorenzo. The

events which took place at the Golden Gate are described in the apocryphal Gospel, the Protevangelium of James and in a work derived from it, the Pseudo-Matthew (3:6), as well as in *The Golden Legend*. The meeting of Joachim and Anna at the Golden Gate was a popular subject with artists, including Giotto and Gaddi.

28 The Church of St Paul, the basilica of San Paolo Fuori le Mura. St Paul's body was buried beside the Via Ostiense and a small shrine was erected over his grave. The Emperor Constantine built the first basilica over the tomb, which was consecrated by Pope Sylvester I in 324. It became such a popular place of pilgrimage that it was enlarged in 395. It was sacked by the Lombards in the eighth century and by the Saracens in the ninth century. In July 1823 a devastating fire almost entirely destroyed the basilica.

29 St Paul's feast day, shared with St Peter, is 29 June. His Conversion is commemorated on 25 January. The Feast of the Holy Innocents is 28 December.

30 St James in Galicia. The relics of St James the Greater were, and still are, revered in the cathedral of Santiago de Compostela in north-west Spain. The pilgrimage *ad limina sancti Jacobi* was one of the three great medieval pilgrimages, the others being to Rome and Jerusalem. Wey himself undertook all three. His journey to Compostella in 1456 is described in Chapter 15. Details of the indulgences available to pilgrims there are given at the end of that chapter.

31 St Bridget. Wey had a special interest in St Bridget and was thoroughly conversant with her writings, quoting from them five times in Chapter 5.

32 Herod and the Innocents. The account of the massacre of the children of Bethlehem of two years old and under, ordered by Herod the Great, is to be found in Matthew 2:16–18.

33 St Lawrence: San Lorenzo Fuori Le Mura. A Roman deacon martyred in 258 by being roasted on a gridiron. During the reign of Constantine a chapel was built over his tomb, which was later enlarged into the present basilica.

34 Pope Pelagius II (579–590).

35 Lawrence and Stephen. These two saints appear together with Christ, St Peter, St Paul, Hippolytus and Pelagius in a sixth-century mosaic on the chancel arch.

36 St Mary Major, Santa Maria Maggiore. This major basilica church (see Chapter 7) was begun by Sixtus III (432–440). It has been altered many times since. It contains some of the oldest Christian mosaics in Rome, dating from the fifth century.

37 Pope Gregory (see n2 above).

38 St Matthew. The place of his martyrdom is not known for certain. Salerno Cathedral claims that his body was brought there in the tenth century by Robert Guiscard and now lies in the cathedral crypt.

   St Luke. Translated relics are claimed by both Constantinople and Padua.

   St Jerome. In Chapter 7 Wey describes the site of St Jerome's original burial in Bethlehem and his subsequent translation to Rome.

   Romula and Redempta. It was appropriate that these two should lie beside the altar of the more famous virgin and martyr, St Agatha, whose dates are uncertain, but who was born (possibly at Palermo or Catania) and died at Catania.

39 Pieces of cloth and hay from the manger. See Chapter 11 for the discovery of these relics by St Helena in Bethlehem and their removal to Constantinople.

Wood from the Holy Cross: see Chapters 6 and 7.

40   Cosmas and Damian. According to legend they were twins of Arab origin, who practised as doctors without pay. In Chapter 9 Wey says their bodies are in Venice.

41   St Gregory (c.540–604). Together with Ambrose, Jerome and Augustine, one of the four Latin Doctors of the Church. Tradition stressed his importance as one who taught the efficacy of prayer and the sacrifice of the Mass in freeing souls from Purgatory. It was said that his prayers delivered the soul of Trajan from Purgatory. Paintings of the Mass of St Gregory, which show him saying Mass while the suffering Christ appears above to confirm the faith of the ministers in the Real Presence, were popular in the fifteenth and sixteenth centuries, especially in Germany and Flanders. The story does not appear in *The Golden Legend*.

42   St Sebastian: San Sebastiano. St Sebastian was a soldier martyred in Diocletian's reign (284–305). A basilica was built over the site in the fourth century. Pilgrims came here to invoke his name against the plague, and his cult became so popular that in the fifth century a crypt was excavated around his tomb. The basilica was altered in the thirteenth century and rebuilt in the seventeenth century.

43   Pope Sylvester and Pope Gregory: see above.

44   St Kalixtus. The Catacombs of San Callisto lie between those of Domitilla and those of Sebastian and cover an extended area near the Appian Way. Almost all the third-century popes were buried there. It is famous for its paintings. Originally a slave, Callistos became Pope in 217. He died five years later.

45   Christ's footprint. Wey had a special interest in visible traces of Christ's time on earth (see also Chapters 7 and 9).

46   Church of the Holy Cross; Santa Croce in Gerusalemme. This was the site of the Sessorian Palace where Constantine's mother, St Helena, lived. It was built in the third century and remained an imperial palace until the sixth century. In the fourth century Helena went on a pilgrimage to Jerusalem, returning in 329 with a fragment of the True Cross, which she kept in the palace. She died in that year and the legend began that it was she who had found the True Cross. The cult was not introduced to Rome until the seventh century. Constantine converted part of the palace into a church and a chapel to house the relic. In the twelfth century Pope Lucius II adapted the church and built a campanile. A number of other relics connected with Christ's Passion are also displayed in the church.

47   Saint Helena, Constantine's mother. See above and Chapters 9 and 14.

48   The crown of thorns: see Chapters 7 and 9.

49   The Holy Cross and the arm of the Good Thief. For the Holy Cross, see above; for the Good Thief, St Dismas, see Chapters 7 and 9.

50   The Three Fountains. The traditional site of St Paul's martyrdom, in c.65 or perhaps 67 AD, Ad Aquas Salvias, is about 3 miles south of Rome on the left bank of the Tiber. The place is commemorated by the church of St Paul at the Three Fountains, Tre Fontane. The present sixteenth-century church, designed by Giacomo della Porta, replaces two chapels built on the spot where, according to tradition, fountains had spouted from the earth at the places where St Paul's severed head had bounced three times. Excavations in the nineteenth century revealed traces of a seventh-century building. The sites of the three fountains are marked by three shrines.

51 St Anastasius. One of the buildings at the place, known in antiquity as Ad Aquas Salvias, where St Paul was executed (see above), is the church of Saints Vincent and Anastasius, the abbey church of the neighbouring Trappist monastery. The origins of this church go back to the seventh century when Pope Honorius I (625–638) built a convent to house some oriental monks. It was rebuilt in brick in the thirteenth century.

52 The Ladder to Heaven, Santa Maria Scala Coeli, is another of the buildings Ad Aquas Salvias (see above). The name of the church records one of St Bernard's ecstatic visions when, while celebrating Mass in the crypt, he had a vision of the souls in Purgatory ascending into heaven, released by his intercession.

53 The Church of the Annunciation of the Blessed Mary. The Church of the Sanctissima Annunciata is to be found close to the north end of the Ponte Vittorio Emanuele II. It is very close to the Ospedale Sancto Spirito. The present facade dates from the eighteenth century.

54 Blessed Mary Aracoeli (Altar of Heaven) and St Helena. See also Chapter 14. In Chapter 9 Wey states that St Helena's body is displayed in Venice – and it was until 2006/7.

The church of Santa Maria d'Aracoeli was built on the ruins of the temple of Juno Moneta. In the eighth century it was called Santa Maria de Capitolio. Its present name, which dates from the twelfth century, refers to the legend that it was here that the Virgin and Child appeared to the Emperor Augustus after he had asked the Tiburtine Sibyl whether there would one day be a greater man than himself.

55 St Luke: see below. See also Chapter 9, and the essay "The Icon of Our Lady of Philerimos", p. 228.

56 The Church of St Mary of the People, Santa Maria del Popolo, was founded in 1099 and rebuilt in the fifteenth century, being completed in 1477 after Wey's visit. St Gregory: see above. For paintings by St Luke, see above.

57 St Mary Rotunda. The Pantheon, built by Marcus Agrippa, was consecrated as a church by Boniface IV in 609 with the dedication of Santa Maria ad Martyres. It was, however, popularly called Santa Maria Rotonda or La Rotonda.

58 St Luke: see above.

59 The Bridge of St Angelus, Ponte Sant Angelo.

60 The Church of the Blessed Mary of the Portico used to stand on the site of the present Anagrafe on the north bank of the Tiber opposite the Isola Tiberina. When Rome was struck by the plague in 1656 the Romans prayed incessantly in front of the eleventh-century enamel image of the Virgin kept in the church. When the epidemic ceased it was decided to build a new sanctuary a little to the north to house the holy image. This is the church of Santa Maria in Campitelli, which was begun in 1661, and where the image is preserved in a Baroque glory above the high altar.

Quintus Aurelius Symmachus had been consul in 485. He was unjustly executed in 525 leaving three daughters, Rusticiana (the wife of Boethius), Proba and Galla. Galla's life and a brief account of her death are given in the Dialogues of St Gregory. She was widowed in the first year of her marriage and she decided to become a bride of Christ. She joined a community of consecrated women who lived near the basilica of St Peter. She died c.550.

61 The Church of St Bartholomew below-the-Bridges; San Bartolomeo. Two bridges, Ponte Cestio and Ponte Fabricio, connect the Isola Tiberina with the south and north banks of the Tiber

respectively. The Church of St Bartholomew stands on the island to the east of them, i.e. downstream – hence Wey's phrase "below the bridges". It is a site of the greatest medical and historical interest. Perhaps because of its boat shape, legend connects the island with the arrival of Aesculapius in Rome in 293 BC from Epidaurus in the form of a snake (see Chapter 9). A temple was built on the site where the snake hid. Under the Republic heartless owners could leave sick slaves in the sanctuary to seek the god's help for their recovery. If they recovered, the owners could not reclaim them into slavery. The pagan temple gave way to the Church of St Bartholomew. According to tradition, Rahere, courtier to the English King, Henry I, was nursed in the hospital attached to this church when he was suffering from malaria, a disease usually fatal at that time. Rahere vowed, if he was spared, to found a priory and hospital on his return to England. King Henry enabled him to fulfil this vow by granting him land in Smithfield in London where the church of St Bartholomew the Great and Barts Hospital still stand. One may assume that Wey was aware of the connection.

62 St Peter in Chains; San Pietro in Vincoli. The church, probably built on the site of a much older predecessor, was consecrated by Pope Sixtus III (432–440). See n75 below.

63 The Church of St Sylvester. There have been two churches of this name: San Sylvestro al Quirinale and San Sylvestro in Capite. Wey is probably referring to the latter, in the Piazza San Sylvestro, which was part of the Monastery of St Sylvester and became in recent times the Central Post Office.

64 St Praxes the Virgin. Santa Prasseda (Praxedes) was, according to tradition, the sister of Pudentiana (Santa Pudenziana – see below). The church was built by Pascal I in 822 on the site of a private house where Christian services were held in antiquity. It was altered in the thirteenth century and given additional decoration in the seventeenth and nineteenth centuries. There are fine mosaics in the chancel. In the right aisle is St Zenon's Chapel, which contains an oratory built in the thirteenth century to house a piece of the scourging column.

65 St Potentia the Virgin. Pudenziana was the sister of Praxedes (see above). By a doubtful etymology her name is derived from that of Pudens, a senator who lived in a house here and who gave hospitality to St Peter. In the second century there was a bathhouse on the site. In the fourth century a church was established in the baths. Neither Pudentiana nor her sister Praxedes was martyred but both are remembered for preparing the bodies of martyrs for burial. Although there have been subsequent repairs and additions, much remains which Wey would have seen, including parts of the fourth-century mosaic.

66 St Vivian is also known as Bibiana and Vibiana. Her feast day is 2 December. Little is known of her. Her *Acta* are a medieval romance much read and admired in Europe in the Middle Ages, especially in Germany and Spain, where many churches are dedicated to her. Since 1969 her official cult has been confined to her basilica on the Esquiline. "Falling sickness" was the name formerly given to epilepsy.

67 The Church of St Vitus and St Modestus. Together with Crescentia they were fourth-century martyrs. Sometimes Vitus was revered separately, sometimes with Modestus, as here, and sometimes, notably in Sicily, with Crescentia as well. In legend Modestus was the tutor and Crescentia the nurse of St Vitus. Their usual feast day was 15 June. St Vitus was invoked by those who suffered from epilepsy and nervous diseases, including St Vitus's dance (Sydenham's chorea) and from the bites of mad dogs and snakes.

68   The Church of St Martinus; San Martino ai Monti. Founded in the fifth century, it was dedicated to St Martin by Pope Symmachus (498–514). Pope Sergius II rebuilt it in the ninth century and added the name of St Sylvester to St Martin in the dedication.

69   San Lorenzo in Lucina, founded in the fourth century on the site of a *titulus* in the house of a woman called Lucina, was rebuilt or altered several times between the twelfth and seventeenth centuries. Three external features from the medieval church remain: the bell tower, the porch and the two lions flanking the door.

70   The Tullianum prison is the name given to the underground execution cell, the lower chamber in the Mamertine Prison. The Mamertine Prison consisted of two rooms, one above the other, hollowed out of the Capitoline Hill, and lies beneath the Church of San Giuseppe dei Falegnami. The list of famous prisoners who died here includes Jugurtha (104 BC), Catiline's fellow conspirators (65 BC) and Vercingetorix (46 BC). In the Middle Ages a legend arose that St Peter had been imprisoned here, hence the name San Pietro in Carcere, St Peter in Prison. The lower chamber, here described by Wey as "the Church of St Nicholas in Prison", was built at the end of 4 BC out of huge blocks of tufa arranged in a vault. It was used as a cistern or a tomb. Legend tells how Peter and Paul caused water to spring miraculously from the earth here so that they could baptise their gaolers. The spring and the pillar to which the prisoners were chained are still visible.

     By contrast, the Church of St Nichola in Carcere lies south-west of the Capitoline Hill and south of the Theatre of Marcellus, close to the Tiber. It was built in the eleventh century on the ruins of three ancient temples which stood side by side overlooking the Forum Holitorium. The word *carcere* in this dedication refers to a Byzantine gaol which occupied the left-hand temple in the seventh and eighth centuries.

71   St Alexis; Sant' Alessio. The church is on the Aventine. Inside it, on the left, is the staircase described by Wey. St Alexis was the son of a patrician family who set out for the Holy Land as a mendicant. He returned to Rome to die, but his family did not recognize him and he spent his remaining years beneath the staircase of his father's house. The legend of "the Beggar beneath the Stairs" was one of the main themes of the mystery plays in the fifteenth century.

72   Church of St Sabas; San Saba. When the monks of the Great Laura in Palestine, a religious community founded by St Sabas in the fifth century, were dispersed in the seventh century by the Persians and then by the Arabs, many of them took refuge in Rome in a building inhabited a century earlier by St Sylvia, the mother of St Gregory the Great. Towards the end of the tenth century the monks from the east constructed the present church on top of their earlier, seventh-century, oratory. Altered over the centuries, the building was restored in 1911. Some parts of the building which Wey would have seen still survive (Birch, *Pilgrimage to Rome*, p. 101).

73   Titus and Vespasian: see above. Wey here is echoing the medieval view that the destruction of the Temple in Jerusalem by the Romans was a manifestation of God's vengeance upon the Jews for the Crucifixion. Many stories calculated to stir up anti-Semitism were current in Wey's time (see Chapters 7, 9, and 12). Chapters 11 and 15, however, show that Wey was not as bigoted as some of his contemporaries.

74   The Church of St Gregory; San Gregorio Magno. Legend tells how St Gregory, in the sixth century, converted his house into a church and convent. The church was rebuilt in the twelfth

century and dedicated to St Gregory. The present building was restored in the seventeenth and eighteenth centuries. To the right of the chapel at the head of the south aisle is a little cell containing an ancient throne which passes for the one used by the saint.

75 The Church of St Peter in Chains. Wey appears to have confused two sites, San Pietro in Vincoli and San Pietro in Carcere. The well and the stone are in the latter church. In the former, consecrated by Sixtus III in the fifth century, are displayed two sets of chains, one of which bound the Apostle in Jerusalem and the other in Rome. The legend about the miraculous joining of the two sets dates from the thirteenth century.

76 The Church of SS Cosma e Damiano attracted the sick and suffering. Birch (*Pilgrimage to Rome*, p. 39) says that it was built on the site of a temple of Castor and Pollux which had been a pagan healing place. In Chapter 9 Wey says their bodies are in Venice.

77 The Church of St Gregory. In view of the reference to "the lance with which he slew the dragon", "St Gregory" is probably a misprint or a misreading for "St George". In 749 Pope Zacharias led a procession from St John Lateran to the church, then dedicated to St Sebastian, but which is now called San Giorgio in Velabro, to transfer part of the skull of St George. He changed the dedication to San Giorgio at the same time.

78 The Basilica of the Holy Apostles, Santi Apostoli, rebuilt in the eighteenth century, goes back to the sixth century when the Popes Pelagius I and John III dedicated it to house the relics of the Apostles Philip and James the Less. A porch built by Sixtus IV in the fifteenth century survives.

79 St John before the Latin Gate contains Romanesque frescoes of the twelfth century (Birch, *Pilgrimage to Rome*, pp. 137–40).

80 St Agnes outside the Walls and St Constantia. Saint Agnes has been venerated in Rome since the fourth century, but the early legends of her martyrdom vary considerably. Constantine, at the request of his daughter Constantia, built a church to commemorate Sant'Agnese whose relics lay buried in a catacomb on the Via Nomentana. Repaired by Pope Symmachus, the church of Santa Agnese fuori le Mura was entirely rebuilt in the seventh century by Pope Honorius I (625–638), who incorporated the virgin martyr's tomb within it. The apse was decorated with a fine mosaic which is still there today. Both Sigeric and Nikolas of Munkathvera visited it.

81 Agnes in Agony. Sant'Agnese in Agone. A small oratory was built in the eighth century on the spot where St Agnes was thought to have been martyred. It was rebuilt by Pope Innocent X. Borromini was in charge of the work from 1653 to 1657.

82 Quo Vadis? This church on the old Appian Way commemorates the legend of how Peter was fleeing from persecution in Rome and met Christ on the road. He asked Him, "*Quo vadis Domine?*" ("Whither goest thou, O Lord?"). Christ replied, "To Rome, to be crucified a second time", and disappeared leaving his footprints in the road. Ashamed, Peter turned around and returned to Rome, where he met his death.

83 Saint Mary of the Well. Santa Maria in Vallicella was rebuilt in the late sixteenth century. Its predecessor, supposedly founded by Gregory the Great in the sixth century, stood in the district called Pozzo Bianco, after the white well, a marble drain top from imperial Rome, which stood in front of the church.

84 St Mary of the Greek School is now called Santa Maria in Cosmedin. It started as a chapel for the Greek community below the Aventine on a site formerly occupied by a temple to Ceres.

This temple later became the Statio Annonae, once the headquarters of Rome's vital food supply organization. The word "School" refers to a charitable guild established (inter alia) for the relief of refugee Greeks from Asia Minor. (Compare the *scuole* in Venice described by Wey in Chapter 9.)

85 St Mary of the Way. The church of Santa Maria in Via was founded following a miracle when an image of the Virgin, painted on a tile, fell into a well, which then overflowed. The image reappeared. Pilgrims visited the well to drink the water and to venerate the Madonna del Pozzo.

86 Santa Maria sopra Minerva was founded in the eighth century near the ruins of a temple of Minerva. Begun in 1280, it is the only medieval Gothic church in Rome. It was modified towards the middle of the fifteenth century. It contains many notable works of art, including the tomb of the painter Fra Angelico, who died in 1455, only three years before Wey's visit to Rome.

87 San Pietro in Montorio. The present church was built at the end of the fifteenth century on a site where, according to a medieval legend, St Peter was crucified.

88 San Tommaso di Canterbury. The original church founded by Offa, in 775, was destroyed in 817. Rebuilt in 1159 it was then dedicated to St Thomas à Becket, who had stayed in the adjoining hospice. This hospice was started in 1362 by John and Alice Shepherd as a hostel for English pilgrims, so Wey himself could have stayed there.

89 There are now several churches in Rome dedicated to St Andrew, but the one most likely to figure in Wey's list is Sant'Andrea delle Fratte, founded in the twelfth century. It takes its name from the thickets, *fratte*, which grew in what was then the north-eastern limit of the city.

90 San Stefano Rotondo on the Coelian Hill, consecrated in the fifth century, could have been one of these.

91 St Eustace, according to legend, was a general under Hadrian. He was said to have been converted, as was St Hubert, by a vision of a stag bearing a crucifix between its antlers. He and his family were said to have been roasted to death in a bronze bull.

92 The church of San Crisogono, which was started in the fifth century and rebuilt in the twelfth century, contains several features Wey could have seen, including the belfry, added in the twelfth century, the floor of the nave (thirteenth century) and the underground church.

93 The basilica of SS Giovanni e Paolo commemorates two brothers who had served Constantine but were beheaded, under Julian the Apostate, in their own home on 26 June 362. It stands on the Coelian Hill and Wey could have seen its twelfth-century porch and campanile.

94 Santi Nereo ed Achilleo. While there was a fourth-century basilica with this dedication over the two saints' graves in Domitilla's catacombs, it had fallen into disuse by the end of the eighth century. Leo III then replaced it by rebuilding a little church previously called Titulus Fasciolae and giving it the dedication which it still bears.

95 Santi Quattro Coronati. The original fourth-century church lasted until 1084. Ruined by Robert Guiscard's troops, it was rebuilt in a smaller form by Pope Pascal II (1099–1118). From the twelfth to the fifteenth centuries it belonged to Benedictine monks, who added a cloister in the thirteenth century. It passed to Augustinian nuns in the sixteenth century. The identity of the four martyrs has not been firmly established.

96 One of these three churches is possibly that of San Martino ai Monti, founded in the fifth century, but completely altered in the seventeenth century.

97 San Clemente is one of the oldest Roman basilicas, founded in the fourth century and dedicated to the fourth Pope, Clement. It was rebuilt in 1108. Much still remains which Wey could have seen, including the Cosmati floor, the ambones, frescoes and the famous apse mosaic. A Mithraeum has been found beneath the basilica.

98 San Marcello was another fourth-century church. It was burned down in 1519 and completely rebuilt in the next two centuries.

99 La Madalena. The present rococo church is largely of the eighteenth century, but records show that in 1320 there was a small oratory here, together with a hospital, which belonged to a confraternity called The Disciplined.

100 St Vivian: see above.

101 The church of Santa Balbina was probably a fourth-century house converted into a place of worship. Thoroughly restored in 1926, it contains some thirteenth-century Cosmati work and frescoes.

102 Saint Prisca. According to one tradition she was baptised by Peter himself and was the first woman to be martyred in Rome. Another says she was the wife of Aquila, who is named by St Paul in his Epistle to the Romans 16:3: "Greet Priscilla and Aquila, my helpers in Christ Jesus". The church of Santa Prisca was rebuilt in the seventeenth and eighteenth centuries but its origin goes back to the second century, making it one of the earliest places of Christian worship in Rome. A Mithraeum has been found on the site (see note 97 above).

103 Saint Suzanna was thought to have been martyred in the house of Pope Caius where a sanctuary was probably established in the fourth century. The church of Santa Suzanna was rebuilt by Leo III in the ninth century and restored by Sixtus IV at the end of the fifteenth.

104 The Hospital of the Holy Spirit. The church of Santo Spirito in Sassia, built in the eighth century for Anglo-Saxon pilgrims, was sacked in 1527 and rebuilt in the sixteenth century.

105 Absolution: see Chapter 15.

15

The 1456 Pilgrimage to Compostella

SYNOPSIS

This chapter deals with Wey's pilgrimage to Santiago de Compostela in 1456 – a short journey compared with those of 1458 and 1462. He left Plymouth on 17 May and arrived back there on 9 June.

TRANSLATION
(Roxburghe, pp. 153–61)

An Account of the Pilgrimage Made by Master William Wey, Bachelor of Sacred Theology, Sometime Fellow of the Royal College of the Most Blessed Mary at Eton, to St James in Spain[1]

In the name of my God, I, William Wey, Fellow of the Royal College at Eton, in the Year of Our Lord 1456, inspired by divine grace and with the leave[2] of my King and Founder, Henry the Sixth, set out on a pilgrim journey on my own account to St James in Compostella in Spain. Leaving the Royal College on 27 March and arriving at the port of Plymouth on the last day of April, I waited there until 17 May. On that day six pilgrim ships set sail in company: one ship was from Portsmouth, another from Bristol, another from Weymouth, another from Lymington, another called the *Cargreen* and a Plymouth ship called the *Mary White*.[3] We were at sea until 21 May, when we came to the port of La Coruña about noon. The first place which we saw in that area of Spain is called Ortyngez, the second place we saw is called Cappryze (on the opposite quarter is the island called Sesarke); the third place we saw is called the Delavale Tower.[4] When these had been sighted the sailors lowered one sail and we entered the port of La Coruña. From there we went to St James in Compostella on the eve of the Feast of the Holy Trinity.

There I heard from the clergy of that Church of St James of Compostella that there is an archbishop who has under him in that church seven cardinals, a dean, a precentor, five archdeacons, a chancellor and two judges, all of whom have mitres and staffs. In addition there are eighty canons of that church. There are also twelve parceners;[5] three of them hold one prebend jointly. Moreover there are twelve parceners of the Holy Spirit and four *duplarii*, who receive a double stipend. These cardinals and bishops receive fifty ducats each year; and, if they are all in residence, a canon will receive twenty ducats each year. These cardinals do not wear amices or furred hoods in the choir, but merely surplices.

At Vespers for the Holy Trinity[6] there were six rectors choral in scarlet capes holding in their hands long staffs covered with silver. They sang the versicle and the *Benedicamus*.[7] Two cardinals in pontificals and wearing mitres, with pastoral staffs and a thurible in the right hand, censed the high altar with one hand and then, in similar fashion, the clergy in the choir. In the procession before Mass on the day of Holy Trinity there were nine bishops and cardinals in pontificals. The clergy of that church enquired if there were any gentlemen from England present. When the reply was given that there were, they were chosen before all other nationalities to carry the canopy over the Body of Christ. There were six there who carried the canopy and the names of four of them are Austile, Gale, Lile and Fulford.[8]

The Archbishop of St James at Compostella has twelve bishops under him, apart from those who are in his church. In the whole kingdom there are three archbishops: first the Archbishop of Compostella; second the Archbishop of Seville, which is a great Spanish city; the third is the Archbishop of Toledo. The last two have canons, not cardinals, under them. The offerings to St James in Compostella are divided into three. The archbishop has one, the canons, cardinals and bishops have the second and the third is reserved for the church fabric.

Next I came to the port of La Coruña where we stayed three days. We used these days in three activities. First in conversation throughout those days with a Jew,[9] then on the Wednesday we had a procession and a St Mary Mass with music, while on Corpus Christi we had a procession in the Franciscan church,[10] followed by a sermon in the same church by an Englishman, a Bachelor of Sacred Theology, whose text was 'Here am I, for thou calledst me.'[11] He concluded from his text that all the Englishmen present could say these words to St James, "Here am I, since by God's grace thou calledst me to come here and visit thy place." There was no other nation which had a conversation with a Jew, processions, a Mass and a sermon except the English.

In the port of La Coruña there were eighty ships with topcastles and four without. They included English, Welsh, Irish, Norman, French, Bretons[12] and others. The total of English vessels was thirty-two. We left the port of La Coruña on 28 May, and had vessels sailing ahead of us and astern in the Spanish sea. On 3 June we returned to the port of La Coruña and on 5 June we set out to sea again from La Coruña, arriving in Plymouth on 9 June. The first part of England to be recognized and sighted by our crew is called the Browsam Rock;[13] the second is called Long Ships, and there are three rocks; the third is called Popyl Hopyl,[14] the fourth Mount's Bay and the fifth the Lizard, of which it is commonly said:

> Be the man ne'er so hard,
> He'll quake by the beard
> Ere he pass the Lizard.

The highest mountain in Spain is called Sturies[15] and it always has snow on top. The University of Spain is called Salamanca.[16] There are five regions in Spain: the region of Spain, the region of Castile and León, and the region of Portugal, which are Christian; the region of Granada and the region of Balmaria[17] are both Saracen regions. Of these regions the Saracen King of Granada was captured by Lord Henry, King of Castile and León, in the year of Our Lord 1456. In this year he captured the largest city of Granada, which is called Málaga. (It is from here that the figs known as Figs of Malike come.) He held that Saracen king in custody in his kingdom and he wrote under his own seal to that king's cities and towns and to those living in them. As a token of his victory the King of Castile and León sent the King of Granada's crown, which was made of gold or gilded, to St James in Compostella. This crown was placed on the head of the seated image of St James[18] in the middle of the high altar on the day of the Holy Trinity in the year of Our Lord mentioned above, being a year of Indulgence at St James.[19]

In the same year a great tower built by the French at Bordeaux, using St Peter's bell-tower as a fortress, was swept away from the land.[20]

In the same year a man from the county of Somerset, who had vowed to make the pilgrimage to St James because of a great infirmity which he had, on arriving at the port of Plymouth, came to me for advice. Because he was afraid he would die from that infirmity he wanted to know if he could return home after making the vow. He believed that he could not escape this infirmity and therefore he preferred to die at home rather than on the way to St James. I advised him to go to St James telling him that it would be better to die on that journey rather than at his home, on account of the indulgences granted to those on pilgrimage to St James. Despite this advice he began his journey back to his own country. After travelling 20 miles in one day with great pain and distress, when he reached the inn where he intended to spend the night, he was healed from the infirmity which he had suffered for a long time. Realizing that he was completely cured he started his journey back to Plymouth, covering in the half day following as great a distance as he had completed in the whole of the previous day. He re-embarked and came to St James. I met him in the house of the Franciscans[21] at La Coruña where he told me this story on Corpus Christi Day.[22] I asked him if he had confessed about his journey homewards and he told me that he had.

Another miracle! One of those sailing on our ship had his purse cut from his belt.[23] He lost his valuables and all the money he had. He immediately made a vow to St James that if he recovered his property he would go to him stripped.[24] After he had made this vow, a Breton, who had cut his purse, was caught in the act of cutting another man's purse.[25] The pilgrim's purse was discovered in the thief's pocket, and so, with St James's help, he got it back. Immediately be set off for St James, stripped, as he had vowed. At that time the ship in which he had previously sailed was carried towards England with a favourable wind, but for four days it was so tossed about at sea that the sailors brought her back to La Coruña.[26] Three days later the sailors set sail again now carrying with them in their ship that pilgrim who had been robbed earlier and whom they had previously sent off on his pilgrimage.

The Song of the Spanish Children Who Danced before Pilgrims for Shillings and Pennies

St James of Compostella, grant you to return to your land.
St James, good Lord, grant you true forgiveness,
Fine weather, a good road, and a fair wind. Fare ye well.
Of your generosity give those who are here a shilling.[27]

The Things Which Follow I Heard in Spain[28]

Let all faithful Catholics who shall read the present letter and devoutly consider its contents understand that the most holy Apostle, James the son of Zebedee, moved by divine grace, visited Spain. In his lifetime the Patron Saint deigned to come to this place and, in addition, stayed here in order to spread and proclaim the Catholic faith to the unbelieving people at that time. In this very place the aforementioned Apostle stood, preached and taught. He led some to the Catholic faith, converting them from the great heresy which was rooted in their hearts. He then went back again to Judaea and there, in the city of Jerusalem, preached Christ's passion and the most holy faith to the people, namely Jews, Gentiles and other pagans. For this he suffered temporal death,[29] following the way of all flesh for the love of our Saviour, Jesus Christ.

After his death, by the workings of divine grace, his disciples took the saint's most blessed body and bore it to a certain port there called Joppa.[30] Here, by divine grace, they found a ship completely ready to sail. They placed the blessed Apostle's body in it and crossing the sea with great joy and blessing the name of the Lord arrived at this place in seven days. This place, where the aforesaid Apostle had declared the faith as I have related, is rightly described as the "harbour". This came about because it was the divine will that the whole of Spain which could not be converted in his lifetime should be taught the faith through his death. The Apostle's disciples arriving at this port carried from the vessel the most holy body they had brought. They sang continually the verse, "Thy ways are in the sea and thy paths in the great waters."[31] Praising the name of the Lord, they laid him on a stone which is today called "The Boat". The body lay on top of a second stone set in the same place. Nowadays this stone is called "The Patron". At once these stones accepted the body in a miraculous fashion. The first stone became hollow like a tomb, the other turned into a sort of seat. Pilgrims to Rome and elsewhere, who visited the body, broke these stones and carried pieces away with them, and as a result very many miracles occurred.[32] Because of this the stone which is called "the Boat" was thrown into the river, while the other stone, which is called "the Patron", was placed beneath the altar of St James at Padrón. The city is now called Padrón for love of him. Accordingly the Most Blessed Pope Gregory the Third,[33] taking cognizance of the truth and acting most devoutly towards holiness, made it known, bearing in mind that the Apostle's arrival both in life and in death had been shown to be a blessing, and so that the memory of his arrival should not perish and so that pilgrims should attain the reward for their great toil, by the authority of the most holy and indisputably powerful pontificate entrusted to him, granted to all, collectively and individually, who were truly penitent and had confessed and who gave some alms, as far as they could, from whatever they had, and who visited the aforesaid place and its stations joyfully and prayerfully, namely in the Church of St Mary of Iria,[34] which was one of the first churches in the whole of Spain, in which a bishop was first made and where there were twenty-eight holy bishops[35] who are buried in the same place, together with many relics of saints, both male and female, which are still there in like manner, to all who came there fifty-eight Lents of indulgence, as is more fully described in the privileges of the aforesaid church.

In the church of St James at Padrón, where the aforesaid stone – known as "the Patron" – is set beneath the altar, twenty fifty [sic] Lents. In the place where "the Boat" is, twenty-five Lents. In the place which is called "the Spring of St James",[36] where the Apostle stood and preached in his lifetime, twenty-five Lents. Moreover, all the aforesaid indulgences have been granted by the Holy Apostolic Fathers to those who visit the aforesaid places even if they have no presents to offer since those who have nothing can give nothing. In total all the indulgences come to 126 Lents of indulgences from the penances laid upon them.

These are the Relics Which Are Kept in the Aforementioned Places[37]

First and foremost the holy stone which is called "the Patron", on which the body of the Blessed James, son of Zebedee lay. This stone is now beneath the altar of St James in the church at Padrón.

Also "the Most Holy Boat". This is in the river. Pilgrims approach it and touch it physically in summer when the water level is low and the river dry.

On the hill in Padrón is the spring where St James set his staff, together with the great stone on which he stood when he first preached in Spain.

Also these are the relics which are kept in the church of St Mary of Iria at Padrón. First, on the altar in the chapel of St Martin, are the relics of the tunic of Our Lord, Jesus Christ, together with the relics of St Paul and St Andrew, Apostles, St Stephen, St Saturninus, St Romanus, St Isidore, St Emilianus, St Leocadia and St Eugenia. This altar was built in honour of St Mary and all saints.

The following are the relics which are kept in the church at Compostella where rests the body of St James, son of Zebedee. First and foremost the body of St James, son of Zebedee, nephew of the Virgin Mary, brother of St John, Apostle and Evangelist, whole and uncorrupted.[38] Next the body of St Fructuosus, bishop, the body of St Athanasius, the body of St Cucufatus, the body of St Theodore, a disciple of the Apostle himself, and the body of St Silvester, martyr and companion of the Apostle.[39] Moreover the head of St James, son of Alphaeus, Apostle,[40] is displayed to all in the treasury of the aforementioned church most clearly.

These are the Indulgences Granted by the Holy Fathers to the Aforesaid Church at Compostella

Whoever has come on pilgrimage to the church of St James, son of Zebedee, at any time, has one-third of all his sins remitted. If he should die on his way there, while there or during his return, provided he repents of his sins, they are all remitted to him. Moreover, all who go on any Sunday in the procession of the church of St James have, for each procession and ministration of the sacrament, forty days of indulgence, and similarly throughout the whole week. If it is a feast day they have 300 days in addition to the aforesaid indulgence of a third of all their sins. Moreover, on the eve of St James's Day and on the day itself and the feast of the dedication of his church, all who have gone there on pilgrimage have 600 days, both on the eve and on the day itself, in addition to the aforementioned indulgence of a third part of all their sins.

Likewise, all who hear Mass said by an archbishop, bishop or cardinal at the altar of St James have 200 days indulgence for each Mass, in addition to the aforesaid indulgences. All these privileges, listed above, have been granted and confirmed, in the manner described, to St James's pilgrims, who have confessed and are truly penitent, by bulls issued by the Holy Fathers of the Apostolic See.

Likewise Pope Callixtus[41] granted that, for the whole of the year when the Feast of St James falls on a Sunday,[42] those who come there on pilgrimage and are truly penitent and have confessed should be absolved from punishment and guilt. Again, by a bull of the Pope, St Callixtus, who was strongly devoted to St James, when the Feast of St James falls on a Sunday, all pilgrims who come to the mother church at Compostella in Galicia on pilgrimage, both on the

Eve and on the Day itself, are granted full indulgence from all their sins. This privilege applies throughout the whole year starting on the first day of January right up to the last day of the month of December next following, inclusively. Again by a bull of the aforesaid Pope Callixtus, which has been confirmed by his successors, it is granted and enjoined that anyone who doubts and does not firmly believe these remissions, privileges and indulgences of the aforesaid church at Compostella shall incur the grave sentence of excommunication by apostolic authority.

The aforesaid indulgences have been confirmed and granted by the lord Pope, Innocent the Second, and by Leo of blessed memory and by other Supreme Pontiffs.[43] The Supreme Pontiffs have graciously granted, moreover, to this same church at Compostella that on the Feast of the Apostle and on his translation and at any time, anyone who intends to go to the aforesaid church on pilgrimage may have the right, from the day that he leaves home on his journey, to choose a confessor, who shall have the power, by apostolic authority, to absolve, even in "papal cases", the pilgrims themselves, while they are on their way thither, or there or returning thence. Moreover it is contained in the said bull that any pilgrim coming to the church at Compostella who, having made his confession and being repentant, dies on the way there or there or returning thence, shall be completely absolved from all his sins. Amen.[44]

COMMENTARY

Of Wey's three pilgrimages, this was the one undertaken first but described last. Written after he had retired from Eton, it is the most polished of the three narratives. It was much shorter both in distance and duration than the two subsequent journeys. Since he was travelling in a Jacobean Holy Year he had many fellow pilgrims travelling with him to Compostella. Constance Storrs, for example, in her *Jacobean Pilgrims from England to St James of Compostella*, lists fifteen ships, which carried 970 pilgrims from England to Spain in 1456.

In this chapter Wey gives the names of four of his fellow pilgrims, all probably West Countrymen. This, together with some anecdotes about his adventures en route, gives an interest not found in the other two accounts.

NOTES

1   William Wey's word *quondam* – "formerly" – shows that this account of his pilgrimage to Compostella was written in Edington Priory, after he vacated his fellowship at Eton, probably at the age of sixty, in 1467. Although it was the first of his three pilgrimages, it was the last to be written up, but Wey gives such a wealth of precise information – exact dates, times and details of indulgences etc. – he was probably using notes made at the time.

2   A contemporary copy of the letter from Henry VI in 1457 giving special permission to William Wey, notwithstanding the Statutes, to absent himself from the College to go on pilgrimage "to Rome, to Jerusalem and to other Holy Places", is still preserved at Eton College. This document refers to Wey's extended pilgrimage in 1458 when he was away for thirty-nine weeks. The letter giving him leave for the pilgrimage to Compostella in 1456 has not survived. Clergy in the diocese of Exeter were usually given three months' leave to travel to Santiago (*ad limina Sancti Jacobi*). This was a generous amount of time but it took account of possible delays caused by bad weather in the Bay of Biscay.

3   For a list of ships licensed to carry pilgrims to Spain in 1456, see Storrs, *Jacobean Pilgrims*, p. 181. Cargreen is a village on the west bank of the Tamar in the parish of Landulph, see Davey, "Smugglers and Pilgrims", p. 22.

4   Ortyngez, Cappryez, Sesarke and Delavale Tower are probably Cabo Ortegal, Cabo Prior, Islas Sisargas and the Torre de Hercules. See Davey, *William Wey*, p. 52.

5   Parceners shared the duties and the emoluments of a prebendary. In this case twelve parceners discharged the functions of four prebendaries. Conversely, a *duplarius* was granted a double stipend.

6   Trinity Sunday in 1456 fell on 23 May. Vespers was sung on the evening before. Wey therefore completed the 75-kilometre journey from La Coruña to Santiago de Compostela between noon on 21 May and the evening of the 22nd.

7   *Benedicamus Patrem et Filium, cum Sancto Spiritu: laudemus et superexaltemus eum in saecula;* i.e. "Let us bless the Father and the Son, with the Holy Ghost: let us praise and exalt him for ever." This is one of the closing verses of the Benedicite, a canticle, based on Daniel 3:57, used as a thanksgiving after the Mass.

8   The identities of these four gentlemen are discussed in Davey, *William Wey*, pp. 64–100. They were probably John Austile, Thomas Gale, Sir John Lile and Sir Baldwin Fulford. All being armigerous, they are properly described by Wey as *generosi*.

9   There was a small but important Jewish community in La Coruña in the fifteenth century. The beautifully illuminated Kennicott Bible, now in the Bodleian (MS Kennicott 1), was completed for them there in 1476. As a bibliophile, Wey might have found a common interest with their leading members. See Davey, "The Pilgrim and the Jew", pp. 23–5.

10   The foundations of the Franciscan church in La Coruña can be seen today in the Jardines de la Maestranza beside the Paseo Marítimo. See Davey, "The House of the Franciscans", pp. 13–16.

11   I Samuel 3:5. The preacher was probably Wey himself. See Davey, *William Wey*, pp. 55–8.

12   For examples of reciprocal piracy and kidnapping by Cornish and Breton sailors involving pilgrims to Santiago, see Huchet, *Les Chemins de Compostelle en Terre de France*, p. 112; Davey, "Pilgrims and Pirates: Boscastle to La Coruña", pp. 34–7.

13　"Browsam Rock" is probably the Brisons.

14　"Popyl Hopyl" is probably the Runnel Stone; see Davey, *William Wey*, pp. 49–50.

15　"Sturies": the Asturias. The Asturian Kingdom in the north of Spain was Spain's Christian refuge in the ninth century. The mountain described by Wey is the Picos de Europa, the highest range in the Cantabrian Cordillera. The highest peak, at 2,648 metres (8,688 ft) is the Torre Cerredo, between Oviedo and Santander. It is only 20 miles from the sea, from which the snow-covered summit is easily visible.

16　The university at Salamanca was founded in 1215.

17　"Balmaria": possibly Almería.

18　The present, seated statue of St James, above the high altar in Santiago Cathedral, which is traditionally hugged by pilgrims, was carved in 1211.

19　In any year when St James's Day, 25 July, falls on a Sunday, the whole year is considered to be a Holy Year and special indulgences are given.

20　Today the church of St Pierre in Bordeaux is 200 metres from the banks of the Garonne, but it seems likely that land reclamation and flood defences have altered the course of the river in the past five and a half centuries. In Wey's time it could have been much closer to the river. The Bordeaux city archives have no record of the disaster described by Wey and it must remain uncertain whether the inundation was caused by an exceptionally high tidal surge or by flood water coming down the Garonne. Church towers, especially in the bastide towns of Aquitaine, were often fortified during the Hundred Years War.

21　The House of the Franciscans: see note 10 above.

22　Corpus Christi Day is the Thursday after Trinity Sunday. In 1456 it fell on 27 May.

23　A Breton cutpurse: see note 12 above.

24　The Latin word *nudus* normally means naked, but that is scarcely likely here. It might stand for *nudis pedibus*, "bare-footed", or, more likely, it means "with only the bare essentials" (cf. Virgil, *Georgics*, 1. 299).

25　Purses at this time were carried by means of loops through which a waist belt was threaded. Cf. the advice given in Chapter 9.

26　The timing of the return voyage to England is repeated by Wey from page 212. The original departure from La Coruña for home, with Wey on board but without the robbed pilgrim, was Friday 28 May. After a day's fair sailing there were four days of storms and the ship returned to La Coruña on Thursday 3 June. On Saturday 5 June, the ship set off again for England. By this time the pilgrim, who had lost and then recovered his purse, had arrived at La Coruña and was able to sail home with Wey. When Wey uses the words "three days later" he was counting inclusively.

27　For a longer discussion of this song, see Davey, *William Wey*, pp. 60–63.

28　This section of the 1456 Itinerary falls into three divisions:

   1.　The first is a version of a "Life of St James" where Wey appears to be using copies of documents seen or distributed at Santiago de Compostela and Padrón.

   2.　The second section is a concise list of the relics to be seen in Padrón, in St Mary of Iria and in the Cathedral of St James. This list was probably based on Wey's own notes taken at the time of his visit and incorporated straight into his narrative, since the mention of the two sacred stones and spring of St James at Padrón duplicates information given just a few lines before. Wey's notes continued with lists of the relics held in St Mary of Iria and the Cathedral of St James. This punctilious interest is in accord with William Wey's practice on his other pilgrimages. There are similar lists for Venice in Chapter 9 and Rome in Chapter 14.

3. The final section, the "Table of Indulgences", may be a transcript of an official schedule distributed or publicized by the authorities in Compostella (see Vázquez de Parga, *Las Peregrinaciones a Santiago de Compostela*, Vol. 1, pp. 151–2). As with relics, Wey was most diligent in recording the indulgences available to pilgrims at each of the shrines he visited; for further examples, see Chapters 9 and 14 *passim*.

29   According to tradition, St James made a visit to Spain at some time between the Crucifixion and his death in 44 AD. This story, however, is not now widely accepted. He is said to have made only seven converts before his return to Jerusalem where he was the first of the Apostles to be martyred by Herod Agrippa I. Then, two of James's disciples, Theodore and Athanasius, took his body to Jaffa and placed it in a stone ship which sailed miraculously across the Mediterranean, through the Straits of Gibraltar, northwards along the Iberian coast and up the River Sar to Padrón, known by the Romans as Iria Flavia. The two stones, one called the Boat (*Barca*) and the other the Padrón, became objects of veneration. The stone which Wey says was placed beneath the altar of St James is still to be seen under the altar in the parish church.

30   Jaffa is also known as Joppa.

31   Wey's phrase, *In mare vie tue et semite tue in aquis multis*, is an echo of Isaiah 43:16, where the Vulgate has *Haec dicit Dominus, qui dedit in mari viam et in aquis torrentibus semitam*.

32   Wey himself built an annexe to the church at Edington to contain his own relics and souvenirs. These included six stones which he had collected from various sites. See his "List of Gifts".

33   Gregory III was Pope from 731 to 741.

34   The Collegiate Church of St Mary at Padrón was once a cathedral. It was destroyed by the Arab general Almanzor and later burned down by the Normans. The thirteenth-century Romanesque portal still survives; the remainder of the present church is of later construction.

35   According to tradition, these bodies are those of twenty-eight bishops who took refuge in Iria Flavia from the Saracens. The other saints' relics are listed below.

36   The Spring of St James can still be seen.

37   Wey has just described the relics at Padrón in the previous paragraph. This is another example of Wey's duplication of material, probably collated from several sources.

38   The relics of St James are now contained in a nineteenth-century silver casket, kept in a crypt under the high altar.

39   Fructuosus, Bishop of Tarragona, was martyred in 259. His feast day is kept on 21 January.
     Theodore and Athanasius: see note 29 above. Their relics can still be seen in Santiago Cathedral.

40   The reliquary containing the head of St James the Less can be seen in the Treasury of Santiago Cathedral.

41   Pope Callixtus is said to have given this privilege to Compostella in 1122. Confirmed by his successors it is said to have been made perpetual in 1179 by Pope Alexander III by the bull *Regis aeterni*.

42 Holy Years at Santiago de Compostela are still celebrated with great ceremony. The Holy Door at the east end of the cathedral, which is walled up in other years, is formally opened by the Archbishop on 31 December and resealed a year later just before the start of New Year's Day. Holy Years occur in a complicated but regular cycle at intervals of six, five, six and eleven years. The year of Wey's visit, 1456, was a Holy Year.

43 See note 41 above.

44 Compare the final paragraph of Chapter 14 for a similar dispensation for pilgrims to Rome.

The Gifts of William Wey
to the Chapel at Edington

SYNOPSIS

This document is not a legal will but it does describe Wey's wishes for the disposal of his property at Edington. It is of interest since it lists, inter alia, some of the souvenirs Wey brought back from his pilgrimages.

TRANSLATION
(Roxburghe, pp. xxviii–xxx)
Written on a flyleaf at the beginning of Bodleian MS 565
in a contemporaneous hand

These be goods of Master William Wey, his gift to the chapel made in the likeness of the Sepulchre of Our Lord at Jerusalem.[1]

First, as for the altar, an her[2] and a canvas; four altar cloths, embroidered; two altar cloths, plain; two towels for the stages;[3] four towels to be used for wiping.[4]

Also two cloths of blue baudekyn.[5] Also two cloths of oworke[6] stained,[7] in that one is Our Lord with a spade in his hand,[8] in that other is Our L...... [half a line scratched out here]. Also three other right well-painted cloths of oworke; in the first is a crucifix in the midst; in the second Our Lady giving Our Lord suck; in the third is the Assumption of Our Blessed Lady.[9] Also two other cloths of linen cloth with three black crosses in each of them.[10]

Of Vestments

First, a pair[11] of vestments of green,[12] the orphrey[13] red. Also a pair of red vestments of the flex of red velvet, orphrey red silk. Also a pair of green vestments of baudekyn with borders of gold, the orphrey of red baudekyn.

Also a pair of vestments of white bustian,[14] the orphrey of green. Also beside that two albs and two amices and two girdles.[15]

Of Corporas

First, four corporas cloths. Also four corporas cases,[16] the first of cloth of gold, with Joachim and Anna,[17] the second of embroidered black silk, the third of white fustian,[18] the fourth of green *wyke*.[19]

For the Hanging of the Sepulchre Without and Within

First two curtains of blue buckram.[20] Also a cloth decorated with the Temple of Jerusalem, the Mount of Olivet and Bethlehem. Also a chalice of silver and overgilt weighing — ounces, made fast with a device of silver in the foot. Also three pair cruets of pewter.[21] Also three dishes of pewter. Also a paxbrede[22] with a crucifix. Also the vernicle[23] and a crucifix in paper closed to boards, the which came from Jerusalem. Also a reliquary of boxwood, in the which be these relics: a stone of the Mount of Calvary, a stone of Sepulchre, a stone of the Hill of Tabor, a stone of the pillar that Our Lord was stretched to, a stone of the place where the cross was hid and found, also a stone of the holy cave of Bethlehem.[24] Also a sacring bell[25] hallowed, written about "Jesus John *pyt ney*".[26] Also two prickets of lateen.[27] Also two standing candlesticks of lateen. Also a quire of paper[28] with the painting of Our Lord, His Passion. Also two pillows[29] of silk.

Other Goods Belonging to the Sepulchre

First a cloth decorated with three Marys and three pilgrims.[30] Another with the appearing of Our Lord Christ Jesu unto His Mother. Also a *mappa mundi*. Also a *mappa* of the Holy Land with Jerusalem in the midst.[31] Also two leaves of parchment, one with the Temple of Jerusalem, another with the Holy Mount of Olivet. Also a desk covered with black, and thereupon the books, one of *Matters of Jerusalem*,[32] the second folio,[33] *To every bayok*. Another of *Saint Anselm, his work*, the second folio *Meditacio vii*. Another *About the Life of the Holy Fathers*, the second folio *-rat amicus abbatis*. Also a stone in the which is the depth of the mortice of Our Lord's cross.[34] Also four questions[35] ordained to the Sepulchre.

Other Things of the Holy Land Made in Boards

First, in a board behind the choir, the length of Our Lord's Sepulchre, with the height of the door, the breadth of the door, the length of Our Lord's foot, the deepness of the mortice of the cross and the roundness of the same.[36]

Also by the clock house of the Sepulchre of Our Lord with two houses at the ends of the same.

Also in the chapter house there be three things, the Chapel of Calvary made in boards, the Church of Bethlehem, made with boards; the Mount of Olivet and the Vale of Jehoshophat, made with board.[37]

My will is that these afore-written be not aliened from the Chapel of the Sepulchre, neither from the Holy Monastery of Edington.

COMMENTARY

This document is written in Middle English, not Latin. The spelling is erratic in the extreme, but most of the words can be interpreted.

It raises the question of how Wey was able to procure the many possessions listed. Some of them would have been expensive. This question is addressed in the Introduction.

In the version presented here, only the spelling of unusual or obscure words has been kept. In other cases modern spelling and orthography have been used with a consistency which does not feature in the original. For example "our" is used throughout in place of *oure, ovre* and *owre,* and "crucifix" for *crvcyfyxe, crwcyfyxe* and *crucyfyx.*

NOTES

Much information about vestments can be found in Hope and Atchley, *English Liturgical Colours.*

1   The Chapel. Once settled in Edington it seems Wey had an extension built to the church there and likely traces of this are still visible. Inside the church, on the south side of the chancel, are the very handsome surroundings of a doorway which led through the exterior wall of the church into a room which now no longer exists, but whose foundations can be seen in the grass outside. This was probably Wey's chapel "made in the likeness of the Sepulchre". The decoration of the inside

doorway indicates a likely date of construction of about 1460–70 which coincides with the years of Wey's retirement at Edington.

2   *Her*. Possibly a hearse cloth or pall. One is recorded at All Saints, Bristol, in 1457: "an herse clothe steynyd with lettres of golde" (Hope and Atchley, *English Liturgical Colours*, pp. 117 –18).

3   Towels for the stages. Wey's *tuellys* appears elsewhere as *tuallium, tuala*. The word refers to the two altar hangings for the two stages (tiers or levels) of the altar, the upper and the lower. These are also variously described as the "dorse and redorse", "overdose and netherdose" and "reredos and frontal". The "reredos", originally a textile hanging, was later made of wood or stone.

4   Towels for wiping; i.e. purificators. these were cloths with which the celebrant in the Mass wiped the vessels and his own lips and hands.

5   Baudekyn. One of the group of textiles known as "cloth of gold". It was woven with a warp of gold thread or wire and a woof of silk. It came originally from Baghdad. Later the name was given also to rich silk brocades, shot silks and even plain silken webs. The word was also used to describe a canopy made of such material and then for a canopy generally, hence "baldaquin", "baldachin" and "baldachino".

6   *Oworke*. An obscure word. It appears to be a type of textile of intermediate value since it occurs in a sequence: "cloths of baudekyn"; "cloths of oworke"; "cloths of linen" (see note 19 below).

7   Stained means decorated in colour. The name of the London Livery Company, "The Painters and Stainers", preserves the connection.

8   Our Lord with a spade: see Chapter 7, note 111.

9   Assumption of the BVM: see Chapter 7, note 88.

      Oliver in *Lives of the Bishops of Exeter*, p. 359, lists similar items: "1 front *de lineo* stained *cum scriptura Honor Deo*" and "1 front *cum tuello annexo* stayned *cum Crucifixo, Maria et Johanne, Petro et Paulo*."

10   This "cloth with crosses" would have been used as a Lenten veil. Close parallels from this period are: "1 veil for Lent to be drawn before the high altar of linen with black crosses", London, St Stephen Coleman Street, 1466; "Three linen cloths stained with crosses for Lent", Cambridge, St Mary the Great, 1504; and "1 linen cloth stained with the Cross and other tokens of the Lord's Passion to cover the cross in the choir", Exeter Cathedral, 1506 (Hope and Atchley, *English Liturgical Colours*, pp. 48, 50).

11   Pair. A "pair of vestments" meant, in Wey's time, a suit of vestments containing up to six garments, as shown in the Inventory of All Saints Church in Bristol dated 1469/70 (Hope and Atchley, *English Liturgical Colours*, p. 192).

12   Green, red and white were three of the four principal liturgical colours, the fourth being black. Other colours are found, but they can be classified under these four headings (Hope and Atchley, *English Liturgical Colours*, p. 3).

13   Orphrey; from the Latin *aurifrigium*. An ornamental band attached to the edge or other portion of a vestment. They were often sumptuously embroidered.

14   Bustian; also spelled bustyan, bistyan and bustany. According to the *OED*, "A cotton fabric of foreign manufacture used for waistcoats and certain church vestments. Sometimes described as a species of fustian but sometimes mentioned as distinct from it". Hope and Atchley, *English Liturgical Colours*, suggest that *bustian* is probably a variant for *fustian*, which was "a coarse

twilled cloth, probably with a linen warp and a cotton woof. In England it was later imitated with wool."

15 Albs, amices and girdles. Together with the stole, maniple and chasuble they could form a suit or "pair" of vestments (note 11 above). The alb was a garment reaching to the heels with tight sleeves, normally made of white linen and girded around the waist. The amice was a linen hood tied around the neck and thrown back in the manner of a collar (Hope and Atchley, *English Liturgical Colours*, p. 251).

16 Corporas or *corporale*: a cloth on which the host was laid and consecrated. The corporas cases mentioned here are also called *burses* (Latin *bursa* a purse).

17 Joachim and Anna, see Chapter 7, note 55.

18 Black silk and white fustian; see notes 12 and 14 above.

19 *Wyke*. Meaning uncertain. As with *oworke* (note 6 above) it appears from its context to be a textile, ranked below silk and fustian. It may be an alternative spelling of "wick", the cotton used in the making of candles, and so here referring to a cotton cloth. Perhaps the modern "candlewick" used in bedspreads is connected with this.

20 Buckram. Originally a fine, thin cloth from Bukhara; "some there is white, made of bombase, so thin that a man may see through it." Later the name was given to a coarse material chiefly used for linings, cloths for poor folk etc. (Hope and Atchley, *English Liturgical Colours*, p. 253).

21 Cruets of pewter. The vessels in which the wine and the water for the Mass are brought to the altar.

22 Paxbrede; also called pax board or *osculatorium*. A small plate of ivory, metal or wood kissed by the celebrant, and sometimes by members of the congregation, at the Mass, to convey the "Kiss of Peace".

23 Vernicle: Chapter 7, note 47 and Chapter 14, note 16.

24 Six stones from:

(a) The Mount of Calvary; Chapter 7, note 116.

(b) The Sepulchre. In Chapter 7 Wey says that a stone lies on top of the Sepulchre "attached to it with cement to prevent it being opened" – doubtless to protect it from souvenir-hunters.

(c) Hill of Tabor. The Greek and Latin name for the hill, *Itabyrium*, fortified by Josephus against the Romans. It is about 6 miles east of Nazareth. It seems unlikely that Wey himself travelled that far north so he probably did not collect the stone himself from the site. He does however include Tabor in the gazetteer in Chapter 12 (list A number 78 and list B number 221).

(d) The Pillar; there were two. For the pillar in Caiaphas's house, see Chapter 7, note 104. For the pillar from Pilate's house, see Chapter 7, note 109. The latter was protected by a wooden grating.

(e) Where the Cross was found; Chapter 7, note 110.

(f) Bethlehem; Ch. 7, notes 140–142.

In Chapter 15 Wey describes how pilgrims to Compostella visited Padrón and broke pieces off the two stones "the Boat" and "the Patron". To protect them "the Patron" was subsequently placed for safety under the altar of St James's church in Padrón, where it can be seen today. "The Boat" was thrown into the river, but still pilgrims waded in to touch it when the river ran low. Chapter 15, note 32.

25   The sacring bell, also called the *Sanctus* bell, is rung at the most solemn portions of the Mass.

26   Jesus John *pyt ney*; if the last word represents *nos* or *nous* the inscription could mean "Jesus, John, pity us", but it may be simply a mistranscription for "pity me".

27   Prickets of latten. A pricket is a candlestick with a spike. Latten, also spelled latin, is an alloy closely resembling brass.

28   Quire: "A set of 4 sheets of parchment or paper doubled to form 8 leaves" (*OED*).

29   Pillows: cushions placed under books used on the altar.

30   Three Marys and three pilgrims. This souvenir perhaps had a special meaning for William Wey. See Chapter 9, note 16, and Davey, *William Wey*, pp. 79–81. According to John 19:25, the three Marys were the BVM, Mary Magdalene and Mary the wife of Cleophas. Chapter 7, note 106.

31   *Mappa* of the Holy Land. This is probably the *Mappa Terrae Sanctae* in the Bodleian, MS Douce 389. See Davey, *Pilgrimage*, pp. 88–90.

32   "Matters of Jerusalem". *The Itineraries*, Bodleian MS 565.

33   The second folio. One way of identifying a book at this time was by giving its title and also the first few letters at the start of the second folio. "The earliest considerable catalogues to record the opening words of the second leaf of each book (*secundo folio*) are those of Dover (1389 AD) and Durham (1391). This very good method of distinguishing books became the almost universal one" (Ker, ed., *Medieval Libraries of Great Britain*, p. xx). Wey uses a different convention towards the end of Chapter 6, when he gives references to books by *Lincolniensis* (Robert Grosseteste), *Magister Historiarum* (Petrus Comestor) and Bede by quoting chapter numbers. Chapter 6, notes 30–32.

34   The mortice is mentioned in Chapter 3, line 85. See also Chapter 7.

35   The Questions. Chapter 9, note 85; Chapter 11, notes 63 and 64.

36   Length, height, breadth, depth etc. Wey was conscientious in recording such dimensions.

37   The models made in boards. A rather later example of these is the model of the Church of the Holy Sepulchre in the Bodleian Library (Library Object 605). This model, dating from the seventeenth century, is made of olive wood, ivory and mother-of-pearl inlay, and comes apart for easier transport (illustration in Davey, *Pilgrimage*, p. 30). There is a similar one in the Museum of the Order of St John in Clerkenwell.

Wey's models were "made with boards" – i.e. of thin strips of wood. When one recalls the difficulties of Wey's return journey from Jaffa to Venice, 2,300 miles in a galley with a sleeping space of 6 ft × 1½ ft and restrictions on the amount of luggage carried, to say nothing of the rest of the route across Europe from Venice to Eton, whether by horse, mule or barge, it seems impossible that Wey could have brought his models back ready assembled. Possibly he bought them in "flat packs for home assembly". Even that would have presented problems of weight and bulk. Perhaps it is more realistic to assume that Wey brought back sketches, which, together with his measurements, enabled him, or a craftsman in Eton or Edington, to construct them.

APPENDIX II

Essays

THE ICON OF OUR LADY OF PHILERIMOS

In describing his voyage home from his 1462 pilgrimage to the Holy Land, William Wey wrote,

> We reached Rhodes on 19 August. There I heard that there is a castle and a small town, called Philerimos, six miles from Rhodes. There is a painting there of the Most Blessed Mary which was sketched by St John the Evangelist when he was on the island of Patmos 150 miles from Rhodes. This was afterwards painted by others. It is the first picture which was made in honour of the Most Blessed Mary and many miracles occurred there.

It was a dangerous time in the Eastern Mediterranean because the Turks were attempting to avenge the defeats inflicted on them in the "County of Greater Wallachia" by Lord Flak, known to posterity as Vlad the Impaler, the model for Bram Stoker's fictional Count Dracula. The Grand Master believed that an attack on Rhodes was imminent. He summoned the Knights and ordered them to lay in stores of wheat and wine to withstand a siege of two years. On the north side of the Grand Master's Palace there were huge underground storerooms on three levels, so vast that Suleiman the Magnificent's doctor, Ramadan, who described the second great siege of Rhodes, said they could hold all the inhabitants of the city together with their possessions. There were ten huge circular silos for storing grain, three of which can still be seen.

Wey and his fellow pilgrims did not wait to see if the Turks would arrive. They reached Cande (Heraklion) in Crete on 5 September and Motys (Methóni) on the 20th. They arrived in Venice on 11 October, setting off for England two days later and getting to Dover on 1 December.

*

For many years now my wife and I have been following Wey's route from Eton to the Holy Land, endeavouring to see as many as possible of the sites he names and the relics and shrines he describes. His account of the Icon of Our Lady of Philerimos especially intrigued us and we decided to try to track it down. In 1998 we were in Rhodes and while there visited Philerimos, a few miles outside Rhodes town. A Christian basilica was built over the pagan temple of Athena Ialysia in the fifth or sixth century and the foundations of the latter and the distinctive baptistery of the former can still be seen. The basilica later became a single-aisled Byzantine chapel and later still the sanctuary of this church became the entrance to a medieval successor built to house the icon of Our Lady of Philerimos. The church was enlarged in the fifteenth century and has been restored in recent times. The *castrum*, castle, which Wey mentions, still stands nearby, although this too has been altered over the intervening centuries.

We went to Rhodes with a number of questions arising from Wey's narrative. While we were there we called at the office of Ms Anna Maria Kasdagli, director of the 4th Ephorate of Byzantine Archaeology of the Dodecanese, who received us with the greatest kindness. Not only did she answer all our questions about the buildings, sites and coins mentioned by Wey, but when we came to the icon of Our Lady of Philerimos she gave us a photocopy of an entry from a recent Maltese publication, *The Order's Early Legacy in Malta*, by Canon John Azzopardi. In this (pp. 20–23) he describes the history of the icon up to 1941. It was the most precious possession of the Knights Hospitaller, being already an object of veneration at Philerimos before the Knights conquered the island in 1306–09. The Rhodians believed that it was painted by St Luke and brought to Rhodes from Jerusalem in about the year 1000. Its fame as a wonder-working image was known all over the Aegean. During the sieges of Rhodes by the Turks in 1480 and 1522 the icon was moved inside the walls of Rhodes for safety.

The Turks attacked Rhodes in June 1522 and, after an epic siege, the Grand Master and 180 surviving brethren left the island on 1 January 1523. The icon went with them to France and Italy during their seven-year exile, being venerated between 1524 and 1527 in the collegiate church of SS Faustino and Giovita at Viterbo. In 1529 the Order settled in Malta and the icon was placed in the church of St Lawrence at Birgu, where it escaped damage when the church was destroyed by fire in 1532. After the building of Valletta it was transferred first to the church of the Virgin of Victories and subsequently to the conventual church, where it had its own chapel. After Napoleon evicted the Knights from Malta in 1798, the Grand Master, Ferdinand von Hompesch, was allowed to take the icon, together with the other two principal relics, the hand of John the Baptist and a splinter from the True Cross, away from the island.

These three relics were presented on 12 October 1799 to the Tsar of Russia, Paul I, who had been elected Grand Master by a few rebel Knights, by the Count de Litta, the Order's representative. After the death of Paul I in 1801 the icon was transferred to the Winter Palace in St Petersburg. When this palace was stormed in the Bolshevik Revolution of 1917 the icon survived because it was in a church 40 kilometres away, at Gatchina, where it had been taken, together with the other relics, for a celebration in honour of the Knights on 12 October. The Dowager Empress, Maria Feodorowna, escaped to her native Denmark, with the help of the British Royal Navy, via Yalta, on board HMS *Marlborough*, taking these relics with her. It seems that the empress might have intended to entrust them to the Russian monastery of St Pantaleimon on Mount Athos, but, in fact, before she died in 1928, she gave them to her daughters, the Grand Duchesses Xenia Alessandrowna and Olga Alessandrowna. They in turn passed them to the president of the Synod of Russian Orthodox Bishops in Exile, Archbishop Antoniye of Kiev and Galizia. After a brief spell in the Russian Church in Berlin they were transferred, in 1929, to Belgrade where, in April 1932, they were officially consigned to the custody of King Alexander I of Yugoslavia. They stayed in the chapel of the royal palace until 1941 when, because of the threat of the Nazi invasion, they were sent to the Orthodox Monastery of Ostrog in Montenegro.

At this point Canon Azzopardi's account concludes with the words, "Nothing has been heard of them since." Ms Kasdagli, however, told us that she had heard a rumour that the icon was still in Montenegro.

We decided the next stage would be to write to the archivist of the Sovereign Military Order of Malta at its present headquarters in Rome. In a most helpful reply the Order's archivist, Dr Valeria Maria Leonardi, told us that while it had been assumed for a long time that the icon had been destroyed in the bombardment of Belgrade in 1941, an article had recently appeared, in *L'Osservatore Romano* of 24 March 2001, by an art historian, Giovannella Berte Ferrarsi, in which she claimed that she had discovered the icon in the National Museum of Montenegro in Cetinje. I wrote to the director, Petar Ćuković, enquiring if the icon was indeed in his Museum and could be seen by the public. He answered by return, in English, and, in addition, most kindly telephoned me to say that the icon was on display to the public in the Museum in Cetinje.

My wife and I had already arranged an itinerary following Wey's progress down the Adriatic from Venice to Dubrovnik visiting all the places he mentions: Poreč,

Rovinj, Pula, Zadar, Sibenik, Trogir, Split, Hvar and Korčula. To see the icon meant extending our journey to Montenegro so we added four more places named by Wey: Kotor, Budva, Antibari and Ulcinj – this last almost on the Albanian border. From Budva it would be only a short distance over the mountains to Cetinje, the former capital of Montenegro when it was a kingdom. Getting from Dubrovnik to Budva was not easy but we eventually achieved it by taking a taxi, which made the frontier crossing from Croatia into Montenegro, which was then part of the joint Serbia–Montenegro state, all that was left of the old Yugoslavia, much simpler. There was a bus from Budva to Cetinje but no scheduled service back. This struck us as strange but we later found out the reason. One simply waited at the bus stop in Cetinje hoping that an entrepreneurial bus operator would arrive to take one back!

On 4 June we left Budva on the 9.30 a.m. bus to Cetinje. It was a spectacular drive over the mountains, which were covered with forests. Once in Cetinje we had difficulty in finding our way to the Museum, although we had taken the precaution of telephoning the director's office the day before to confirm our visit. After one set of misdirections from a shopkeeper, we stopped a student who spoke some English and who pointed us in the right direction. We arrived first at a museum which we later discovered was the former royal palace. There one of the staff redirected us to the National Museum of Art, where we reported to the front office and were taken up to Petar Ćuković's office. We were greeted royally and were soon escorted, with our own personal interpreter, to the special room where the icon is on display. We were not disappointed. The director had been at great pains to display the treasure in a fitting manner. The colour chosen for the surrounding decor was "Klein" blue, and the director explained to us his reasons for selecting this tone. The icon was covered by a sheet of glass to protect it from overenthusiastic lips, but the sympathetic manner in which it was displayed respected it both as a religious icon and as a work of art.

The icon measures approximately 15½ × 12 inches (44 × 36 cm) and depicts the face of the Virgin looking to her left. Mr Ćuković said that experts had variously dated it to between the ninth and eleventh centuries. Because of its age and fragility it is very dark and the features are not immediately or easily distinguishable. The director explained that the eight white triangles which jut out around the Virgin's halo are actually the tips of a Maltese Cross, something which is not at first sight apparent. The icon is "dressed" with precious stones, principally rubies and sapphires, whose monetary value is enormous – another reason for the security which surrounds the icon and its gallery. A copy of the icon was commissioned by Tsar Nicholas I in the early nineteenth century and is now displayed in the Basilica of Santa Maria degli Angeli at Assisi; a photograph of the original was taken in 1932.

On returning to the director's office for coffee Mr Ćuković informed us, to our surprise and delight, that the other two relics, so prized by the Knights Hospitaller, the hand of the Baptist and the splinter of the True Cross, were in St Peter's Monastery, only a short distance away. We spent the rest of the day on our own personal tours, with English-speaking specialists, of the other four museums which form the historical and artistic heart of Cetinje and, late in the afternoon, in the treasury of the Monastery of St Peter Petrović, we saw these relics also. A small casket contains the Baptist's hand, which still has one arm of a broken Maltese Cross attached to it.

The director told us what had happened to the relics after 1941. They had remained in the Monastery of Ostrog until 1952 when they were taken to the State Treasury in the new capital of Montenegro, Podgorika. They remained there until 1978, when they were placed in their present homes in Cetinje.

If anyone wishes to see these relics they would be well advised to inform the museum authorities of their interest. As mentioned above, there are five museums on a "campus" in Cetinje and guided visits, organized by travel agents in Croatia to Montenegro, steer groups mainly to the Palace of King Nikola I. While this houses a most interesting collection, including, incidentally, a portrait of the Dowager Empress who rescued the relics, the Museum of Art and the Monastery of St Peter do not appear to figure on the usual itinerary. We cannot speak too highly of the welcome we received from the director and all his colleagues, and we are most grateful to them for their kindness and hospitality.

WEY'S SERMONS AND SYON MONASTERY

In view of Wey's extensive knowledge of St Bridget's writings and the gift of his *Sermons* to the Bridgettine Monastery at Syon, I began a most interesting quest to see if the volumes of Wey's *Sermons* still exist, and, if they do, to discover if any of his four sermons, described in *The Itineraries*, are included in them.

Syon Monastery was the only house of the Bridgettine Order to be founded in England. St Bridget was born of noble parents in about 1303. In 1316 she married Ulf, who was to become Lord of Narke. Eventually Ulf and Bridget went on pilgrimage to Compostella. On the return journey Ulf became seriously ill and vowed to enter a monastery if he recovered. He lived to return to Sweden but died in 1344 before he could fulfil his promise. After a series of divine revelations St Bridget founded the Order of Bridgettine Sisters.

In England there was considerable interest in this Order. In 1408 two priests were sent from the abbey at Vadstena in Sweden, where the first house of the Order had been opened, to report on the possibility of a foundation in England. Money was a problem, which was solved by using possessions sequestrated from French monastic cells, the alien priories, which suffered as a result of the wars between England and France. Early in 1415 King Henry V laid the foundation stone of the new monastery at Twickenham. Five years later, on 28 January 1420, the new community was solemnly enclosed, the first professions taking place on 21 April 1420.

The original site was soon found to be unhealthy and too cramped for the growing community. In 1426 work began on a new set of buildings at Isleworth, which were completed in 1431. The full strength of the foundation was intended to be 60 sisters, 13 priests, 4 deacons and 8 lay brothers, giving a total of 85 which is the number of the 13 Apostles (including St Paul) and the 72 Disciples of Christ.

The monastery's estates were scattered over fourteen counties and at one time included the priory of St Michael's Mount in Cornwall (lost under Henry VI and restored by Edward IV).

F.R. Johnston in *Syon Abbey* writes:

> The convent possessed one of the finest libraries in England, many of the volumes being presented by the brothers themselves when they were professed. Good use of it was made in the preparation of sermons and for literary work. Its resources were also available for friends of the community such as the Oxford Chancellor, Thomas Gascoigne, who was a keen student of St Bridget's *Revelations* and the author of a life of the saint.

The monastery suffered much in the 1530s and was finally suppressed on 25 November 1539; some members of the community were pensioned; others, splitting into groups, went to Denham in Buckinghamshire and to Antwerp, moving later to Termonde.

On the accession of Queen Mary some of the survivors returned to England and in 1557 they were solemnly re-enclosed. This state did not continue for very long. When Elizabeth became queen the Monastery was again suppressed and the members left England, under the protection of the retiring Spanish ambassador, in 1559.

There followed three centuries of exile until 1861. After twenty-two years in Flanders (Termonde, Hemstede, Mishagen, Antwerp and Malines) the community moved to Rouen in France. In 1594 the twenty-two sisters and seven brothers moved to Lisbon. In Portugal they suffered various setbacks including a fire in 1651, when most of their archives were destroyed, and the earthquake of 1755, when their buildings were razed to the ground.

In 1809 some of the community returned to England, eventually settling in Staffordshire, but this group died out through lack of postulants. A smaller group of four choir sisters and three lay sisters remained behind in Lisbon. Ten postulants joined them in 1816 and 1817. Eventually in 1861 the community returned to England, settling in a convent at Spettisbury in Dorset. In 1887 they moved to Devon, first to Chudleigh and then, in 1925, to Marley, South Brent. In the period 1986–87, sadly, three sisters died and the building at Marley, now known as Syon Abbey, was much too large for the order's foreseeable needs. Enquiries were made of other enclosed orders to investigate the possibility of sharing accommodation. These enquiries came to nothing and the decision was made to remain on the site but in other buildings. Accordingly the stables and other farm buildings were converted between December 1989 and October 1990. The new monastic buildings were blessed on 2 February 1991. The new small chapel contains the large painting of Our Lady which had been left by its owner for safe keeping at the Lisbon monastery, while he went on pilgrimage to Compostella, but which was never collected on his return.

So much for the travels of the members of the Order. What about their books? Did they survive these peregrinations?

In *Medieval Libraries of Great Britain: A List of Surviving Books* by N.R. Ker, over ninety books which once belonged to Syon are listed. There is only one volume of *Sermones dominicales* of the fifteenth century listed there (p. 186). In Ker it is given the press mark P 51, whereas the *Sermones etc* listed by Bateson have the press mark Q 14, so they are probably not the same. It has to be said that there were several volumes of sermons by various authors in the library.

At the time of Ker's *List* (2nd edn 1964) this volume of *Sermones* was in the possession of Mr J.S. Cox of Morcombelake. By the time of Ker's *Second Supplement* the owner had moved to the Channel Islands, where he had a printing company. The Society of Antiquaries was able to confirm that Mr Cox had been a fellow of the Society. His son, Dr Gregory Stephens Cox, who lives in Guernsey, informed me that his father had died and that his library was now in his possession. Dr Cox told me that his father had always been most helpful to research scholars who wished for information about his books and that he was pleased to continue the tradition. He informed me that this particular volume was not William Wey's book of sermons.

In Ker's *List* (p. 187) Syon Abbey is shown as still having five of its original books. As the sisters at Syon Abbey had recently moved into their new, smaller, accommodation, I thought it likely they would have placed their books elsewhere. I therefore wrote to the Devon County Librarian asking if he knew their whereabouts, and he informed me that "the library formerly of Syon Monastery has been deposited with the University of Exeter". I accordingly visited the University Library and was given access to the collection. Again William Wey's *Sermons* could not be found and one must wonder if they still exist.

WILLIAM WEY'S OWN BOOKS

William Wey fully appreciated the value of books. Not only did he own some splendid volumes himself, three of which can still be seen in Eton College, but he made sure that they would find suitable homes after his death.

Wey left three (1, 2 and 3 below) to Edington Priory in Wiltshire, where he spent the last years of his life. One of these was *The Itineraries* (1), now in the Bodleian Library, Oxford (Bodleian MS 565). He gave two other volumes (4 and 5), titles unspecified, to Exeter College, Oxford, in 1457. These are recorded in the Register of the Rector, Fellows etc. for summer 1457 but they are no longer there. The next group of books (6, 7 and 8) was donated to Eton College. They are still there. Finally he gave Syon Monastery two volumes of his own sermons (9 and 10). The present whereabouts of these books is unknown.

The Ten Books

1   *One of materys of Jerusalem*; the second folio *"to every boyok"*.

2   *Synt Anselme ys works*; the second folio *"meditacio vij"*.

3   *De vita sanctorum patrum*; the second folio *"-rat amicus"*.

4, 5 recorded in the *Exeter College Register, uni adducenti duo volumina Collegio a Willelmo Wey missa, iiis iiiid*: "[Payment] to the person who brought the two books which were sent by William Wey to the College, three shillings and four pence."

6   Chrysostom, *Opus Imperfectum in Matthaeum* (Eton Coll. MS 42).

7   Jerome, *In Danielem*; Berengaudus, *In Apocalypsim* (Eton Coll. MS 76).

8   P de Natalibus, *Secunda Pars Catalogi Sanctorum* (Eton Coll. MS 99).

9, 10 *Sermones de festis principalibus et sanctis cum aliis multis sermonibus generalibus.*

These volumes are listed in *The Catalogue of Syon Monastery Library*, Corpus Christi College, Cambridge, MS 141, pp. 162 and 164. See also Mary Bateson, *Library of Syon Monastery*, p. 244. The entry reads:

> *Willelmus Wey in suis sermonibus dominicalibus super euangelia. Q 14.*
> *Idem in sermonibus de principalibus festis et aliquibus sanctis cum aliis*
> *sermonibus generalibus. Q 14. fo. 236.*

There also appear to have been four tables. The entry in Bateson reads:

> *Wey Q 14. q. 12. Sermones dominicales super Euangelia per totum annum. Item sermones de festis principalibus et sanctis cum aliis multis sermonibus generalibus. fo. 236. Tabula docens principia et foliaciones sermonum dominicalium et festivalium fo. 276. Item. Tabula secundum ordinem alphabeti super sermones praedictos. fo. 277. Item tabula notabilium sermonum predictorum. fo. 280. Item Tabula narrationum in sermonibus dictis contentarum. fo. 285.*

ANDREA MOROSINI OF VENICE, WILLIAM WEY'S *PATRONUS*

Andrea Morosini's voyages were not always uneventful. In 1463, the year after Wey's third pilgrimage, Morosini again carried pilgrims to Jaffa. The two pilgrim galleys which sailed from Venice that year were the *Contarina*, whose *patronus* was Ser Andrea Contarini, and the *Morosina*, whose *patronus* was Ser Andrea Morosini. Hostilities had broken out between the Turks and the Venetians. The Turks had already taken the Peloponnese, as Wey discovered when his galley put in at Methóni on 27 June 1462 when he wrote:

> *Audivi eciam quod Turcus adquisierat Lamoreiam, quae est in Grecia, quam possederunt Greci.* ("I heard also that the Turk had taken Lamoreia, which is in Greece and which was occupied by Greeks.")

The Turks were now threatening not only Rhodes but also the important Venetian fortresses of Methóni and Coroni, known as "the eyes of the Serene Republic". It was vital for Venice to deploy reinforcements quickly to protect them. When the *Morosina* and the *Contarina* put in at Candia with pilgrims on their way back to Venice from Jaffa, the Governor seized his opportunity. The two large galleys, which were, in any case, going in that direction, would serve his purpose well as troop ships. They were at once requisitioned by the Governor to carry soldiers to the "island of *Amorea*". This is Wey's *Lamoreia* – the Peloponnese – which was then known as the "Morea", a term still found.

On their eventual return to Venice the two *patroni*, Andrea Morosini and Andrea Contarini, claimed compensation and were awarded fifteen "large *lire*" each by the Senate on 26 September 1463. This episode is described in *The Calendar of State Papers; Venetian, 1202–1509*.

William Wey himself gives tantalisingly few names of people he met during the course of his itineraries. One he does mention was John Tiptoft, Earl of Worcester, who was a fellow pilgrim to Jerusalem in 1458. Two Venetian galleys carried pilgrims that year. Tiptoft's was the *Loredana*, and the Venetian records confirm that its original *patronus* was Ser Antonio Loredano, who stood down in favour of his kinsman, Baldesar Diedo, so that he could act as personal escort to Sir John Tiptoft. The names of Wey's galley and his *patronus* are not known. The *Loredana* went to the Holy Land again in 1459. On that voyage the Venetian Senate, which was anxious that their city's fragile relations with the Turks should not be compromised by contact with the Knights of Rhodes, who were continually engaged in hostilities with the Turks, forbade the officers and crew of the galley to land on Rhodes.

There is a little more information about William Wey's *patronus* for his second Jerusalem pilgrimage four years later. In his account for 1462 Wey mentions him twice:

> *et tunc xxviij die Julii equitavimus ad portum Jaff et vespere intravimus in galeam…Patronus meus Andreas Morason tardatus erat per duos dies super terram apud Jaff, quousque solvisset novo domino Jerusalem l. ducatus.* ("then, on 28 July, we rode to the port of Jaffa and boarded our galley that evening… My *patronus*, Andrew Morason, was delayed two days ashore at Jaffa until he paid the new lord of Jerusalem fifty ducats.")

and

fideles et catholici viri istarum civitatum, et regni Hungarie, ad locum maris, ubi edificatur Venecia, venerunt, et ibi edificabant civitatem. Sic quidem magna pars generosorum Venecie traxerunt originem ab Hungariis, ex quibus dominus Andreas Morason patronus meus duxit originem. ("faithful Catholic men from these cities and from the kingdom of Hungary came to the place on the sea where Venice is built and built a city there. Thus a large part of the nobility of Venice derive their origins from the Hungarians. Lord Andrew Morason, the *patronus* of my galley, traced his descent from them.")

The year 1464 saw Andrea Morosini's name again in the Venetian records. As already noted, relations between Venice and the Knights of Rhodes were not always smooth, since Venice tried to avoid action which would disrupt her trade, whereas the Knights had little compunction about fighting the Turks and vice versa.

Three Venetian galleys, en route from Alexandria in 1464, laden with goods and carrying several Moors as passengers, were forced by a storm to take refuge in Rhodes harbour. The Venetians had felt compelled to accept the Moors as passengers since, being already at war with Mahomet II, they did not wish to offend the Sultan by refusing these merchants a passage, and so find themselves at war with him too. This was a real possibility as they had discovered that Mahomet II had already sent ambassadors to the Sultan urging him to attack Venice. Although they knew that the presence of Moors on the galleys could anger the Hospitallers, the Venetians sought the safety of Rhodes' harbour. The Grand Master of the Hospitallers, Pedro Raimondo Zacosta, using the presence of the Moors on board the Venetian galleys as an excuse, gave orders to seize the ships. In the ensuing fight many Venetians were wounded and some were killed. The Moors and their property were seized and imprisoned. Zacosta ignored all the Venetians' pleas for their release.

When the Sultan heard of this, he held the Venetians responsible and accused them of complicity with the Knights of Rhodes. In a tit-for-tat action he seized as hostages the Venetian nobles, citizens and merchants in Syria and Egypt, together with their property, and imprisoned them, in irons and under sentence of death, in Cairo.

The Venetian Senate had to take speedy and robust action. They ordered their captain-general, another Loredano, Jacopo, to proceed to Rhodes and take whatever steps were necessary, preferably not military, though that option was not excluded, to secure the release of the Moors. The situation was extremely delicate. Venice wished to avoid giving offence to a number of interested and belligerent parties but also had to consider the safety of some of its wealthiest and most distinguished citizens.

On arriving at Rhodes Jacopo Loredano spent three days in fruitless diplomatic negotiations, but the Grand Master, "instigated by incredible obstinacy and avarice", was obdurate. The Venetians alleged further that he went so far as to send an embassy of his own to make an agreement with the Turk. Jacopo Loredano lost patience and "resorted to other remedies". Zacosta gave in, releasing the Moors and restoring as much of their property as could be found.

At this point the actions of Jacopo Loredano seem to have caused annoyance, or worse, to certain Englishmen in Rhodes. Anxious to keep on good terms with King Edward IV and the English Knights of St John, the Doge, Christopher Moro, wrote a lengthy letter to King Edward describing the whole of this episode in detail and apologising if "anything disagreeable" to the King occurred. Copies of it were sent to "the Lord Robert, Prior of St John's of Jerusalem in England", the Earl of Warwick, and "the Reverend Lord Brother John Langstrother, most worthy Preceptor of the Order of St John of Jerusalem." This letter, dated 9 September 1465, is to be found in the *Calendar of State Papers: Venetian, 1202–1509* (p. 115, para. 397).

The Venetians were not yet out of the wood. To secure the release of their citizens they were convinced that they would still have to pay, "according to the Barbary fashion", a considerable ransom. They estimated that the damage done to them would "exceed the sum of many thousand ducats".

Unfortunately for Ser Andrea Morosini (Wey's Andrew Morason), he had arranged at this time to carry a cargo of timber, arrows and other equipment to Rhodes. The Venetian Senate, smarting from the action of the Grand Master, forbade Morosini, by a decree dated 28 September 1464, "to go to Rhodes or to any other place belonging to the Knights of St John" (Newett, *Canon Pietro Casola's Pilgrimage*, p. 83).

The Doge, who wrote the letter to King Edward IV, was Christopher Moro, whose election and coronation in May 1462 were depicted in such brilliant detail by William Wey, who was an eyewitness of the ceremony. The Grand Master, Pedro Zacosta, was the *Dominus magister de Rodys* whose orders for the defence of Rhodes and its provisioning were described by Wey while he was there in August 1462.

These events and the persons involved in them well illustrate the hazards faced by pilgrims like William Wey in the Eastern Mediterranean at this time.

The Morosini Family and Pilgrims to the Holy Land in the Fourteenth and Fifteenth Centuries

William Wey's *patronus* was not the only member of the Morosini family to be involved in the transport of pilgrims to the Holy Land in the later Middle Ages. The Venetian records show that for more than a century the Morosini were concerned with this traffic.

In April 1382 the senate ordered that about a hundred pilgrims going to the Holy Sepulchre should be taken on an unarmed galley belonging to Ser Andrea Morosini (Newett, *Canon Pietro Casola's Pilgrimage*, p. 36).

In April 1384 Ser Dardi Morosini was given leave to take a group of seventy or seventy-one, and Ser Andrea Morosini sixty-four, men and women pilgrims to Jaffa (Newett, *Canon Pietro Casola's Pilgrimage*, pp. 37 and 38).

In 1494 Don Alvise Morosini travelled as one of the "deputies", gentlemen apprentices who were the equivalent of midshipmen, on Canon Casola's galley. This young man caused much annoyance by returning late to his ship at the end of his run ashore in Rhodes (Newett, *Canon Pietro Casola's Pilgrimage*, p. 211).

More than thirty years after William Wey's second Jerusalem pilgrimage, yet another member of the Morosini family was engaged in the transport of pilgrims to Jaffa. Wynkyn de Worde's *Information for Pilgrims* was published at Westminster in about 1498 (see E.G. Duff, *Fifteenth Century English Books*). This book, number 225 in Duff's list, is described as being in the Advocates' Library in Edinburgh. Duff gives the following extract:

> The seuen and twentye daye on the monthe of Iune there passyd from Venyse under sayle out of the hauen of Venyse atte the sonne goyng downe certayn pylgrymes towarde Ierusalem in a shippe of a marchauntes of Venyse callyd Iohn Moreson. The patron of the same shippe was callyd Luke Mantell, to the nombre of xlvi pilgryme, every man payeng, some more, some less, as they myghte accorde wyth the patron. Some that myghte paye wel payed xxxij dukates, and some xxvi and xxiiij for meete drynke and passage to porte Iaffe.

Other Members of the Morosini Family

Wey's *Dominus Andreas Morason, generosus*, was Ser Andrea Morosini, a member of a distinguished Venetian family. Five hundred years before Wey embarked on Andrea's galley, the Morosini were famous benefactors of Venice, and two hundred years after Wey's death a member of the family became Doge.

In 982 Giovanni Morosini gave the island of *San Giorgio Maggiore* to the Benedictines.

The tomb of Doge Marin Morosini, who died in 1253, is in the Basilica of San Marco, and the tomb of Nicola Morosini, bishop of Torcello, who died in 1305, is in the cathedral on the island of Torcello.

In Venice, in the Campo Santo Stefano, which is also called the Campo Morosini, is the seventeenth-century Palazzo Morosini. The Palazzo Loredan, the home of the family which produced Tiptoft's *patronus*, mentioned above, is on the other side.

In the seventeenth century the Morosini family were visited at their house, the Casa Corner-Martinengo-Rava, by the astronomer Galileo Galilei.

Portraits of the Morosini family by Jacopo Tintoretto and his son, Domenico, are included in a painting of the Resurrection on the altar to the left of the high altar in the church of San Giorgio Maggiore. A series of Baroque monuments of the Morosini family, which were formerly in the church of San Clemente, are now kept in the Museo Diocesano in Venice.

Francesco Morosini, the elder, was a governor of Candia. A fountain, bearing his name, which he had built in 1628, can still be seen in the Plateia Venizélou in Herakleion. He was also responsible for the rebuilding, in 1626, of the fortress which guarded the harbour of Ierápetra and which had been damaged in an earthquake. His tomb, described as that of "the patriarch, Francesco Morosini, who died in 1678", is in the church of San Nicola da Tolentino. It was designed by Filippo Parodi.

On 5 September 1669 the Venetian commander of Candia surrendered to the Turks, who had started their siege of this "last bastion of Christendom in the eastern Mediterranean" twenty-one years before, in 1648. His name also was Francesco Morosini. This younger Francesco was perhaps the most distinguished member of this ancient family in the seventeenth century, being Doge from 1688 to 1694. His sword, a gift from Pope Alexander VIII, is in the Treasury of San Marco. As the admiral who conquered the Peloponnese in 1694, Francesco Morosini has two rooms devoted to him in the Museo Correr. The gate of the Arsenale is flanked by two colossal lions, sent by him from Piraeus as spoils of war and placed there in 1692. In the Palazzo Ducale is a huge triumphal arch, erected in his honour by

Antonio Gaspari in 1694, while his sepulchral seal, cast by Filippo Parodi in 1694, is in the pavement of the nave of the church of Santo Stefano.

The most lasting mark made by Francesco Morosini in Athens can be seen on the Acropolis. It was this Morosini who gave the order in 1687 to a young Austrian artillery officer to shell the Parthenon, which was being used by the Turks as a gunpowder magazine. The result is visible today.

Bibliography

Arocena, Felix. *Los Himnos de la Liturgia de las Horas* (Madrid: Ediciones Palabra, 1992).

Azzopardi, Canon John. *The Order's Early Legacy in Malta: the Sovereign Military Hospitaller Order of St John of Jerusalem of Rhodes and of Malta* (Valletta: Said International, 1989).

Bandinel, B., ed. *The Itineraries of William Wey* (London: The Roxburghe Club, 1857).

Barnes, R., and Branfoot, C., eds. *Pilgrimage; the Sacred Journey* (Oxford: Ashmolean Museum, 2006).

Bateson, Mary. *The Library of Syon Monastery* (Cambridge: University of Cambridge Press, 1898).

Birch, D.J. *Pilgrimage to Rome in the Middle Ages* (Woodbridge: Boydell & Brewer, 1998).

Brommer, P., and Krümmel, A. *Klöster und Stifte am Mittelrhein* (Koblenz: Görres Verlag , 1998).

Brown, Rawdon, ed. *Calendar of Venetian State Papers 1205–1509;* Vol. I. (London: Longmans, Green, Reader & Dyer, 1864).

Butler's Lives of the Saints, 4 vols, ed. H. Thurston and D. Attwater (Aberdeen: Burns & Oates, 1956).

Cambridge Medieval History (Cambridge: Cambridge University Press, 1911–36).

Corpus Christi College, Cambridge. *The Catalogue of the Library of Syon Monastery* (MS 141).

Davey, Eileen. *Northern Cyprus* (London: I.B. Tauris, 1993).

Davey. Francis. *William Wey: An English Pilgrim to Compostella in 1456* (London: Confraternity of St James, 2000).

Davey, Francis. *Pilgrims and Pirates. Confraternity of St James* (CSJ) *Bulletin* No. 63.

Davey, Francis. *Smugglers and Pilgrims. CSJ Bulletin* No. 69.

Davey, Francis. *The Pilgrim and the Jew. CSJ Bulletin* No. 72.

Davey, Francis. *The House of the Franciscans. CSJ Bulletin* No. 74.

Davey, Francis. 'William Wey', in *Pilgrimage, the Sacred Journey* (Oxford, Ashmolean Museum, 2006).

De Voragine, Jacobus. *The Golden Legend*, selected and edited by C. Stace (London: Penguin, 1998).

Duff, E.G. *Fifteenth Century English Books* (Oxford: Oxford University Press, 1917).

Emden, A.B. *A Biographical Register of the University of Oxford to AD 1500*, 3 vols (Oxford: Oxford University Press, 1959).

English Hymnal (Oxford: Oxford University Press, 1906).

Gunnis, R. *Historic Cyprus* (Nicosia: Rustem, 1992).

Harrison, F.L. *Music in Medieval Britain* (London: Routledge & Kegan Paul, 1958).

Hope, Sir W. St J., and Atchley, E.G.C.F. *English Liturgical Colours* (London: SPCK , 1918).

Huchet, P. *Les Chemins de Compostelle en Terre de France* (Rennes: Editions Ouest-France, 1997).

Hymns Ancient and Modern (London: W. Clowes and Sons, n.d.).

Johnston, F.R. *Syon Abbey: A Short History of the English Bridgettines* (Eccles: Eccles and District History Society in association with Syon Abbey, 1964).

Kempe, Margery. *The Book of Margery Kempe,* ed. B. Windeatt (London: Penguin, 1985).

Ker, N.R. *Medieval Libraries of Great Britain* (London : Royal Historical Society 1964).

Kollias, Elias. *The Knights of Rhodes; the Palace and the City* (Athens: Ekdotike Athenon S.A., 1998).

Kollias, Elias. *The Medieval City of Rhodes and the Palace of the Grand Master* (Athens: Ministry of Culture Archaeological Receipts Fund, 1998).

Latham, R.E. *Revised Medieval Latin Word-List* (Oxford: Oxford University Press, 1994).

Mitchell, R.J. *John Tiptoft* (London: Longmans, 1938).

Mitchell, R.J. *The Spring Voyage* (London: John Murray, 1965).

Mone, F.J. *Hymni Latini Medii Aevi,* 3 vols (Freiburg im Breisgau, 1855).

Newett, M.M. *Canon Pietro Casola's Pilgrimage to Jerusalem in the Year 1494* (Manchester: Manchester University Press, 1907).

Ohler, N. *The Medieval Traveller*, trans. C.Hillier (Woodbridge, Boydell & Brewer, 1989).

Oliver, G. *Lives of the Bishops of Exeter* (Exeter: Roberts, 1861).

Orme, Nicholas. *Medieval Schools* (New Haven CT: Yale University Press, 2006).

Orme, Nicholas. *The Minor Clergy of Exeter Cathedral 1300–1548* (Exeter: Exeter University Press, 1980).

Oxford Dictionary of the Christian Church (ODCC), ed. F.L. Cross and E.A. Livingstone (Oxford: Oxford University Press, 1997).

Prescott, H.F.M. *Jerusalem Journey* (London: Eyre & Spottiswoode, 1954).

Prescott, H.F.M. *Once to Sinai* (London: Eyre & Spottiswoode, 1957).

St Augustine's Abbey (The Monks of). *The Book of Saints* (London: AC Black, 1989).

Storrs, C.M. *Jacobean Pilgrims from England to St James of Compostella, from the Early Twelfth to the Late Fifteenth Century* (Santiago de Compostela: Xunta de Galicia, 1994).

Tate, R.B., and Turville-Petre, T. *Two Pilgrim Itineraries of the Later Middle Ages: Purchas's Pilgrim and Master Robert Langton* (Santiago de Compostela: Xunta de Galicia, 1995).

Vázquez de Parga, Luis, Lacarra, José M., and Uria Ríu, Juan. *Las Peregrinaciones a Santiago de Compostela,* 3 vols (Madrid: Consejo Superior de Investigaciones Científicas, 1948).

Webb, Diana. *Medieval European Pilgrimage* (Basingstoke: Palgrave, 2002).

Weir, Alison. *Lancaster and York: The Wars of the Roses* (London: Pimlico, 1998).

Index